Praise for Philip Delves Broughton's
Ahead of the Curve

"[Delves Broughton] makes a better writer than corporate drone. If you're thinking of following in his footsteps, I'd invest in this book first."
—Bryan Burrough, *The Washington Post*

"*Ahead of the Curve* is a cautionary tale for those who believe that the grass—and their future paycheck—would be greener if only they could jump the fence into the rarefied world of the Masters of Business Administration."
—*The New York Times*

"[A] horrifying and very funny memoir . . . It is hard to account for the odd position that Harvard holds in the American imagination, and Mr. Delves Broughton's excellent book only deepens the puzzle."
—Andrew Ferguson, *The Wall Street Journal*

"A fascinating book . . . a disturbing meditation on American business, the limits of meritocracy, and the terrible personal sacrifices people are willing to make in pursuit of a buck. Even better, once done, you'll think—with good reason—that you might know as much about business as any B-school grad."
—*The Boston Globe*

"Informative, wry, and well-written, Delves Broughton's book will make rewarding and pleasurable reading for anybody wishing to understand why American business is the way it is."
—John Cassidy, staff writer for *The New Yorker* and author of *Dot.Con*

"Engaging . . . an insightful account of HBS life. . . . [Delves Broughton] has put his class notes to good use by providing an excellent layman's guide to the big ideas of the literature."
—*The Economist*

"An important exposé of life in the most famous educational institution in the world. Delves Broughton deftly chronicles the pathologies, shrewdness and effectiveness of an elite whose training and attitudes shape not only our modern economies but also our civilizations."
—Rory Stewart, author of *The Prince of the Marshes* and *The Places in Between*

ABOUT THE AUTHOR

Philip Delves Broughton was born in Bangladesh and grew up in England. He graduated from New College, Oxford, in 1994 and received his MBA from the Harvard Business School in 2006. From 1998–2004 he served, successively, as the New York and Paris bureau chief for *The Daily Telegraph* of London and reported widely from North and South America, Europe, and Africa. His work has appeared in newspapers and magazines around the world. He lives in Connecticut with his wife and two sons.

AHEAD

OF THE

CURVE

Two Years at
Harvard
Business School

PHILIP

DELVES BROUGHTON

PENGUIN BOOKS

PENGUIN BOOKS

Published by the Penguin Group

Penguin Group (USA) Inc., 375 Hudson Street, New York, New York 10014, U.S.A. •
Penguin Group (Canada), 90 Eglinton Avenue East, Suite 700, Toronto, Ontario, Canada
M4P 2Y3 (a division of Pearson Penguin Canada Inc.) • Penguin Books Ltd, 80 Strand, London
WC2R 0RL, England • Penguin Ireland, 25 St Stephen's Green, Dublin 2, Ireland (a division
of Penguin Books Ltd) • Penguin Group (Australia), 250 Camberwell Road, Camberwell,
Victoria 3124, Australia (a division of Pearson Australia Group Pty Ltd) • Penguin Books India
Pvt Ltd, 11 Community Centre, Panchsheel Park, New Delhi – 110 017, India • Penguin Group
(NZ), 67 Apollo Drive, Rosedale, North Shore 0632, New Zealand (a division of Pearson
New Zealand Ltd) • Penguin Books (South Africa) (Pty) Ltd, 24 Sturdee Avenue, Rosebank,
Johannesburg 2196, South Africa

Penguin Books Ltd, Registered Offices: 80 Strand, London WC2R 0RL, England

First published in the United States of America by The Penguin Press,
a member of Penguin Group (USA) Inc. 2008
This edition with a new afterword published in Penguin Books 2009

10   9   8   7   6   5   4   3   2   1

THE LIBRARY OF CONGRESS HAS CATALOGED THE HARDCOVER EDITION AS FOLLOWS:
Broughton, Philip Delves.
   The curve : two years at Harvard Business School / Philip Delves Broughton
      p.   cm.
   Includes index.
   ISBN 978-1-59420-175-2 (hc.)
   ISBN 978-0-14-311543-4 (pbk.)
   1. Harvard Business School. 2. Business education—Massachusetts. 3. Business students—
Massachusetts. 4. Management—Study and teaching (Higher)—Massachusetts. I. Title.
   HF1131.H4B76   2008
   650.071'.17444—dc22   2007042746

Printed in the United States of America

For Margret

There are two types of education. One
should teach us how to make a living
and the other how to live.

—John Adams

CONTENTS

PREFACE

I did not go to Harvard Business School planning to write a book about the experience. In fact, after ten years as a journalist, I went there to recover from writing, to stop looking at the world around me as a source of potential stories. I wanted to learn about business in order to gain control of my own financial fate and, more important, my time. I was tired of living at the end of a cell phone, prey to an employer's demands. A master's in business administration, I hoped, would be my path to greater knowledge about the workings of the world and broader choices about the life I might lead.

I say this only to make clear that this book was never intended as an inside raid. In many ways, I loved my two years at Harvard. My classmates were smart and considerate. The faculty was, for the most part, inspiring and committed. The facilities and the speakers who came to spend time with us were quite extraordinary. As a catbird seat for viewing capitalism, there is no better place. For me, and everyone I knew, Harvard changed the view of our futures and the possibilities available to us through business.

But it was an intense time, far more intense than I'd ever imagined. The work load, especially in the first few weeks, was crushing as we struggled to learn the functional areas of business, finance, accounting, operations, marketing, and organizational behavior. As the months passed, the pressure to find jobs, the "right" jobs, became a separate education in itself, beyond what occurred in the classroom.

This book is my attempt to describe my experience and that of my classmates in this cauldron of capitalism. Reading through the diary I kept during my two years there, I was surprised by the emotions the experience drew out of me. I had expected a more neutral time at business school, a period of study and preparation for a different career. Instead, we MBA students spent much of our time discussing our ambitions and the kinds of lives we wanted for ourselves and our families. This debate looms large in the book, alongside accounts of what we learned in class, what the many famous speakers said, and how we went about deciding what to do for work. To have the opportunity to study at Harvard Business School is a great gift. Any gripes, criticisms, or anxieties I express should be taken for what they are: high-class problems.

In 1960, five thousand MBAs graduated from American universities. In 2000, the number had risen to a hundred thousand. The MBA course now comes in all kinds of flavors. There is the classic two-year, full-time residential course, which I took. But you can now study for an MBA part-time, online, at night, or in multiple international locations. Where capitalism goes, the MBA follows. The number of MBA applicants in the Middle East, China, and India is soaring. Survey after survey has shown that MBAs tend to receive higher salaries and better jobs. Those three precious letters have become a calling card, and in some cases a requirement, for success in business.

While I attended Harvard Business School (HBS, as I shall often refer to it), between 2004 and 2006, the school's alumni included the president of the United States, the secretary of the U.S. Treasury, the president of the World Bank, the mayor of New York City, not to mention the CEOs of General Electric, Goldman Sachs, and Procter and Gamble. HBS alumni filled 20 percent of the top three jobs at the Fortune 500 companies. The newly fashionable private equity and hedge fund industries were stacked with Harvard MBAs, who were received like gods when they returned to campus. It was daunting and thrilling to join such a powerful lineage.

The school believes that the kind of leadership required to succeed in business can also be applied to other spheres—politics, education, health care, the arts. I did not come from a business background and instinctively resisted this notion that businesspeople should be running everything. It was a question that came up repeatedly over the next two years, and it cuts to why a book on the Harvard MBA should be of interest to a broader audience than those who either have an MBA or are considering getting one. The language, practices, and leadership styles taught in the MBA course affect all of us. Business schools no longer produce just business leaders. MBAs determine the lives many of us will lead, the hours we work, the vacations we get, the culture we consume, the health care we receive, and the education provided to our children. Since 2000, the Harvard MBA in the Oval Office has made decisions of global and historical consequence. In short, the MBA, its content, and the network of people who hold it, matter. And it has ambitions to matter even more.

Finally, this book is just one person's view. No single MBA could ever be representative of the nine hundred students in the Harvard Business School class of 2006. Everything in this book occurred as I describe it. But I have altered the names and changed details to conceal the identities of some of my fellow students. I did this for two reasons. The first was privacy. The Harvard Business School classroom is a safe learning environment, a place to experiment and make mistakes. My classmates did not know that one day I would write a book about our experiences. While my own embarrassments and humiliations fill this book, theirs are their own concern. The second reason for concealing some identities is that it allows me to describe what we went through with greater honesty than if I had to worry about the reputations of people I like and admire. The professors, since their role as teachers is a public one, appear as they were, as do the speakers who came to campus. My intention in combining these approaches is to give as accurate a picture of my time at HBS as possible.

When my class graduated in June 2006, we received an open letter from the dean of the school, Jay Light. "As you join other HBS alumni around the world," he wrote, "I hope you'll stay connected to the School and continue to share your thoughts and perspectives on your years here." Here are mine.

Chapter One

LET'S GET
RETARDED

Well, don't we all feel like jumping to
the end of the world sometimes?

—MICK JAGGER

"I don't know what you think of Philip, but right now, for you, he's just
Philip."

The dean of Harvard Business School and ninety of my classmates
were looking straight toward me. At that very moment, I was trying to
corral a collapsing chicken salad sandwich and looking very "just Philip"
indeed. We were a few weeks into the MBA course, and Dean Kim Clark
had come to our classroom this lunchtime to introduce himself and take
questions. He was a gaunt, devout Mormon in his late fifties who spoke
with the authority of the prophets, quiet but commanding.

"When I first came into this classroom as a young professor to teach,
there was a guy called Jack sitting there. He's now Jack Brennan, head of
Vanguard. Over there was a former Dartmouth football player, Jeff. Jeff
Immelt is now the chief executive of General Electric. Over there was
Donna, Donna Dubinsky who became the CEO of Palm."

A switch seemed to have been flipped in our windowless basement classroom. You could feel the hum of ambition. Ninety students in five rows arranged in a horseshoe facing the blackboard, all of them, even the one now licking mayonnaise and chicken off his pencil, thinking: Will I be the one they mention in twenty-five years? Will a future dean address the class of 2031 saying, "In that seat was Susan. She was shy of speaking in class but now she's running the largest hedge fund in the world. Tom over there became CEO of Google. And Philip. Well. How many billions should one man have?"

We were all looking at each other, wondering.

I first set foot on the campus of Harvard Business School one sultry evening in August 2004. My wife, Margret, and our one-year-old son, Augie, were staying in New York until our possessions arrived from France, where we had been living for the previous two and a half years. I knew no one at the school among the students or on the faculty. For the first time in a decade, I had neither an employer nor a job title and no monthly paycheck. Around two hundred students with little or no background in business had been summoned early to the business school for a course formally known as Analytics, less formally as Math Camp. The goal was to bring us up to speed with the remaining seven hundred members of our class who would arrive in three weeks. They, the school assumed, had spent enough time over the past few years handcuffed to their laptops churning out financial models and corporate PowerPoint presentations to know the basics. We, on the other hand, would have to undergo a compressed version of the first-year course known as the RC, the required curriculum. We would be introduced to the HBS case method of teaching and, it was hoped, be less intimidated when the first year proper began.

After registering, I was given a folder containing the case studies for the first week and told to report in fifteen minutes to a conference room in Spangler, the vast neo-Georgian building that forms the heart of the campus, to meet my study group. I went outside into the treacly warmth, found a bench close to the tennis courts, pulled out the first of hundreds of cases I would soon confront, and began to read. The entire HBS curriculum is made of case studies, business situations drawn from real life. The question you are expected to answer in each one is: What would you do? There are no right or wrong answers to these problems. In many cases the actions taken by the case protagonists turn out to be disastrous. The only thing that matters is how you think about the problems, how you deal with the paucity of information, the uncertainty. The hope is that long after the minutiae of accounting or bond pricing have faded to a blur, you will be left with a distinctive way of thinking and making decisions. Cases are written by members of the faculty and can range in length from a couple of pages to more than thirty. They generally include a dramatic narrative that sets up the situation, an analysis of the business under discussion, and several pages of exhibits, charts, tables, pictures, and any additional text required to illustrate the problem. My first case began: "Once upon a time many, many years ago, there lived a feudal landlord in a small province of Western Europe. The landlord, Baron Coburg, lived in a castle high on a hill. He was responsible for the well-being of many peasants who occupied the lands surrounding his castle."

The baron had two peasants, Ivan and Frederick, whom he ordered to farm two different plots of land. He gave them seed, fertilizer, and oxen, but told them to lease a plow from Feyador the plow-maker. They returned a year later with different amounts of wheat, their oxen a year older, and their plows in different states of disrepair. The case concluded: "After they had taken their leave, the baron began to contemplate what had happened. 'Yes,' he thought, 'they did well, but I wonder which one did better?'"

It was an accounting case, and the challenge was to help the baron answer his question by drawing up income statements and balance sheets for the two farms. Why any medieval baron given the choice between rape and plunder and bookkeeping might choose the latter beat me. But this was Harvard Business School, where even the medieval barons were different. On one of the tennis courts in front of me, two students were just beginning their warm-up. One wore a blue bandanna, the other no shirt. They began to hit, gently at first, each standing a few feet from the net, knocking the ball back and forth. I paused to watch them, hypnotized by their metronomic hitting. Slowly they worked their way deeper into each half of the court, their arms whipping through the air, the ball dropping closer and closer to the baseline. I wondered how many hours had gone into training those perfect forehands, that unerring focus on the ball traveling through the air. Within the rectangle of the court, everything was happening exactly as it should. I tucked my case study back in the folder and made my way to Spangler to meet my study group.

Sitting around a large blue table were two military veterans, a former employee of the New York City mayor's office, a Taiwanese management consultant, and a very nervous blond woman, freshly sprung from a Boston mutual fund company. The vets seemed too big for the room, their biceps bursting out of skin-tight T-shirts, while the blonde seemed terrified and small. The New Yorker, Justin, it turned out, had grown up a few blocks from my wife. All of them, it became clear as we set to work on the baron, knew far more about business than I. They had flipped open their laptops and were ready to go. Before arriving at Harvard, I had only ever used one of the programs in Microsoft Office. That was Word. I had never opened the spreadsheet program, Excel, or the presentation program, PowerPoint. For the first few days, I decided I would stick with my trusty pencil and paper and focus on what was being said, rather than try to master new software. J. P. Morgan, after all, had never had Excel and he used to run most of the U.S. economy. I looked back at the baron's problem. It didn't seem that complicated: a couple of bushels here, a couple there, fertilizer, oxen, plows that undergo some wear and tear, and an exploitative feudal landlord.

"Ivan," I volunteered after a few moments. Everyone looked up. "Ivan's the better farmer." I quickly explained my calculation.

"You forgot to depreciate the oxen," said Jake, an ex-marine.

I went back to work. "Frederick," I said a moment later.

"Did you put the full value of Ivan's plow under 'cost of goods sold'?"

asked Jake. At this point, I decided to shut up. My entire knowledge of accounting came down to my assigned summer reading. What with having to move from Europe and everything, this reading had been skimpier than I had hoped.

"Is the baron the equity holder or a lender?" inquired Jon. He had just returned from leading combat teams into terrorized areas of Baghdad. He seemed by far the least anxious in the room. "And does anyone get charged for depleting the land with fertilizer?"

For the next hour, I scribbled away while the same handful of numbers chattered in my head like garbled code. "Twenty pounds of fertilizer are worth two bushels of wheat, an ox valued at forty bushels with ten years' worth of work in him works for a year. Ivan still owes Feyador for the plow . . ." The numbers kept shifting beneath me. First Ivan was the better farmer, producing two thirds of a bushel more per acre than Frederick. Then Frederick nudged ahead by five sixths. It was like one of those children's puzzles where you roll balls around a flat surface trying to get them to stay in holes, and just when you think you have all six in, the first one rolls out again.

"I've done some ratios," said the blonde. "Net sales over assets shows Frederick is the better farmer." The others nodded. But the peasants aren't selling anything, I thought. They are simply turning their goods over to the feudal landlord. So perhaps feudal tribute over assets might be the better ratio. This wasn't helpful.

Next up was "The Case of the Unidentified U.S. Industries." It was our first foray into finance. From the moment I was accepted by Harvard Business School, I had been dreading finance. I was eager to learn about it, but I worried that I would be so far behind the class technically that everything would sail over my head. That first evening did nothing to boost my confidence. We were given a list of twelve industries, from a basic chemical company and a supermarket chain to a major airline and commercial bank, and an unlabeled set of balance sheet percentages and ratios. We were to match the industry to the correct set of numbers.

I had gotten the gist of ratios during my summer reading. You compared numbers from financial statements to develop insights into the quality of a business. Take inventory. Companies that need to hold inventory are constantly trying to balance the cost of storing inventory with the need to keep up with supply. It's like any household. You want enough food to feed the family, but you don't want so much it's spilling out of your cupboards and going rotten before you get a chance to eat it. But then again, you might want to buy occasionally in bulk, getting things cheaper, rather than running out every day to the overpriced corner store. Or perhaps you're a real foodie and like to buy fresh food every day. The point is that different households will have different ways of managing inventory. The only crimes are waste and undersupply. To analyze inventory management in a set of financial statements, you might start with the figures for "cost of goods sold" and "inventory." "Cost of goods sold," or COGS, is simply the cost to the manufacturer of the goods it has sold in a given period. "Inventory" is the cost to the manufacturer of the goods it is waiting to sell. Divide COGS by inventory and you get a pretty good idea of how fast the company is shifting product. A ratio of one tells you that the company holds exactly as much inventory as it sells in the period covered by the balance sheet. In a fresh foods market, for a balance sheet covering a year, you would expect an extremely high ratio as inventory is replenished on an almost daily basis. But in a high-end jeweler's, that ratio might be below one, as each item is held for a long time before it finds a buyer.

"The supermarket's going to have the highest inventory turnover," said Jon.

"Or the meat packer," said Jake.

"The commercial bank will probably have the most current assets and liabilities for deposits and withdrawals," said the Taiwanese. I could tell Justin was as baffled as I was, from the way he kept tugging at his hair and chin.

"Wow," I exclaimed. "I wonder who could make 16.7 percent profit margins. Jewelry stores?" I was just trying to say something.

Everyone kept scanning the numbers, trying to find meaning. We looked at debt over assets. A company with lots of fixed assets, like factories, would most likely have more debt than an advertising agency, whose main assets were human beings. It is one of the least appealing features of company accounts, and perhaps their greatest flaw, that humans appear only as costs on income statements, never as assets on a balance sheet. Unlike a factory, humans, of course, can get up and walk out the door at any time, hence banks' reluctance to lend to advertising agencies, law firms, or architectural practices. No chemical plant is going to say to hell with it, default on its loan, and go join an ashram.

We squinted at net sales over net assets, trying to figure out which companies were generating the most sales from their assets. Again, the ad agency, with nothing but some rented office space and few assets, should have had a high ratio, indicating lots of sales from few assets, whereas the manufacturer would have had a lower one. After an hour, we thought we had nailed down half of them. After two hours, we were up to eight. As the third hour rolled by, it felt as if we would never get there. Just when we thought we had identified the airline, it started to look like the automaker again. Or could it be the maker of name-brand quality men's apparel?

I was beginning to feel what would become a familiar set of sensations. The life-sapping effect of fluorescent lighting. The vague stench of Styrofoam and Chinese noodles drifting up from the waste basket. Dehydration and itching skin. The realization that half the people in the room were checking e-mail and surfing the Web, which explained why any question lingered in the air for seconds before stimulating an answer. Through the window, I could see the hulking shadow of Harvard Stadium in the blue-black night. What had begun as a rat-a-tat exchange of thoughts had slowed to dreamlike speed. Words and ideas drifted between us in slow motion. It was nearly midnight when we gave up.

The air was still hot and thick when I walked out to my car. I drove home to our new apartment in West Cambridge, ten minutes from the business school. There was no one on the streets, and for the first time in a decade I wasn't living in a major city. My dog, Scarlett, greeted me at the door. She had been waiting patiently on the steps in the dark, and the moment I arrived she burst out to pee on the sidewalk. The lock on the front door was broken. It was unsettling sleeping in an empty apartment in a town I barely knew. My life had been reduced to school and this room with an air mattress on the floor and a picnic table from Costco in the corner. I lay there hearing every single noise, a tree branch scratching against my window, the cars passing outside, their lights shining on the ceiling above me. It took me hours to get to sleep that night as a single question churned around my mind: What have I done?

We rejoined the battle the next morning at seven. The Spangler meeting rooms were jammed with Math Campers struggling with the as-yet unidentified industries. Their enthusiasm for the task was staggering. The halls rang with discussions of profit margins and leverage ratios. Banks, I heard someone say authoritatively, tended to have huge short-term liabilities—otherwise known as the money in their customers' accounts, which could be withdrawn at any time—and similarly huge amounts of receivables, or loans made to its customers. For banks, loans are assets, while the money it holds for its customers is a liability. It took me a while to get this straight. The money they have is a liability, whereas the money they have given away is an asset. But once I had figured it out, I looked at my unidentified industries and there it was, leaping out at me, the bank! Finally I had something to offer my group. I raced into the room with my discovery, but they had already figured this out. It was a relief to go to class.

There are two main classroom buildings at HBS, Aldrich and Hawes, which contain thirty or so almost identical classrooms. Aldrich is named after Senator Nelson Aldrich, a lavishly mustachioed Rhode Islander, whose daughter married John D. Rockefeller, Jr. Rod Hawes graduated

from HBS in 1969 and made his fortune in insurance. He built and sold
Life Re Corporation of America and has since diverted much of his fortune
into philanthropy. In each of the classrooms ninety or so seats ascended in
five semicircular rows, divided by two aisles. A few of the rooms had tall
windows looking out onto campus, but most had none at all. Sitting in these
windowless, temperature-controlled, mercilessly lit rooms was like being in
a casino, with no sense of the world outside, immune to time and nature.
We were each allotted two laptop widths of space along the curving desks
and a swiveling office chair upholstered in purple. When we arrived in class
at our assigned seats, we had to slide a white laminated card printed with
our names into a slot in front of our place so the professors could identify
us. Tucked under each desk were plugs for our computers. To my right was
Laurie, an Alaskan with a doctorate in chemistry who previously ran a
research center for a biotech company. To my left was Ben, a former
employee of the New York City Parks Department. Laurie would spend the
two weeks of Math Camp in a state of staring-eyed terror. Despite her obvious brilliance, she dreaded being called on by a professor. Give her a mole-
cule to decompose, she said, she would decompose it, recompose it, and tie it
up with a bow. Ask her for an accounting ratio, and she dissolved into a
puddle. Ben was much calmer. He wore a beard and sandals and had spent
the previous two weeks hiking the Appalachian Trail. Like me, he seemed
allergic to his computer and took his notes in longhand. But he evidently
had one of those clear, logical minds that would lend itself well to this
place. Occupying the lower two thirds of my view was the thick buzz-cut
neck of a former marine. For several hours a day, for the next two weeks,
his surreal muscles flexed and twitched inches from my face, distracting
me from the weighted average cost of capital and decision trees.

The professors stood in the pit, with a desk for their notes and three sets
of blackboards and projector screens to play with. The more adventurous
ones could play videos or use a polling gizmo. Students could vote on any
issue by pressing one of the buttons built into their desks, red or green, and
see the results instantly displayed on a screen up front. The professors could

stand close to the front or roam up and down the aisles and rows, spurring their students to talk.

Harvard Business School had adopted the case method of teaching from the Harvard Law School. Classes begin with a cold call, in which the professor picks out a student to introduce the case we prepared the night before. This can be a harrowing experience for the student, lasting anywhere between two and fifteen minutes. Once the cold call is over, any student can raise his hand to comment. A comment can be a question, a response to something the professor or another student has said, or an example from one's own experience that clarifies the current problem. The only requirement is that the comment advance the class's learning.

Our first professor, David Hawkins, was a bluff Australian who had swum in the Olympics in the early 1950s and still had the broad shoulders and blond hair of a Bondi Beach lifeguard. Arriving in class, he unfolded his newspaper and read out a story from the front page of *The Wall Street Journal.* It was about a company that had been ordered to restate its earnings because of years of accounting errors. He then rested on the edge of his desk and leaned back, his mouth falling open as he thought. In one hand was a scrunched-up piece of paper, scrawled with his notes for the day's class. In the other he held a piece of yellow chalk that he would soon be hurling from one blackboard to another to highlight a specific point. "You see," he said after a moment's pause, "accounting really does matter. Now, on to this baron." He hunched his shoulders and began shuffling around the front of the room, dragging one leg, baron-like. "How can it be so hard to tell which of these blasted peasants is the better farmer?" A sense of relief washed over the class. As students were called on to explain their numbers, it became clear that no one had cracked this case. In fact, cracking it was not the point. The purpose of the baron case, Hawkins explained to us, was to demonstrate the difficulty of divining economic truth from even the simplest-seeming situation. In accounting, it was more important to use common sense than to cling to rules.

During Analytics, the teaching was more casual than what we would face in the RC, but the schedule was identical. Classes began at 8:40 A.M. and each one lasted an hour and twenty minutes. There was a twenty-minute break between the first and second class. On Monday, Wednesday, and Friday there was a third class after lunch, at 1:10 P.M. On Tuesdays and Thursdays we were free at 11:40 A.M. We were then expected to spend a minimum of two hours preparing each case. In addition to accounting, Analytics included crash courses in finance and TOM, that is, Technology and Operations Management. The three subjects were the most mathematical we would be obliged to take during the first year, so we needed to get comfortable with them.

After Hawkins's class came finance with Mihir Desai, a young Indian professor, tall and elegant with long, delicate fingers. He ingratiated himself with us immediately by saying that the ideas in finance were simple. It was only the explanations that got complicated. We were not to spend his class staring into our computers tinkering with spreadsheets. Rather, we were to learn finance in such a way that we could explain it to our mothers. Desai promised to come down hard on any Wall Street mumbo jumbo and encouraged us to strip away any preconceptions we might have. Those of us who thought we knew any finance were to relearn it from the bottom up. Those of us who knew nothing were setting out on a great adventure.

I met up with Justin for lunch. He had grown up in New York, where his father ran a successful investment business. After graduating from college, he had taught in Los Angeles as part of Teach for America and then worked in the New York City mayor's office. He had come to HBS in large part because the people he most admired in public service had come from successful careers in business. An MBA would be useful whatever he chose to do next. I asked him if he knew what that might be.

"Not yet," he said. "I'm going to be looking. If you find anything, tell me." All around us we heard the same conversation. Where are you from? What did you do? Why did you come to HBS?

After lunch, we had Technology and Operations Management, taught by Frances Frei, an energetic woman with a boyish thatch of spiky brown hair and a uniform of men's shirts and dark pants. Our first case with her involved constructing a decision tree, a means of assigning probabilities to the outcomes of certain investment decisions. If I drill for oil in a certain spot, I will have to spend $10 million with two possible outcomes. There is a 30 percent chance I will find nothing and a 70 percent chance I will make a $20-million find. You multiply the percentages by the outcomes to get zero and positive $14 million. So the estimated value of this investment is $14 million minus the $10-million drilling cost, to get $4 million. The usefulness of decision trees depends on the accuracy of your probabilities, but the idea is not to find certainty but to deal more comfortably with uncertainty, to find handholds, however tenuous, in the otherwise sheer rock face of financial decision making.

In the classes that followed, Frei hustled us on to regression analysis, a means of weighing the importance of different factors on a particular outcome. The case we studied dealt with a bank trying to use customer data to decide what to do about its online services. The bank knew all kinds of things about its customers, from their dates of birth and zip codes to their average balance size and use of online banking. Using Excel, we were required to organize and graph this data to establish behavioral patterns among customers. If they lived close to a branch, were they more likely to visit it? Did their age influence their likelihood of using online services? To what extent? Did customers' behavior vary by zip code? The bank wanted to use this data to help decide on the size of its investment in further online services, which were cheaper to offer than fully staffed branches. As an Excel virgin, it took me hours to organize thousands of cells of data into neat graphs. But even as I flailed about, I could feel my excitement building at the amount I might learn here. Why did banks send me different mailings from those it sent my neighbor? How did you decide how much money to invest in a project with uncertain outcomes? Having spent most of my life interpreting the world through words and language, it was startling to witness the power of numbers, models, and statistical tools. The full range of my ignorance was becoming apparent, and the prospect of spending two years acquiring an entirely fresh perspective invigorated me.

On the final day of Math Camp, study groups were pitted against one another in a mock financial negotiation. The subject was the acquisition of a tractor company, and my side was the potential acquirer. We met into the night, preparing our strategy, trying to decide what we could get away with paying. The next day, some groups dressed up in suits to try to assert themselves over their opponents. In our group, the military guys took charge and turned out to be convincing liars and brutal tacticians. We did very well. By the end of Analytics, I was exhausted. I had been working from 7:00 A.M. to midnight every day just to keep up. When Margret, my wife, and Augie, our one-year-old son, arrived, I was delighted to see them. But I was also tired and testy. I had been warned about the HBS bubble, in which even the most trivial tasks assumed the most absurd proportions, and it was absolutely true. And this was just the dress rehearsal.

The first year of the MBA course at Harvard Business School is called the required curriculum, or RC. It is broken down into ten courses, five each semester, intended to cover the fundamentals of business. The first semester courses are finance 1, accounting, marketing, operations, and organizational behavior. The second semester brings finance 2, negotiations, strategy, leadership and corporate accountability, and a macroeconomics course called Business, Government, and International Economics, known to all as "Biggie." During the second year, the EC, or elective curriculum, we could choose from a wide variety of courses or pursue independent research.

We would be graded on a forced curve, based on our performance against one another. At the top of the curve would be the academic cream. At the bottom, the stragglers. If everyone gets 95 percent on a test and you get 94 percent, too bad. You will be at the bottom of the curve. In each subject, the top 15 to 25 percent of the class receives a 1, the middle 65 to 75 percent a 2, and the bottom 20 percent a 3. Fifty percent of our grade would be determined by how we participated in class, the quality and frequency of our comments. The remaining 50 percent would be based on our performance in midterms and end-of-term exams. Halfway through each semester, our professors would provide evaluations of our class contributions so we would know how we were doing. After two years, the top 5 percent of the class would be awarded Baker Scholarships, the highest academic honor. The next 15 percent would receive honors. If at any point our academic performance fell below a certain level, we would be warned. Consistently poor performance was known as "hitting the screen," and would result in suspension or expulsion. If we attended every class, prepared our cases, and spoke in class, this should not be a problem. Except, I wondered, how was I, with no experience of business, supposed to compete academically with students who had studied finance or business at university and then spent several years honing their skills?

I first saw the class in its entirety at the end of August, when they arrived for a one-week course called Foundations, intended to ease us into the RC. We gathered in the Burden Auditorium, a cavernous hall half buried in the middle of campus, with seats sloping steeply down toward a stage. As the students poured in, Analytics suddenly seemed very cozy. The director of the RC program, a short, thick-shouldered man called Rick Ruback, took the stage. He spoke in a Boston accent and told us that we should think of him as the plant manager, the man walking the shop floor making sure the employees aren't bunging up the machines with chewing gum or taking illicit cigarette breaks. He was not to be confused with the chairman of the MBA program, who acted as a kind of company president, offering advice and oversight, nor the chief executive officer, the dean, Kim Clark. He said that our class consisted of 895 students, chosen from 7,100 applications, reflecting a 12.6 percent acceptance rate. We were very fortunate to have gotten in, he said. Thirty-four percent of our class was women and 32 percent international. The average age was twenty-seven, which put me, at thirty-two, on the high end. The course chairman, Carl Kester, followed Ruback and said how happy he was to welcome a diverse class.

Within our ranks were Olympians and consultants, gay activists, the former
assistant to J. Paul Bremer, the head of the Coalition Provisional Authority
in Iraq and a Harvard MBA, and even the "former Paris bureau chief of
The Daily Telegraph." Me.

Next came the dean. I had read his biography on the school's website.
He had arrived at Harvard as an undergraduate and never left, acquiring
his doctorate and rising through the ranks of the business school. He had
been a scoutmaster and a bishop in the Mormon Church, and had seven
children. He wore a pair of half-moon spectacles on a chain around his
neck and spoke in a sepulchral whisper. He oozed seriousness of purpose
and offered us three pieces of advice: work hard; be humble, or rather "cul-
tivate the habits of humility"; and when you pass the dean on the street or
on campus, don't panic. Apparently some foreign students don't understand
him when he says, "How's it going?" He said it's fine just to reply, "Hi," or
"How are you." He also warned us not to become cynical.

After Clark, we heard from Margie Yang, the CEO of Esquel, a Hong
Kong shirt manufacturer. HBS had been reevaluating how it taught business
ethics since Enron collapsed under the leadership of one of its most fêted
MBAs, Jeff Skilling. Yang's talk was part of the school's response. She told us
that when doing business in as lawless a place as China, it was more important than ever to have a set of values to anchor you. But any business person
operating in China over the past thirty years who told you he hadn't done
ethically dubious things, she said, was lying. Ethical lapses, she said, were
sometimes necessary to survive. Her larger point seemed to be that behaving
ethically in business was less about following a graven set of principles than
about adapting to changing situations in as decent a way as possible. Business ethics were dynamic rather than static, and until you tried to do business in a place like China, there was no use pontificating about the subject.

Finally a second-year student rose to welcome us and to reiterate the
importance of values to our future in business. He told us that simply by
getting into HBS, "You've won." From now on, it was all about how we
decided to govern our lives. There was something creepy about his

Kennedyesque cadences and his well-practiced call to arms. But what he said would be repeated throughout my time at Harvard. HBS was a brand as much as a school, and by attending, we were associating ourselves with one of the greatest brands in business. We were now part of an elite, and we should get used to it. I struggled with this idea. It seemed so arrogant on the part of the school, and somehow demeaning to those of us who had just arrived. Regardless of who we were when we arrived, or what we might learn or become over the next two years, simply by being accepted by HBS, we had entered an überclass. It was HBS, not anything that came before it, that conferred the "winner" tag on all of us. At the end of Analytics, Frances Frei had explained that now that we were at Harvard, the professors were at our disposal. They would help us to learn and build businesses. They would even help our children get into HBS, if needed. It was a brutal acknowledgment of the legacy admissions system, whereby the children of alumni are preferred, and it immediately set me thinking: How many in this room were here simply because someone had pulled strings? What kind of capitalism is going to be taught here? The meritocratic, level-playing-field, competitive version? Or another kind?

From Burden, we walked to our first class of the RC, called Learning to Lead. The case we studied in this class dealt with a small family-owned ice cream company whose chairman was in trouble. His underlings could not agree, and the company's profits were in free fall. The atmosphere had changed dramatically since Analytics. People were suddenly full of confidence, eager to speak and to make their mark. The battle for classroom air time had begun. Students now talked about "take-aways" rather than lessons, "going forward" instead of the future, and "consensus building" rather than agreeing. I had always been uneasy when talk turned to consensus building, which seemed like the prelude to a dismal group compromise. "Philip, why aren't you helping us build consensus? Come on, let's just build some consensus here." I kept wondering what a young Bill Gates or Rupert Murdoch would have made of this course. Not much, I imagine.

The following day we played "Crimson Greetings," described to us as "a game to bring fun to all kinds of learning." The entire class was divided into separate "universes," in which six or seven teams of around ten students competed in building and running a greeting card business. The goal was to run the most profitable business. We would have to purchase supplies, manage inventory, design and manufacture the cards, decide on a price, and then sell the cards in a series of timed sessions over the next two days. After each session, each universe gathered with a professor to measure, evaluate, and discuss its performance. The academic content of the exercise, however, was secondary to the larger purpose, which was for the students to get to know one another.

We began in a classroom on campus watching a video of a stilted Englishman. "Your assignment will be to develop the operations of a greeting card company and to make it profitable," he said. He spoke with the robotic menace of a Bond villain and could easily have been dispatching us to drive poisoned umbrella tips into enemy agents. We then made our way over to a gymnasium across the road from the business school. A room packed with 895 type-A personalities engaged in a business game sounds roughly like the African jungle. The lions roar, the birds squawk, the apes pound their chests, and the alligator snaps his jaws. My group contained three management consultants, from Austria, Indonesia, and Canada; a Korean banker from Los Angeles; a Chinese shoe marketer from Texas; an Argentine central banker; an Argentine engineer; a Lebanese American investment banker; a biotech executive from Boston; and Linda, a small, angry New Yorker who had been a management consultant and managed a software company but who said her real passion was racial and sexual equality.

Our first task was assigning roles. Linda quickly seized control. She was an expert negotiator, she said, so she would purchase supplies. She would also help with sales. Gunther, the Austrian, rallied to her side. The rest of us were left to divide up the production and distribution roles. One person had to check for quality. Another had to make sure we delivered our cards on time. I volunteered for the four-man production team, alongside the

Argentines and the Lebanese American, cutting up paper, applying glue and glitter, and writing festive greetings.

First, we had to design a Christmas card. We gathered as a team to decide on a simple yet elegant drawing that could be produced at speed. We settled on a tree, drawn as a triangle and flecked with silvery glitter. Inside the card would be the nondenominational "Season's Greetings." Linda scampered off to buy supplies while production huddled to lay out our table. I stood at one end with scissors to cut the cards. The Argentines stood poised to dispense glitter and write the message. And the Lebanese American banker picked out a green pen to draw trees. Around us were the rest of the team braced to deliver supplies and finished product, keep tabs on inventory, accounts, and the clock and to check for quality. A horn sounded, and we were off. I cut as fast as I could, and the Argentines glittered like demons. For the next half hour, we churned out cards until the horn sounded again. Then we moved to the side of the gym to debrief and recover, while the organizers inspected our tables and gathered up the records of our performance.

Linda sat down cross-legged and scowled. Her disappointment was obvious. "The group next to us delivered way more cards," she began. "And we wasted a lot of supplies. We need to do a deep dive on production to improve our metrics." The Argentines looked at me, and I could see they were about to burst out laughing. But we nodded seriously.

"The quality wasn't good enough," Linda said, running down the list on the clipboard she had procured with our supplies money. "And we missed out on delivering a batch of cards just before the end. We need to drill down on that." She had strict ideas about the colors for our cards, the kind of decorations we would use, and the negotiations she, naturally, would need to perform to get our supplies at a good price and dig us out of the hole we production losers had dug. The Argentines, Raphael and Ernesto, were now whispering to each other. Linda raised a single tiny digit.

"One conversation, guys. We need to be having *one* conversation."

They fell silent.

Gunther then rose to his feet. "We need to start thinking about the presentation we're going to have to make at the end of this, right," he began. "I think that at the least, you know, we need to build a chart that shows time on the x axis and financial performance on the y, so we can show how we improve performance."

Linda looked up adoringly. Finally, someone who understood.

The Indonesian woman nudged me in the ribs. "What did he say he was putting on the y axis?"

"Financial performance," I whispered back.

"Hey, guys, would you like to share?" said Gunther, wheeling round to stare at us. "If you're gonna talk, you should share." Linda beamed in approval.

The second round of the game involved making a Halloween card. We were struggling to come up with an inscription when I had my first HBS brain wave.

"How about Boo!?" It would be both appropriate and easy to write. The idea was taken up. Production was far slicker the second time around, but Linda circled the table scowling. When we had finished our first batch of cards, she picked them up, flicked through them, and tossed them angrily to the table, shouting, "What are *these*?!" She then screwed up the supply negotiations, bringing us the wrong cards and markers. A Canadian woman, who up to now had been silent, began cursing under her breath.

During our next break, Gunther took up position again beside our whiteboard. "We should have done a GANTT chart!" he exclaimed.

"A GANTT chart!" Linda squealed, shaking with laughter.

"What's a GANTT chart?" I asked Raphael. He shrugged.

"It's a bar chart used to lay out a project schedule," the Indonesian said.

Fortunately, a revolt ensued. On production, our savior was Ernesto, whose hobby was handicrafts. After two rounds, he could crank out beautifully made cards at a blistering pace. He instructed the rest of us in a few basic folding and cutting tricks, and in no time, we were off. When the time came to make the presentation, Linda and Gunther had drafted such a complicated set of time and process charts, they had completely lost sight of our central task. In fact, it wasn't clear at all that we had been making greeting cards. In the meantime, the Canadian and the Korean had been at work on their own presentation, which made far more sense. Since I had an English accent and some experience in public speaking, it was suggested that I present to the rest of our universe. I shared that responsibility with the Chinese Texan. Asked what I had learned from the exercise, I spoke about communication and described the moment when I, an Englishman, had found myself in a discussion with an Indonesian and two Argentines about why "Boo!" was a good thing to put in a Halloween card. I added that we also had the "Martha Stewart of Argentina" on our team. Afterward, Ernesto found me and asked, "Who is this Martha Stewart?"

My experience of Linda and Gunther convinced me that it took just two consultants to screw up a project. One to drive everyone insane, and the other to laugh at her PowerPoint jokes. At the end of the second day of Crimson Greetings, I ran into Justin and we swapped notes. I told him about the "one conversation" put-down.

"Ah, the old 'one conversation' Nazi," he said.

"The what?"

"Every organization has one. They're always the ones who can never stay on point, but they insist that everyone listen to them in silence."

We agreed that it was exhausting to be meeting so many people in such a short space of time. Our faces ached from all the smiling and rote conversation. It was a necessary ritual, but wearing nonetheless. During coffee breaks from Crimson Greetings, I had noticed how many of the class seemed to know one another or at least know people in common. The networks of certain universities and companies ran very deep. For those like me, who knew no one, it was a question of drifting through the crowds until I spotted familiar faces from Analytics. Yet whenever I felt pangs of regret for my old life—the job, the status, the structure—I reminded myself that I had chosen this path for a reason. However uncomfortable I found the bonding exercises or the forced introductions, they were the necessary prelude to something bigger and more important. I reminded myself of the dean's injunction: don't become cynical.

After the lunacy of Crimson Greetings, we returned to our classrooms for the first of six classes studying the roots of modern capitalism. Sitting to my right was a willowy blonde with heavy bags under her eyes. She had spent the past three years toiling at a New York–based private equity firm, specializing in real estate. She said she had come to HBS for the vacation. Pure and simple. She did not expect to learn much, but she was looking forward to sleeping, working out, and taking long vacations. To my left was a former financial journalist who feigned cool by arriving each day without his textbook, but then spent the entire class providing me with his muted commentary on the discussion. In one of these classes, we studied the history of Rolls-Royce and the current state of capitalism in Britain. It was intriguing to hear what others in the class found interesting. During the Second World War, Rolls-Royce was called upon to churn out planes and engines for the war effort. In just a few months, it put together a large network of subcontractors to help it guarantee fast, dependable manufacturing. A woman who had worked as an engineer at Boeing said that outsourcing on such a scale was unthinkable at her old employer, where they preferred to do as much in house as possible. A Frenchman who had run a factory in Russia for a French food conglomerate told us, "Where I used to work it took six or seven months to decide to subcontract, then five months to negotiate with the subcontractor to get the arrangement right, then another six months for the process to start. And we were just making biscuits."

The professor called on me to say whether or not I thought Britain was in decline. I said absolutely not. Or, rather, it depended from what point you started. Of course, Britain no longer had an empire, but it remained a stable, thriving economy. It was one of the richest countries in the world yet retained a broad welfare safety net for the least fortunate. My remarks aroused some opposition. A Russian man said that in his experience, the British were lazy and incompetent. A young American banker who had lived in London for a year said that the Underground didn't work and that the overall level of service from shops, restaurants, airports, and utility providers was terrible. The idea that Britain was still a great country, he said, was a joke. I said that having lived in Britain, France, and the United States, I found things to recommend and object to in all of them, and one could not say one was better than the other: The lack of vacation time in the United States versus Europe. Universal health care in France and Britain versus the $11,000 check I had just written to insure my family privately for the year in the United States. I could see the American banker glowering at me from across the room, but the Frenchman approached me afterward to say he appreciated my standing up for our continent.

"I'm just sorry about the shark," he said. Sharking was a term used to describe students who gratuitously sought to discredit the remarks of others. I had not fully appreciated the banker's hostility, but to the rest of the class, it was clear. I had been sharked.

On the final day of Foundations, we returned to Burden for another talk and slide presentation from Ruback. He showed us the HBS anxiety curve. It placed time on the horizontal axis and stress on the vertical. The line started high, fell as the semester wore on, shot up again for exams, and went off the chart during the recruiting season. His next slide broke down the working week to show us what the faculty expected of us: 55.1 hours per week on academic work, made up of classes and at least two hours of preparation per case. Based on my experience in Analytics, I knew that was a woeful underestimate. It doesn't leave much time for anything else, he said, but that's all part of the challenge. HBS is not about letting everyone do everything. It is about forcing you to make choices. What are your ambitions? What are your obligations? Do they tally? If not, what should you do to change one or the other? How should you spend your time to get what you want?

For many in the class, 55.1 hours a week of academic work sounded like a breeze. They were used to working from eighty to one hundred hours a week at their previous jobs. Much of the first-year material would be familiar to them. I was not one of them. As he wrapped up, Ruback told an anecdote of an MBA student arguing with someone in the HBS administration. As tempers rose, the student burst out, "Why are you treating me like this? I'm the customer, goddamnit." "No, you're not," said the HBS employee. "You're the product." "I guess you're somewhere between," said Ruback, once the laughter had abated. "Sometimes you're the customer, other times you'll feel like the product."

After Ruback's speech, we walked over to Aldrich to meet our sections. The section was HBS's most aggressive act of socialization and network building. For the whole of the first year, you had to attend every single class with the same ninety people. They would be the focus for your academic and social lives. Each section was intended to be a microcosm of the 895-strong class, with the same proportion of men to women, American to international students, the same mix of backgrounds and ethnicity. For the rest of our lives, HBS would regard us as a section. We would be reunited as a section every five years. Fund-raisers would appeal to us as a section. As far as HBS was concerned, I would forever be a member of Section A, class of 2006.

Our classroom, Aldrich 7, was located in the basement, beside the men's lavatories. When we arrived, our name cards were in place. I was sitting halfway down on the left-hand side, facing the blackboards. It was a nice, neutral spot. Not too close to the front, somewhat invisible. Before the class began, we were given access to a database containing photographs and short profiles of the entire class, so when we arrived we could look around and spot the German, the athlete, the UPS employee, the investment bank analyst, the ones who liked yoga, running, or African dance. It was an extraordinary thing, after having grown so used to controlling the extent of one's friends and acquaintances, now suddenly to be plunked into a room full of strangers with the message "For the next year, this is your world—and as far as the HBS network goes, here is where it all begins." But looking around, I found it hard not to feel excited. After ten years of work, this was a second chance at university.

I had been placed between two students from the military. To my right was Bob, who had flown the Stealth bomber. I had met him during Analytics, and he frightened me. He was short and trim with strawberry blond hair and pale blue eyes. He had four children and ate his lunch from a Winnie the Pooh plastic box that he brought from home. He seemed humorless and resolute. Just the man you'd like to have flying billions of dollars' worth of military hardware. He had come to business school because he had grown tired of air force life and wanted greater opportunities for himself and his family. He was thirty-five and had little time to waste.

To my left was Lara, who would be returning to West Point to teach once she had obtained her MBA. While Bob had been dropping bombs on Iraq from far above the clouds, Lara had been running the supplies and accounting division of her unit on the ground. She operated on a drip feed of diet soda, and preferred Mountain Dew for its caffeine rush.

Bob and Lara represented one of the three Ms said to characterize the HBS class: Mormons, Military, and McKinsey. The Mormon thing began with Dean Kim Clark. In our section were four Mormons, including Bob. For many of the international students, and the Americans, this was their first encounter with Mormons, and their suspicion prompted the usual polygamy jokes.

As for the military: five students had served in the military, again including Bob. McKinsey, the consulting firm, seemed to regard the school as its private training and recruitment facility. We began with five McKinsey-ites in our section, and by the time we left, they had converted four more.

Our section chair was Ben Esty, a youthful finance professor who would serve as our link to the administration. He would never teach us a course but would serve as our reference point and guide on official matters. He strode up and down the classroom, flicking the hair out of his eyes and explaining at martial volume how important our section would be to us. We would remember these people forever. They would become our first calls in our business lives, and perhaps even our personal lives. We would be marching through the jungle of the required curriculum arm in arm, hoisting each other across the marshes of ignorance and ineptitude toward the sun-drenched heights of competence and opportunity. It felt like one of those movies where a bunch of misfits, each gifted in his own way—one in explosives, another in disguise, another in forgery or karate—are thrown together to achieve a dangerous mission.

Then we had to play another get-to-know-each-other game. This time we were given ten minutes to huddle in our rows and find something we had in common. It felt like the kind of punishment human resources departments were constantly inflicting on people who would really rather be doing their jobs, a snappy little bonding exercise to pass the time. Bob volunteered to lead our discussion. Eva, a chic Mexican cement company executive, looked horrified and barely spoke. I sympathized. Others in the room, though, seemed to dig it. They were laughing and whispering and plotting, as if they had done this a million times—which in fact many of them had.

First up was the second row in the middle. A man on the far right began: "Hi, I'm Joseph. I'm from New York and used to be a bond trader." He then sat down. For a moment, we thought he had missed the point. Then the person next to him said, "A bond trader? How funny. I used to trade stocks in Milan." The next person rose: "Milan? I once did an assignment there when I was a consultant based in London." And on down the row until the connections game was complete.

Bob rose next and said, "In this row, we all once taught a class." Mission accomplished. As he sat down, Esty said he might want to elaborate a little, to laughter from the room. After the row that came before us, we felt a little dull, out of the loop compared with the giggling consultants and bankers for whom this seemed to constitute thrilling entertainment. Once all the rows had had their turn, Esty asked if there were any questions. A hand rose behind me. It was attached to a small body from which came a scared midwestern voice. "Anyone got any plans to meet up this weekend?" You could see people looking up toward the ceiling. "Perhaps you could deal with that afterward," said Esty. He wished us good luck and dismissed us.

At the back of the class, Misty, an army veteran, shouted "Who's coming to the Red Line for a beer?" A fragmented cheer went up. She stood at the door waving people through as if they were paratroopers leaping from a plane. After the sense of discovery I had experienced in Analytics, I was suddenly despondent. This was what I had left Paris for? Snickering twenty-seven-year-olds who relished HR games? Stampedes for beer? People hoping to kick-start their social life? Outside, on the lawn between Aldrich and Spangler, the Student Association had set up a tent with a bar and a thumping sound system. A song by the Black Eyed Peas was playing. I strained to hear the words. Could that really be the chorus? I listened again while heads bobbed all around me. Yes, it was. "Let's get retarded in here, let's get retarded."

Chapter Two

STARTING
OVER

Far better it is to dare mighty things,
to win glorious triumphs even though
checkered by failure, than to rank
with those poor spirits who neither
enjoy nor suffer much because they
live in the gray twilight that knows
neither victory nor defeat.

—THEODORE ROOSEVELT,
QUOTED ON THE
HBS ADMISSIONS WEBSITE

When I was a child, I was often told the story of my great-grandmother. Daw Ma Ma was Burmese. She lived in Rangoon and was married to an Anglo-French civil servant. When she was thirty-five, her husband died, leaving her with nine children and a meager inheritance. With no prior experience of business, she struck upon the idea of bringing Hollywood films to Burma. Within a few years, she was the country's largest film distributor and owned the biggest cinema in Rangoon, the Palladium. One of my mother's clearest memories of childhood was watching *Ben-Hur* from the family box. Daw Ma Ma's success allowed her to acquire houses and land in Rangoon's fanciest neighborhood, alongside Inya Lake. Here on this compound of stately wooden houses, my mother grew up alongside fifty-two first cousins. Throughout the day, businesspeople, politicians, and diplomats thronged the compound, seeking my great-grandmother's favor. When she died, her house was filled with bouquets from the great men of Hollywood and an enormous white cake sent by the Rank Organisation.

Soon after her death, Burma was taken over by a military junta and Burma's economy slowly fell to pieces. My great-grandmother's businesses were dismantled or acquired by the state, and the compound by Inya Lake was broken up and fell into disrepair. Most of my mother's family left Burma. Some went to America, others to Australia and Scandinavia. My mother met my father, an Englishman, in Bangladesh. Her family was trying to arrange visas to emigrate to the United States. My father was a Church of England missionary at the time, in charge of Dacca's Anglican church. They fell in love, married, had me, and moved back to England. All the various branches of my mother's family have survived, some have thrived, but none has forgotten what Daw Ma Ma created for them in Burma and what they lost. Her success as a businesswoman produced a golden age for my family, and I was reminded of it constantly.

People apply to business school for all kinds of reasons, but they usually can be placed into two broad categories: those who know exactly why they're going; and those who just sort of do. In the first category are those from companies with a long tradition of sending employees to business school. These tend to be Wall Street banks, consulting firms, and large corporations where access to upper management requires an MBA. But they also include people who have a specific career change in mind. They want to give up making engine parts and become investment advisers or financiers. They know what they need to learn, and they arrive on campus with a purpose. The second category includes people who know they want a change but don't know what kind. They hope that business school will provide an answer, or at the very least give them some fresh options. They also feel that two years of navel-gazing at business school is more respectable than lobbing paper balls into their wastepaper bin all day hoping against hope that somehow the glacier of their career will crack and send them sliding off on some exciting new adventure. I fell into the second category. I wanted control over my time, my financial resources, and my life, and I imagined that a general competence in business would stand me in better stead than sticking with what I had been doing up to then.

My path to Harvard Business School was circuitous. After returning to England when I was two, my father took over a parish in Northampton, a godless town best known for making shoes. For most of my childhood the conversation in our home revolved around flower-arranging rotas for the church and parish church council meetings. For a while, my parents supplemented my father's derisory stipend by buying and selling cheap houses and renting them out to a rag bag of tenants. There were Ong and Lo, Korean brothers studying butchery; Christine, an attractive young secretary and dope fiend, who also turned out to be a prostitute; Ian, a John Lennon look-alike and inveterate bum who stopped paying rent and defeated my parents when they took him to court; and a series of dubious students from Nene College, the local fourth-rate educational establishment, who appeared to major in petty theft and vandalism.

We also had tenants in the vicarage. There was Mick, a cobbler whose great passion was CB radio. We could hear him in the evenings talking into his microphone: "Iron Duke calling Rubber Duck. Come in, Rubber Duck." And there was Jim, a rather forlorn middle-aged lawyer who kept a stack of pornographic magazines beside his bed. Mick was very good to me. Whenever I asked him to come out into the back garden and dig holes, a peculiar passion when I was five, he would comply, emerging from the house, his hair greased back and a cigarette hanging from his lips, holding a can of Carlsberg Special Brew. Later, after I had been sent away to school, he fell in love and moved out. The last we heard, he had been arrested for breaking into a building site one night and setting fire to a JCB digger.

The larger point of this is that business, aside from Daw Ma Ma's legend, was not a way of life in my family. Rather, it was a necessary evil. It meant the telephone ringing in the evening and my father rising from behind his newspaper, setting down his drink, and, with a heavy sigh, leaving the house to deal with a burst pipe or a police raid on the hooker. It meant the local Indian wheeler-dealers who would come to buy a house with a briefcase full of cash, and the dusty auction rooms where my parents could buy all the furniture they needed for five bedrooms and a kitchen for under fifty quid. At the boarding school I attended as a teenager, I remember looking at the fathers who would come on Sundays to pick up their sons. They sat at the wheels of their BMWs reading the Sunday papers, wearing yellow cashmere V-necks, their cheeks riddled with burst veins. They were my clichéd vision of businessmen: gin-swilling, golf-playing, dull, predictable slaves to money. This prejudice persisted through university, where I was determinedly antivocational, studying classics, Latin and Greek literature, history and philosophy. Shortly before graduation, I tagged along with friends to the recruiting presentations given by the big investment banks and consulting firms. I ate their sandwiches and drank their champagne, but when I listened to the employees describe their work, I knew this was not for me.

One particular business story, however, did capture my attention around this time. It was a biography of the British billionaire Sir James Goldsmith. He had built his fortune over many years in all kinds of ways. As a teenager he incurred large gambling debts, which his father had to pay off. He came to national attention in Britain at the age of twenty when he eloped with the eighteen-year-old daughter of a Bolivian tin magnate. Their escapade was lapped up by the newspapers. When Goldsmith's wife died giving birth to their first child, he turned serious about his work. He was opportunistic, buying and selling pharmaceutical and food companies, frequently risking bankruptcy. His financing was the subject of frequent media investigations. Then, in the 1980s, his moment truly arrived. Using junk bonds, Goldsmith borrowed, bought, and asset-stripped his way to a great fortune. He was the model for Sir Lawrence Wildman, Gordon Gekko's English nemesis in the movie *Wall Street*. Shortly before the markets crashed in October 1987, Goldsmith sold everything he had and retired to the palace he was building for himself on Mexico's Pacific Coast. He appeared on the cover of *Time* magazine above the headline "The Lucky Gambler." Goldsmith's life, as his biographer described it, was a grand adventure, full of risk, daring, and rich human encounters. Nothing like business as I had previously understood it. It got me thinking.

The summer after graduation I spent mooning around my parents' house reading travel books and dreaming of a poet's life on a Greek island: a stone bed, honey and yogurt for breakfast, a few worn tomes on a shelf hewn into the wall, evenings in some harbor-front bar. Only after yet another impatient stare from my father did I finally take a job with a tele-marketing company in London, arranged by my friend William. The work consisted of four of us sitting in a room on Lots Road trying to sell advertising space for a new publication called *The Truck Driver's Hand Book*. We were paid solely on commission, 20 percent of any advertising we sold. William was both naturally good at this and driven to succeed by the financial requirements of a fast-escalating cocaine habit. He would laugh at me as I stared at the telephone.

"Come on, you loser. It's easy. Watch." He would dial an engine parts supplier in Watford, charm the secretary, speak to the owner, and wrap up the call with a confirmed sale. "Go on. Let's see you do it."

I would dial a number as slowly as I could, jabbing wretchedly at the telephone as if it were diseased. The secretary of the firm I was calling would ask me to repeat what I was saying. "Truck Driver's what? No, he's not in. No, he won't be in later. No. Not until next week or the week after. No we don't do advertising anyway." Click. On the tenth day, I made a sale.

In theory, I should have made six hundred pounds for myself. But I celebrated by taking the next two days off and watching a cricket match on television. The owner of the firm, a nasty drunk, withheld the money and sacked me. Business and I were clearly not meant to be.

From this nadir, journalism was an obvious next step. I wrote to the editor of *The Daily Telegraph* and was given a few shifts on the paper's gossip column. I turned out to be good at going to cocktail parties and returning with fifty-word items about how an MP's dog had urinated on a duchess's rose bushes, or a writer had found inspiration for his latest book while sailing with the archbishop of York. This evolved into a ten-year stint on Fleet Street, including six as a foreign correspondent.

My first foreign posting was to New York. I was twenty-five years old and carried all my possessions in a suitcase. Over the next two years, I traveled all over the United States and Latin America—to Terre Haute, Indiana, when Timothy McVeigh was executed; to Florida during the presidential election recounts; to the Arctic to interview Inuit; and to Tijuana to meet policemen and newspapermen who stood up to the local drug cartels. It was exciting and occasionally daring stuff. My telephone would ring well before dawn as my editors in London reached their desks, and I would be dispatched, sore-headed from the night before, to the scene of a plane crash, a dramatic arrest, or a sudden political development. I spent six weeks in Chile after General Pinochet was arrested in London, flew overnight to the Galápagos Islands after an oil tanker went down, interviewed the first female president of Panama over the thrumming of a military helicopter deep in a Central American jungle, and spent a frightening week in a violence-torn Port-au-Prince. But at some point, a poisonous notion entered my brain and began to spread: newspaper journalism was dying. All people spoke about in London were our dwindling readership and the lack of investment by our owners. Those long flights and hours spent in clammy airport departure lounges, breathing the noxious fast food odors, began to feel worthless, and I started looking for a way out.

. . .

One day, I was sent to interview Gustavo Cisneros, a Venezuelan billionaire
and a friend of the then owner of *The Daily Telegraph,* Conrad Black.
Interviewing and writing nice things about Black's friends and potential
friends was part of the job of the New York correspondent. Early in my
posting, I had spent a harrowing day with the television presenter Barbara
Walters, who ten minutes into our interview told me my questions were the
most boring she had ever heard. Later she refused to let the photographer
who accompanied me get within five feet of her, insisting he take his shots
from the other side of the room. Black also sent me to interview Henry
Kissinger in his office on Park Avenue. He growled at me for an hour or so
about geopolitics. Later, I discovered that the tape recording of my interview
skipped every few seconds. In my paranoia, I suspected some magnetic distor-
tion machine in Kissinger's office had done me in. I was missing every fourth
or fifth word Kissinger had said. "The key to peace . . . *click, grumble . . .*
negotiation between the Lebanese . . . *squeal, grunt . . .* Bush needs a strategic . . . *wheeeeeeeeeee."* The piece I wrote was thin on quotes and long on
description and analysis. What the journalism pros call "broad brush."

Cisneros had his offices in a townhouse on the Upper East Side and had
decorated them in accordance with his status as a Latin American pluto-
crat: dark wood paneling, oil paintings of conquistadors on horseback, deep,
comfortable armchairs, and footmen offering perfectly brewed coffee. Cisneros himself was a smallish man. He wore a pale gray suit, white shirt,
and blue, patterned tie. He sat tidily in his chair, using spare hand gestures
to describe an acquisition here, a sell-off there, a sales thrust into new markets somewhere over there. His hair was a slight distraction, boot-polish
black and combed so tightly back over his skull it seemed to be stretching
the creases out of his forehead. His family had made its money in gritty
businesses such as bottling, haulage, and agriculture, but he had expanded
successfully into media and technology. All of that toil and sweat, however,
was occurring thousands of miles from here, on the roads of Latin America

and the production back lots of Miami. Here, Gustavo and I could sit, sip our coffee, and talk big picture—about the impact of globalization, the importance of local brands. If this was business, I could get used to it. As I was escorted out by his secretary, a door in the wood paneling creaked open and I glimpsed a small conference room where a man and a woman, both immaculate and beautiful, were sitting at their laptops and chatting. They looked toward me and smiled and continued their conversation. The secretary said, "Mr. Cisneros only hires Harvard MBAs to work in his private office." I felt I had been given a glimpse of a better world.

Several of my friends had obtained MBAs, mostly from INSEAD, a school just outside Paris, and spoke well of their experience. The few who had been to HBS were dismissive of it. They mocked its self-importance, the earnestness of the students, the very opposite of British insouciance. All, however, said that the MBA had taught them the language of business. For that they were grateful. So, in August 2001, in a gray, windowless cubicle in an office tower close to Penn Station, I took the GMAT, the standardized test in English and math required for graduate business school. I waited a few moments for a computer to spit out my score: 730 out of 800. The average for Harvard was 700. I could do this.

September 11 knocked me off track. Reporting seemed important again. For several weeks, I was pushed to my limits writing and managing a team of other reporters and photographers flown in from London and all jostling to shine on the story. Then one evening, in the middle of it all, I went to a basement dive for drinks with the rest of the British pack in New York. Christmas lights hung all round the room, making everyone's already booze-swollen faces look that much redder. "Sensational story," said one, raising his beer bottle. "Never made so much money off a story in my life." It was the same emotionally indifferent response I heard whenever a big story broke, a political scandal, a celebrity trial, even a terrorist attack killing thousands. The cynicism that once attracted me to journalism was turning me off. Furthermore, the experience of standing beneath the Twin Towers just before their collapse, watching people leap to their deaths, had forced on me the same question it must have forced on millions of others, and it grew louder as the days passed. If everything ended for you right now, would you be happy with the life you have lived? I had never felt the pressure of this question in the same way. For several weeks, I would wake up feeling as if I were being pressed into a corner with a knife at my throat, forced to give an answer. Have you lived the life you should have? Have you done everything you could have? Have you? Have you?

As a reward for my work in New York, I was offered the job of Paris bureau chief. Margret, whom I had met eighteen months earlier, and I were married just before we moved. Marriage and Paris distracted me again from thoughts of upending my career. There was a rambunctious presidential election to report on and all of France to discover, and one year after we were married, our first son, Augustus, was born. But the questions kept nagging at me.

A diplomat at the British embassy in Paris told me that whenever the ambassador invited the local British press over for lunch, he referred to it as feeding time at the trough. At the next embassy lunch, I looked around the table at the hacks who had stayed in Paris long after their staff jobs expired. Each month, they seemed to descend ever farther down the freelance ladder, their clothes deteriorating, their lips stained darker with cheap red wine. There was one who only ever asked one question, but he applied it to any topic: "Ambassador, what does all this mean for Europe?" The ambassador would pull at his cuffs and reply politely across the elaborately set table, but you could feel the ghost of the Duke of Wellington, a former occupant of the residence, cringing at this unseemly rabble. After long evenings of red wine and conversation with friends, I would lie in bed staring at the ceiling, my mind churning with ill-defined fears and desires. I looked up the totem pole at my newspaper and saw middle-aged men complaining about their salaries and the mediocrity of their managers and harking back to their days reporting from the road. I dreaded being called back to work at a desk in London. So I wrote a letter to myself describing my feelings. I wrote that it was exhausting to feel like this, constantly thinking about change. I was thirty-one years old and had one of the most coveted jobs in my profession and yet all I could think of was what would happen next. I was whipsawed between feeling self-indulgent and feeling sensible, worrying that if I let my next career change happen to me rather than making it happen myself, I would deeply regret it. I wrote about Daw Ma Ma and how the memory of what she built magnified my family's sense of loss, wielding a nostalgic grip on us some fifty years later. Business had been her salvation, and business, I felt after avoiding it for so long, might also be mine.

The Harvard Business School website was cluttered with inspiring bait. Theodore Roosevelt's challenge to "Dare Mighty Things" stood out in large crimson letters. Words like *passion* and *leadership* were sprinkled about like punctuation. There were photographs of eager-looking students and bespectacled professors, their hands poised in explanatory poses, exuding wisdom and energy. There on the banks of the Charles River people were daring, leading, imagining, and pursuing. I was drawn to Harvard for two main reasons. The first, I confess, was the name. However famous Harvard is in the United States, it is even more so overseas. It remains, for better or worse, by far the best-known university in America. The second reason was the particular education the business school promised. Even though most business schools teach much the same stuff, the approach and emphasis vary. Among the top schools, Stanford is known as a place for Silicon Valley entrepreneurs. Kellogg, at Northwestern University, is famous for marketing. If your dream is to build or manage a great American brand, Kellogg is the place. Wharton, at the University of Pennsylvania, is for financiers, those with their eyes fixed on Wall Street. Columbia is similarly plugged into all that happens in New York. The Sloan School, at MIT, is for engineers and scientists wanting to turn their ideas into businesses. And Harvard is about general management. It prepares you to manage and lead all the parts of a business without any particular specialization. These descriptions doubtless do all of these schools a disservice, but they are repeated so often that an applicant, forced to choose, can scarcely ignore them.

Over the Christmas holiday of 2003, I wrote application essays for four schools: Harvard, Kellogg, Stanford, and the Haas School at Berkeley. With no sense of what any of them would make of me, I hoped at least one would take me in. I cranked the essays out blind, as honestly as I could. I had no template to work from, no friendly advisers telling me what the admissions offices wanted to hear. The questions were of three kinds: Why do you want to come to business school? Why do you want to come to this business school? And what have you done in your life up to now that makes you think a business education at this school would be worth your time and ours? As an example of my leadership experience, I wrote about running a newspaper bureau on September 11, 2001. To illustrate an ethical quandary, I described the difficulty of staying impartial as a reporter when writing about the victims and supporters of General Pinochet in Chile. My intention in coming to business school, I wrote, was to be able to build and manage my own media company one day, creating and distributing the kind of news and entertainment I could be proud of.

My English referees were baffled by the forms they were required to fill out. "You have to help me with this, Philip," my editor pleaded on the telephone from his home in rural England on Christmas Eve "Where on this scale of one to five am I supposed to rank your leadership qualities?"

The next stage in the process was to be interviewed by alumni. My Harvard alumnus was a Frenchman of formidable girth who had once been the publisher of a business magazine. He hobbled to the door of his apartment on Place Vauban to greet me, his leg in a cast. It was early evening and the spotlights shining on Les Invalides reflected off the ceiling. He had pulled out a chair embossed with the Harvard insignia and the year of his graduation. He invited me to sit on it and then retreated behind his enormous desk.

"So, why Harvard?" His rich voice seemed to emanate from deep beneath layers of gleefully devoured cheese and terrine.

"It's supposed to be the best one, isn't it?"

"I see you read Classics at Oxford. Who was your favorite author?"

"Any of the golden age Latin poets. Virgil, Catullus, Horace."

"What is your favorite work by Virgil?"

"*The Georgics.*"

"Hmm. Most people say *The Aeneid.* I had a man a few years ago who claimed to have gone to the Lycée Louis le Grand here in Paris, the same school I went to. But I spotted that he spelled *le Grand* as one word on his résumé. We all had to learn Latin, so I asked him something about Latin and he couldn't answer. It turned out he was a fraud. So I like to check these things."

He asked me one more question about why I wanted to move on from journalism, and we then spent a pleasant half hour talking about the teaching of classics in English schools and his affection for English books about the French. He must have given a favorable account of me because in April I received an e-mail from Harvard offering me a place.

It was a warm spring day and I took our dog, Scarlett, out for a walk around Les Invalides. We passed the usual gaggle of lost tourists looking for the entrance to Napoleon's tomb, and the restaurants where waiters were unwinding their awnings. I asked myself why it was that all this beauty, this civilization was not enough. Why did I feel the need to toss everything in the air again and start afresh?

Soon after I was accepted, I received a book called *The HBS Survival Guide, Class of 2006*, compiled by the student association. One lunchtime, I found a bench in the Tuileries and cracked it open. "Welcome to the Harvard Business School," it read, "to a rich and diverse community made up of impressive people challenging themselves and each other . . . and to some of the best years of your life!" There followed a list of the book's corporate sponsors. They included five management consulting firms, the Gillette Company, and Wachovia Securities, a bank based in North Carolina. In a chapter called "What to Bring," two students had written: "Don't bring that guitar or piano you were planning on picking up again. Do bring those skis and golf clubs that you will pick up again . . . Don't bring the deal toy you received after 'leading' that hot tech IPO in 1999. Do bring the offer letter you secured after actually leading that dull bond offering in 2003 . . . Don't bring any books from literature or history classes you took in college. I get it. You're smarter than me. You don't need to quote Keats every time I see you in the Aldrich bathroom . . . Don't bring 'I'll never.' Do bring 'I'll try.' Don't bring your cynicism. Do bring all the diverse rest of you. We can't wait to share the experience."

Who were these people? And why did they talk like this? Why can't I bring my cynicism? Or my books? Aren't they part of the "diverse rest of me"? And what in God's name is a deal toy? On another page titled "What to Expect and How to Prepare," I read, "Your calendar will be jam-packed with amazing, fun things to do, and not enough hours in the day to do them all. It will be as if someone dropped you into a Disneyland for future CEOs . . . You can put networking on the bottom of your to-do list, and you'll still end up with a stellar network of friends. That's the real power behind the famous HBS network—international, multi-industry friendships that last." The associate director of MBA Support Services had contributed a long piece that included a two-by-two table describing the physical, emotional, cognitive, and behavioral signals of stress. These ranged from sweaty palms and nausea to crying a lot and wanting to throw things or hit people.

On almost every page was a grainy black-and-white photograph of students with their arms slung around one another, on mountaintops, in bars, in tuxedos, clutching surfboards, or just sitting in a dorm room. A chapter called "Nightlife in Boston" showed two students drinking from a single outsize cocktail. It read, "When you look back at your HBS experience 20 years from now, you won't remember TOM or Finance, but you will remember dancing drunk with friends on that table in Pravda with a bottle of Vodka in each hand!" The HBS archetype was now forming in my head as a wide-eyed, stress-addled philistine with a drinking problem and a future in management consulting.

This was at odds with what I read of Harvard's newly created Leadership and Values Initiative. It had taken me the previous two and a half years to familiarize myself with the peculiar locutions of *Le Monde*. Suddenly, here was another, even stranger language. The Leadership and Values Initiative, I read, would "challenge students to access their moral compass and to apply rigorous ethical standards to their business and leadership decisions such that this process becomes instinctual." Professor Lynn Paine was quoted as saying the school needed to "develop a comprehensive approach to 'leadership and values' that goes beyond the often punitive legal compliance stance" and "foster '[integrity] strategies that can help prevent damaging ethical lapses while tapping into powerful human impulses for moral thought and action.'" It took me several readings to unravel all this. Integrity strategies? Access my moral compass? Did this mean they were going to teach me how not to be a crook? And what if this process of not behaving like a crook was not yet instinctual? What if I had no moral compass to access? Or if it began malfunctioning after two bottles of vodka in Pravda? Was Lynn Paine the problem or the solution?

On our last night in Paris, Margret and I went for dinner at Maceo, a restaurant just behind the Palais Royal. We toasted each other with champagne, shared a bottle of white wine, and ate grilled snapper and chilled tomato soup. Cigarette smoke drifted across the tables along with the sound of people clattering out of the theater and into the streets around us. The reality of returning to America struck us with full force. Like most foreigners who live in France, we had had a mixed experience. But tonight, Paris was as old-fashioned and romantic as the poets and songwriters had promised. We asked each other what we had learned from living there.

"Patience," I told her. There was absolutely no point trying to hurry a Frenchman. The revolutionary spirit lives on and they do what they want in their own time. If it's *pas possible,* only charm, never muscle, can win the day.

"I've learned what I need to be happy," said Margret, by which she meant not material things, but friends, a support network, some kind of professional fulfillment.

"I realized how much I love my own culture," I said. Learning about France by living there had given me only so much satisfaction. I missed the Anglo-American media, the newspapers, television, and films, the burbling radio programs, the sense of humor I always took for granted, the banal obsession with sport. Despite our gripes, Paris had been wonderful to us. We had arrived in February 2002 after our wedding and honeymoon. It was one of those gray, drizzly days we would get to know well. The cobbles round the Place Wagram glistened as we drove in from the airport. Thin, smoking men and women walked briskly to work. From the *Telegraph*'s office on the rue de Rivoli, we stared in dumb fascination as two of the city's gardeners trimmed the trees in the Tuileries to an even height so that in spring they would bloom to form a canopy as flat and green as a Ping-Pong table.

We saw three of those wonderful Paris springs. I had immersed myself in the local politics and interviewed a series of French actresses, each one wearing a tighter sweater than the last. In my final months, I had been blacklisted by the French foreign ministry for asking impertinent questions of the imperious foreign minister, Dominique de Villepin. We had taken the train from Paris to Milan to see *Rigoletto* at La Scala, and eaten the greatest lunch of our lives at Le Grand Véfour, a restaurant founded before the Revolution and tucked into a corner of the Palais Royal. A few weeks before our departure, I had sat beside President Chirac's chief diplomatic adviser at the state dinner for the Queen at the Elysée Palace and drunk wines from great vineyards while discussing France's place in the world. I had a great job. But as I stared into the future, I knew I needed a change. I needed to go back to school and study accounting.

Chapter Three

A PLACE
APART

The Harvard Business School of 2004, when I arrived to begin my MBA, was a very different place from the scrappy little outfit founded in 1908. Just fifty-nine graduate students enrolled for that first year of an as-yet-unproven curriculum regarded with suspicion by most of the university. Other universities taught business to undergraduates at the time, but Harvard was the first to try a graduate course. The rationale for the new school was articulated by the president of Harvard, Charles W. Eliot, in a speech to the Harvard Club of Connecticut on February 21, 1908. "Business in the upper walks has become a highly intellectual calling, requiring knowledge of languages, economics, industrial organization and commercial law and wide reading concerning the resources and habits of the different nations. In all these directions we propose to give professional instruction." The goal of the school was to educate not only future businessmen but also senior diplomats and government officials, who increasingly needed knowledge of business and organizations to do their work.

In its early years, the school struggled to define its purpose and place at Harvard and within the broader business class. In June 1909, Edwin Gay, the first dean of the school, wrote to a friend:

I am constantly being told by business men that we cannot teach "business." I heartily agree with them; we do not try to teach business in the sense in which business men ordinarily understand their routine methods, or in the sense in which you speak of teaching young men to be "money makers" or "to get the better of their competitors." We believe that there is science in business and it is the task of studying and developing that science in which we are primarily interested. It is our aim to give our young business men the breadth of horizon, as well as the equipment of information and grasp of principles which will enable them . . . to be better citizens and men of culture as well as broader men of business.

Gay resolved to adopt the case teaching method from the law school. Rather than hearing lectures, students would learn business by analyzing real situations and discussing them in class. From this, they would derive general principles applicable throughout their careers. The method was known as "learning by doing," and it has persisted to this day. When the first designs for the school were commissioned, Gay's successor, Wallace Donham, said he wanted the business school's architecture to support a "life of plain living and high thinking in surroundings of quiet good taste." He emphasized that it was important for the buildings to help students socialize and become "something more than money-makers." It was one of the great money-makers of his time, however, who put up the money for these buildings. George F. Baker, the president of the First National Bank, had been a towering figure on Wall Street for sixty years by the time the business school's fund-raisers came knocking. Along with J. P. Morgan, he had financed the Gilded Age boom of the late nineteenth century and acted as the de facto U.S. Treasury at a time when Washington's financial expertise was negligible. He was also famously taciturn, hence his nickname The Sphinx. Baker once said, "[B]usiness men of America should reduce their talk two-thirds . . . There is rarely ever a reason good enough for anybody to talk." This barrel of laughs hemmed and hawed about Harvard's request for $1 million of the $5 million needed to build the business school before offering the entire $5 million, if he could have "the privilege of building the whole school." In 1925, in a rare torrent of words, he told a gathering of the Harvard Business School Club that he hoped the school would "graduate some of the greatest men in the world" and "teach them so to conduct themselves as to gain the respect of their fellows and also to keep up their standards of integrity, for thereby they may gain for themselves the greatest happiness that life can bestow."

The first dormitories at the school were named after former U.S. Treasury secretaries Mellon, Dillon, and Gallatin, while the faculty and administration were housed in Morgan, named after J.P. The majestic heart of the campus was Baker Library, with its soaring silent reading room. By 2004, Baker's original campus had expanded to cover over forty-four lavishly appointed acres. The endowment of the business school was edging toward $2 billion. Aside from the nine hundred MBA students enrolled each year, hundreds more businesspeople were cycled through the executive education program. Harvard Business School Publishing was a $100-million-a-year business all by itself. The school employed two hundred faculty members and maintained research offices in Hong Kong, Paris, Tokyo, Mumbai, and Buenos Aires. Graduate business schools had sprouted at universities across the world, churning out tens of thousands of MBAs each year. But year after year, Harvard Business School sat atop or close to the top of the media's business school rankings. It was a behemoth, a global brand. The HBS MBA, I heard it said, was the "union card of the global financial elite."

HBS sits on the opposite bank of the Charles River from the rest of Harvard. Surrounding it is the Boston suburb of Allston, which consists largely of collision repair shops, freeways, and decaying housing stock. It is a brisk ten-minute walk to the charming chaos of Harvard Square, the center of the university, but the psychological gulf is wider. HBS refers to the larger university as "across the river," as in "across the river, they wear tweed jackets, read Marx, and haven't a clue about how the world really works. Here at HBS we know better." In Harvard Square—really more of a pedestrian-choked triangle—you find the usual college town throng of students in khaki shorts and flip-flops, bums, crazies, and panhandlers with Ph.D.s. In one corner of the square you can pay two dollars to play chess with a taciturn Ukrainian. In another you can buy coffee in the same store frequented by John F. Kennedy when he was an undergraduate. The lamp-posts are encrusted with flyers inviting you to watch a play, buy a bike, or donate sperm at the local hospital. There is a newsstand in the middle of the square where you can buy newspapers and magazines from around the world, or join the desultory group of antiwar protesters who seem to have taken up permanent residence there. The streets are lined with bookstores and secondhand record shops, burger and pizza joints, and of course a place to buy Tibetan artifacts and yoga mats.

In the square you might see a visiting president, a rock star, a religious guru, an old friend, or maybe just a creepy Iggy Pop look-alike wearing nothing but cycling shorts and asking for train fare home. In the morning, students run through the square on their way to class, and at night they crowd the ethnic restaurants, spilling out onto alleys, stairways, and ter-races. In the summer, high-school kids and adults on extension courses take over, excited to be at Harvard. In the fall, rowers ply the Charles River readying for the regatta in October, the trees turn the color of the Georgian brick, and the turquoise cupolas on the oldest buildings stand out crisply against the pale New England sky.

Cross the river to the business school and you leave all this behind. The winding flower-lined paths and stately buildings exude a gilded, country-club inertia. When you look through the windows it is a surprise to see young people staring into laptops rather than butlers polishing silver or caddies repairing golf clubs. It feels like a place to contemplate the grand and universal, the clouds scudding across the sky, and the swirling flight of birds. Anything but the pros and cons of activity-based cost accounting. The students are trim and well turned out. All have neat haircuts. The ivy climbing the walls looks as though it has been combed into place. Every blade of grass, every flower and hedge has been tended to, and sprinklers sputter on and off to a regular rhythm.

A friend who had visited Baghdad's Green Zone said that Harvard Business School felt eerily familiar. Whatever hell befell the rest of Iraq, the Green Zone was made luxurious with palm trees, swimming pools, and functioning electricity. Its occupants cocooned themselves from the unfolding horror so that they could focus on the broader mission of rebuilding a country. So, too, HBS smacks of an ivory tower, cut off from the world outside.

The first building you pass as you enter the campus from North Harvard Street is Shad, a hulking brick gymnasium, off-limits to the rest of the university. It is probably best kept that way, as Shad really has no place at a graduate school. It should instead be part of the U.S. Olympic Federation's elite training facility. It houses immaculately maintained basketball, racquetball, and squash courts, saunas, steam rooms, and an indoor running track. The weight-training machines are constantly maintained to keep up with the extreme demands of the student body. Visiting executives stop by just to gawk. The four tennis courts beside the gym are occupied from the moment the long Boston winter relents until it returns.

Beyond the gym lies the heart of the campus, Spangler Hall, completed in 2001 and named after Dick Spangler, class of 1956, who was chairman of the Bank of North Carolina and later president of the University of North Carolina. It contains the school cafeteria, a bar, a sprawling student common area, meeting rooms, an auditorium, a post office, and a general store. The doors swing open at the merest touch, a hint of the luxury to come. The soaring celery-colored walls are hung with monumental pieces of contemporary art, donated by a Canadian investor, Gerald Schwartz, class of 1970. In winter, the gas fireplaces are lit early each morning so that students can loll on the chocolate brown leather sofas and toast their feet while tinkering with their financial projections.

The cafeteria is divided into seven separate stations where chefs in white toques offer everything from made-to-order sandwiches to stir-fries, sushi, pasta, and international specials that change daily. One day it is Scandinavian salmon, the next, a Moroccan tagine, the next, sausage and sauerkraut—a perfectly globalized menu. A spindly little man with a jockey's bowlegged gait operates the espresso machine and prepares infusions of Oriental teas.

Spangler was like no student facility I had ever seen. It felt more like a Four Seasons resort. You half expected to see a tennis coach wandering through, flirting with his pupil, or a bellboy hustling past with a trolley full of luggage. A couple of weeks into the course, I was chatting with a German classmate, Max Verlander. On the surface, he was a rather dour engineer from Frankfurt with a pudding bowl haircut. But beneath lay a devilish streak. We were standing outside the cafeteria looking into the common room, where students lay stretched out on the sofas tapping languidly at their laptops and talking into their cell phones, so certain of their place in the world. Max looked into the room and said, "It's decadent, isn't it?"

Chapter Four

RIDING
THE BOOZE
LUGE

I spent the first weekend of the RC with Margret and Augie. The summer heat was finally abating and we attacked a knot of trees in our small backyard, chopping and disentangling them until they were less of an ugly clump. After living all our adult lives in apartments in cities, it was novel for us to be in a two-family house with a backyard and our very own garage. Even though we knew we had only two years here in Cambridge, the start of business school felt like the start of a steadier time in our lives. I had exchanged the rootlessness of being a foreign correspondent, the frequent, unpredictable travel, for a regular schedule. For the first time since we had been married, we could plan our weekends knowing that I would be around.

After our first section meeting, on Friday, we had had to pick up the rest of our case studies for the semester. These came in four large white plastic bags. All across campus, students staggered home, grimacing under the weight—roughly that of a large load of supermarket shopping. As I tottered along toward the bus stop, Stephen, a friend from Analytics, stopped me to ask me to join his study group. In Analytics, we had been assigned study groups, but now we were on our own. HBS strongly encouraged the formation of study groups, four or five students who would meet for an hour before class each day to discuss the upcoming cases. The study group would allow us to clarify the ideas that had come up as we prepared the cases alone and to warm up our brains each morning. Before coming to HBS, Stephen had worked for the State Department, specializing in Far East Asia. He had worked on trade issues, helping out businesspeople, and eventually he concluded that it might be more interesting, and more lucrative, to go into business himself than to remain a diplomat. I had sat opposite him in Analytics and had watched him closely. He rarely took notes and often spent the classes staring into space with a broad grin on his face. When I asked him how he remembered everything we discussed, he tapped his head: "It's up here. I find it easier just to concentrate on what is being said than to take notes." He had an easy confidence about him, so when he approached me to say he had three others lined up for a study group and would I like to be the fifth, I said yes.

"Who are the others?" I asked.

"The classic HBS lineup. A banker, a consultant, and a consultant turned venture capitalist. And then there's you and me to lower the tone."

We arranged to meet for the first time on Monday morning at 7:30. In order to get to campus on time, I set my alarm for six so I would have time to walk the dog, shower, help with Augie's breakfast, and catch the 6:50 bus to Harvard Square. I reviewed my cases as the bus rattled along the Cambridge streets, glancing over the passages I had highlighted, mentally noting the questions that remained. Waiting on a sofa in the basement of Spangler Hall was Alan, a Princeton-educated Indian with a background in astrophysics and venture capital. Alongside him was his roommate, Ollie, a Chinese American who had rarely seen daylight during his past two years as an analyst on Wall Street. He was sipping green tea from a large Styrofoam cup. After a couple of minutes, Stephen arrived with Michael, a reserved Sean Penn look-alike who had worked for a Hollywood studio and was counting down the days until he could return to Los Angeles.

"Shall we start with marketing?" Stephen said.

The first case was about Black and Decker. The company's power tools division was in decline. Some blamed the firm's decision to start making toasters and kettles as well as drills for diminishing the brand. Others saw the main threat as low-cost competitors from Japan. Either way, the company was now considering beefing up its image with professional workmen by launching DeWalt, a line of bright yellow power tools.

"I think this DeWalt idea sucks," Stephen began. "When you've got the Japanese pounding you on cost and quality, why would you look to yellow tools to save you? It doesn't make any sense."

"I agree," Ollie said. "The first thing I'd do is get out of toasters. They're low margin and they're hurting the brand. I once spent time working on a construction site and the workers used to make fun of each other's tools. They don't want to go to work and have people say things like 'Hey, you bring your wife's tools?' You'd think they'd just pick the tools which work best, but they're actually really image conscious."

"Look at this," Alan said, pointing to the case. "Black and Decker is the seventh ranked brand in the United States. You have to use that. It doesn't make sense to have that kind of brand-strength and then start a separate brand to get away from it."

"But we're still not explaining how they can improve their share in the tradesmen and industrial segments," Stephen said. "If you look at page four, Black and Decker has forty-five percent of the consumer segment but just twenty percent in the industrial tools segment and nine percent in the tradesmen segment. And those two segments are each worth around the same as the consumer segment. When you look at the consumer survey, it says that the users in these segments much prefer the Japanese brands. I can see Black and Decker worrying that those feelings will apply to all their products soon."

"So which option are we going for?" I asked. "Do we just stick with what we're doing and try to improve margins? Create the Black and Decker sub-brand? Or go with this new DeWalt line?"

"I say we go with the sub-brand," Alan said. "We can try it out, use our brand recognition and focus on service and design."

"Sounds good," Stephen said. "What about accounting?" In the next case, the owners and players of a baseball club could not agree about the club's accounting methods. "I couldn't figure out this depreciation thing. Did anyone get a number?"

"Yeah, I calculated that management were overdepreciating the team by five million a year," Alan said.

"I got seven point two million," Michael said. And for the next ten minutes we argued about it.

As we arrived in our section classroom, everyone seemed to feel the moment. We were at the beginning of nine months with these people. A couple of them had come fresh from college and must have looked at Bob and me as weathered veterans of life. There were midwesterners in baggy gray sweatshirts, nattily dressed Asians, Wall Street women in designer shoes and expensive jeans, and the consultants in their chinos and white T-shirts under blue shirts, clicking their pencils and lining up their financial calculators, ready to work. This was the real start of the "transformational experience" HBS promised, the first step on a well-worn path to worldly success.

Our marketing professor was Tom Steenburgh, a barrel-chested man with close-cropped brown hair. He looked like the kind of solidly built salesman I used to see in rental car offices when I traveled around the United States. All he was missing was a bag of golf clubs and an oversized Burberry raincoat. He showed us a video of Black and Decker's come-to-Jesus presentation of the plan to launch DeWalt. Steenburgh told us that people believe anything in sales meetings. The challenge is to be skeptical once you've left. As we considered Black and Decker's difficulty in fending off cheaper, higher-quality Japanese tools, Bob raised his hand. He recommended that the company sell its tools as Made in America, playing on their buyers' patriotism. A former political strategist across the room interrupted to say "going nativist" was neither very appealing nor sustainable if the Japanese tools remained both better and cheaper. His comments, often accompanied by his throwing down his pen in exasperation, quickly became a highlight of the class discussions. Steenburgh emphasized that the answer to resolving Black and Decker's challenge would be found by focusing on what the customer wanted rather than on what the company could offer. The customer, he said, should be the center of any company's universe. "A good product," he said, "doesn't always get you there." You needed marketing, sales, and customer service to sell it.

Financial Reporting and Control (FRC) came next. Accounting did not convey the course's scope. That was merely the financial reporting part, record-keeping to calculate profits and limit tax liabilities. Control was the use of internally gathered data to improve company performance. It was about using accounts to measure efficiency and make company-wide decisions. Eddie Riedl, our professor, was a live-wire accountant from New York who spoke quickly and strutted round the classroom with one hand tucked into his tight gray pants, the other gesticulating with a piece of yellow chalk. After the very briefest introduction, he looked one way and then pointed to me, like a basketball player tossing a no-look pass. First accounting class, first cold call. I could scarcely believe it. I stared down at the six-by-four-inch card on which I had written my notes. Eddie moved to the blackboard, chalk poised, waiting for me to speak.

"So this is a case about a baseball club, the Kansas City Zephyrs, in which the owners and players cannot agree about how profitable the club is," I began. Looking around the classroom, I could see looks of curiosity mixed with sympathy.

"Very good, carry on," Riedl said, drawing up two columns, one marked "Owners," the other marked "Players."

"The players think that the owners are using accounting tricks to reduce their profits and then using these numbers to justify not paying the players more."

"I didn't realize you could play tricks with accounting," Riedl said. "I thought accounting was an accurate reflection of what went on in a company."

There was a ripple of laughter.

"It's a question of perception, I guess," I said. "If you take a look at the way the value of players is depreciated under the tax laws, it doesn't seem to make much sense."

"Great, let's take a look at this depreciation rule."

"So it seems that when you buy a team, you can capitalize the value of your players."

"And what does it mean to capitalize something?"

"I think it means you treat it as an asset, which appears on your balance sheet, rather than an expense, which appears only on your income statement."

"Okay. And what then?"

"So if you buy a team for a hundred million and capitalize the value of players at, say fifty million, you can then charge a depreciation expense over six years."

"And how is that expense different from the salaries you pay your players?"

"It means you're incurring a double expense. There's the depreciation expense, which doesn't make any sense anyway, because, say the team you bought was stacked with talented young players, they're probably going to go up in value over six years as they gain experience, not down. And then there's the annual salary expense as well. The players argue that the only real expense is salary and that the owners are abusing the depreciation allowance to minimize their profits so they can justify lower salaries."

"Philip here clearly sympathizes with the baseball players. Anyone disagree?"

Several hands went up, and I was off the hook. Bob scribbled a note to me. It read, "Well done." It was a relief to have it over, and even more of a relief that Riedl had not pressed me for numbers. I had slaved over the case for three hours the night before and come up short. My calculations, even after the study group, were an incoherent scribble.

Toward the end of the class, Riedl asked us to answer a poll using the red and green buttons embedded in our desks. "If you think accounting is generally useful, press red. If you think it is generally useless, press green." Useful won by a slender margin. Each side then had to make its case. The useful camp said accounting created consistent standards across different companies and businesses and allowed one to compare their performances. It also helped in managing a company to know how money flowed through it and how efficiently it was being used.

The useless camp said accounting was merely the art of manipulating numbers to fit whatever goal you had in mind. It was confusing and deceptive, and described events long after they had happened. There were far more effective ways of examining a company's health and performance than trying to decipher its accounts.

Accounting, Riedl explained, told the story of a company through numbers. But there was book accounting, which management used to manage its internal processes, and tax accounting, which was the preserve of tax specialists focused on exploiting the tax code to reduce tax liabilities. In the case of the Kansas City Zephyrs, the book and tax accounting were blurred, creating this mistrust between the players and owners. The purpose of FRC was not to make accountants of us but to help us look at accounts in a critical way, to search constantly for truth and to sniff out evidence of error or bias.

"There are two mantras in accounting, which we will come back to again and again during this course," said Riedl. He wrote them up and asked us to memorize them. The first was the foundation of accounting:

$$\text{Assets} = \text{Liabilities} + \text{Equity}.$$

The second mantra was:

$$\text{Accounting} = \text{Economic truth} + \text{Measurement error} + \text{Bias}.$$

During this course, Riedl promised, we would spend our time pursuing economic truth and discovering the reasons why it could be so hard to find.

We would see inventory fiddles, the premature booking of unearned income, the accounting benefits of leasing versus owning.

I had imagined accounting would be much drier than it was turning out to be.

Lunch followed in our classroom. Carl Kester, the chair of the MBA course, came in to talk to us about community standards, or rather the house rules. It was the fourth or fifth time we had had these stressed to us. Basically, they told us to be respectful of one another and not to cheat. One of the standards, "no cheering guests," prompted someone to ask why. Kester, a large blond man with the quiet manner of a midwestern loan officer, told us that at some point in the mid-nineties, cheering in class got out of hand. It was perfectly normal for visitors to class, friends or families of students, to receive a welcome round of applause. But it had gotten to the point where sections would coordinate special cheers, waves, and dance routines. One section even had people back-flipping down the rows in class. Faculty hated it, half the students hated it, and the guests hated it. Most of Kester's talk, though, was a warning against forming virtual, online study groups that would be considered a kind of cheating. The school felt that the educational experience of HBS would be undermined if large groups of students traded notes online. Instead of thinking through problems themselves and working with study groups and the section to grapple with the messy problems presented in the cases, students would develop cheat sheets and formulaic answers. Virtual study groups would jeopardize the entire process of repeated decision-making, discussing, and dealing with uncertainty that we were there to learn. It was the human interaction that made HBS so unique and the administration's relentless focus on this process that gave the education its heft.

Over breakfast one day, Ben, the New York City Parks official who had been my neighbor during Analytics, asked me what I thought of the school's mission statement, "to educate leaders who make a difference in the world."

"It seems a bit vague," I told him. "Perhaps it could use the word *business*. And I don't really like the phrase 'make a difference.' It supposes the person making the difference knows better, which isn't always the case. There is a thin line between making a difference and just imposing your will."

"I wonder why the school can't just admit that its job is teaching people how to run profitable businesses?" Ben said. He was quite cross. "Why does it even think that leadership is best taught through courses on business? I mean, if it is really leadership they want to teach, why don't they have us taking history or religion courses or spending the weekends with the Marine Corps?"

LEAD was the course in which some of this would be unraveled. It dealt with the role of human behavior in business. It was about understanding people's motives and psychological needs as well as one's own role in a company and the way to get ahead. The business big shots who came to the school to speak always said this was the most vital stuff we would study, and yet students always held it in the lowest regard. Jeff Immelt, the CEO of General Electric, said in a speech on campus, "I hated organizational behavior at business school. But OB just turns out to be the most important class you can take here. Because the ability to attract people, to pay them the right way, to create culture and values and reinforce them, that's what makes companies great." Yet the perception was that the course was soft, touchy-feely, unteachable. Misty, a former soldier, huffed before the first class that she had learned all she needed to know about leadership from the military.

This general suspicion about LEAD was reinforced by our professor, Joel Podolny, who wore a salt-and-pepper beard and spoke in the whispering, confidential tones of a late-night DJ. The course began with an analysis of Erik Peterson, a recent MBA graduate who had gone on to run a small cell-phone operation based in Hanover, New Hampshire. He had wanted to be a general manager and was thrilled to have the opportunity so early in his career.

But from the moment Peterson arrived at work, he realized he was in deep trouble. He was working like a dog, had no idea who was reporting to whom, and had to deal with an idle, duplicitous subcontractor and an impatient ownership team in Los Angeles. His chief engineer was lazy and a misogynist. The staff were envious of each other's salaries. There were zoning problems and a nitpicking supervisor to deal with. When the president of the company visited, Peterson screwed up, meeting him in a noisy restaurant and letting him roam around the company offices to discover the lousy situation for himself. By the end of the day, Peterson "felt stunned and humiliated." Peterson was a classic malfunctioning MBA and a warning that MBAs could be losers, too.

For some in the section, the discussion of Erik Peterson's problems seemed like a liberation from the tyranny of numbers. Real problems at last! Others recoiled into their seats at the frivolity of the subject matter. Had we really come to business school for low-brow personal development sessions? Podolny sketched out our discussion on the blackboard, creating a spider's web of circles and linking arrows. Did Erik Peterson create his own lack of empowerment? How can one be both a leader and a manager, both inspiring and structured? What could Peterson have done differently? Should he have deluged upper management with information in order to cover his back? Should he have clarified his own powers before accepting the job so he could have taken more drastic action against those who sought to undermine him? What were the critical "choice points"? When everything started to turn sour, should he have turned to his bosses and "opened the kimono"?

LEAD prompted two basic questions: the first was whether leadership could be taught, and the second, whether business was a proper medium through which to teach it. These were questions that applied not just to Podolny's course but to HBS more broadly, given its mission. Some, like Misty, never seemed to get over the idea that a man with a beard and fifteen advanced degrees, who had spent no time leading a tank division, was trying to teach us leadership. Others, like me, found the idea of treating human behavior as a process to be managed, like cash flow or machine operations, flat out disturbing. But I realized that my initial reaction to the course was like that of an earlier generation's toward the idea of seeing a shrink. What do you need all that for? Can't you just talk it out with friends? Sort it out for yourself? Take a long walk and think about it? As the course wore on, I became more open to the idea that while the mysterious qualities of a Napoleon or an Alexander the Great could never be taught, there was still plenty one could learn about managing and motivating others.

LEAD allowed us to take an anthropological approach to companies. Instead of focusing on numbers and financing, we examined the causes and effects of those curious behaviors that occur in business settings. In one case we studied the importance of psychological contracts between employees and employers. On the one hand there are formal contracts, which detail hours, salary, and job requirements. But just as important are the psychological contracts, the unwritten understandings that employees often regard as rights, a set of expectations about one's status and treatment. Companies that underestimate the importance of these often find themselves in deep trouble. We studied a plating company that rewarded its high-productivity employees with extra time off and turned a blind eye to their intimidating and casually racist behavior. This allowed the company to keep wages lower and secure the loyalty of workers who might otherwise have left. Rather than trying to apply some noble set of principles, the manager had looked at what he was trying to achieve, the context in which he was working, and let develop a culture and a way of doing things that worked. But it was a short-term solution. He had let in a slow-working disease which would eventually hurt the company's reputation and ability to function.

Stuart, a chiseled former Wall Street trader sitting in the back row, said that the case reminded him of the investment bankers he knew who earned hundreds of thousands of dollars a year but fussed over whether or not they received a free dinner and a cab ride home if they worked past 9:00 P.M. People who could well afford the meal and the cab would hover around to get the perk, simply to feel they were getting everything the firm owed them. And those who didn't take the perk, or who didn't like eating after nine or didn't need to get a cab home, felt they were losing out. To resolve the issue, his firm tried giving everyone a flat sum of money to use however they liked. Then, of course, those who lived a long way from the office or who had enjoyed wolfing down an enormous Chinese takeout at 11:00 P.M. said they were now losing out. After countless adjustments, Stuart said, the firm still had not figured out a way of keeping everyone psychologically satisfied.

The fourth of the five courses we would be taking this first semester was Technology and Operations Management, taught by a young woman professor from Turkey. Zeynep Ton had recently graduated from the HBS doctoral program and was an improbably chic and energetic guide to the world of factory design, manufacturing schedules, supply chains, and process management. Our first case was about Benihana, the Japanese-inspired restaurant chain. We saw how its founder had deconstructed the mechanics of restaurants to create something unique and highly profitable. By having chefs prepare food at the tables, he could cut back on kitchen space. Customers were rotated in and out of the restaurant at speed. A limited menu meant far less waste. And all of this was packaged and offered up as entertainment, with chefs spinning their knives as they sliced up vegetables and meat and cooked them right in front of the diners. It gave one a strange feeling of power to be able to peel back a business as elemental as a restaurant and see where in the process of serving food one could make and lose money. Later in the semester, I learned a term for that delusional sense of authority, the sense that after a few TOM classes I could reengineer the operations of any business put before me. It was called Beginnihana.

. . .

In no time, I was swamped by the work. As much as I enjoyed the class discussions, there was barely time to get everything done. Any case involving numbers seemed to take me twice the suggested two hours, as I toiled away with pencil and paper, loath to fire up Excel. Several professors told us that the flood of learning was like "drinking from a fire hose." And then there was FOMO, fear of missing out. The trick to HBS, the administration kept telling us, was not succumbing to FOMO. You had to choose exactly what you wanted to do and do it without fretting about what else was going on. I quelled my own FOMO by going to the library each day and reading the newspapers, trying to get my head as far away from the bubble as possible. But FOMO was a persistent stalker on campus, sowing poison in every mind.

To celebrate the end of the first week, my section hosted a party. Everyone was invited to dress up as hip-hop stars, and we poured into a small on-campus apartment sporting fake jewelry, velour leisure suits, baseball caps skewed off to the side, and pimp hats and canes. The centerpiece of the party was a booze luge, a large block of ice with a narrow channel cut through it. You had to stand at the bottom while vodka was poured into the channel and wait for it to come slithering down into your mouth. The music was absolutely deafening, precluding the need for anything approaching a conversation. All we could do was smile awkwardly in the half-light and cheer on whichever sucker had his lips frozen to the luge. "Greg!" we cheered. "You are the *man*! The *man*! Go Greg! Suck it down baby! *Drink, drink, drink*!" On Monday morning, a very befuddled Scottish doctor who sat in front of me told me the whole scene reminded him "of that movie *American Pie*."

Riedl liked to start his classes with an anecdote about his three-year-old daughter. "I got a call this morning from my wife, at seven thirty. I was in the office. 'Good news and bad news,' she says. 'Good news, your daughter said *Dada* this morning. Bad news, she was looking at a can of prunes.'" Despite his best efforts to keep us amused, I dreaded the work for his class. It required hours of head scratching, and Margret became used to the sound of me screaming and hurling my FRC cases against the wall.

In LEAD, we continued to break down human dynamics into groupings and flow charts. At times it seemed like an academic discipline in search of a subject rather than the other way round. We studied a woman called Taran Swan, who had set up Nickelodeon Latin America. She was team-focused, supportive, a great leader. But the case closed with her pregnant and ordered to take bed rest. A Brazilian movieplex manager, who sat in the front row, said of course she should rest. She was a pregnant woman. What was she even thinking trying to cling onto her job? Everyone laughed at his machismo. Then Misty raised her hand. "I mean what's bed rest, right? Is it like when you stay in bed asleep? Or are you, like, actually working from bed? Because sometimes I, like, do my cases in bed. But not all the time, you know. But she could work from bed, make telephone calls and stuff." She seemed oblivious to the eye-rolling all around her. The case concluded with Swan returning to her home in New York and reportedly working sixty-five-hour weeks—from bed.

In another LEAD class, a young American who used to work in freight shipping in the Florida Panhandle was asked to play a factory manager in a simulation negotiation with one of his workers. He hammered away at the worker and threatened his health benefits to get his way. A Frenchman who used to market gin and only ever wore black pointed out to me afterward that a negotiation like that would have prompted a strike in France. Our classmate, on the other hand, was cheered.

Halfway through the second week, three second-years burst into our classroom after our final class of the day and handed out a copy of a letter they said had been sent to our section chair. The letter purported to be from someone in the section complaining that everyone was drinking too much and thus not fully prepared for class. The second-years initiated a discussion and invited contributions from the class. But after a few nervous comments, the doors to the classroom flew open and the whole of last year's Section A, "Old A," came rushing in. It was a prank. They presented a slide show, pulling information from our class cards to make fun of us. They compared a former advertising executive with crazy curly hair to an evil genius, a former World Banker to Glenn Close in *Fatal Attraction*, and mocked a dashing West African financier for his interests in tribal dance and handicrafts. They then played recordings of spoof telephone calls to three people in our section, two to men who were lured into sexually tinged conversations and one to a woman, in which someone pretended to be an angry Indian food delivery man. Everyone seemed to be having a hoot. The head of Old A told us we needed to "fuckin' lighten up our shit." After a month of pious lecturing, the suddenly sophomoric invasion felt quite schizophrenic. Sitting beside me, Bob was gripping his pencil and staring straight ahead. I did not know what to make of it, either. It felt as though HBS had two modes, deadly serious and frat boy, with little in between.

At the Club Fair, that afternoon, an event in which we were invited to join the various clubs on campus, we found long lines in front of the Food and Wine Club, while the Texan and Republican Clubs looked dejected. I bumped into Laurie, the Alaskan biochemist from Analytics. She said she had been the victim of her section's prank because she was the oldest in the class. The pranksters had made the whole class stand up and then said that only whoever was alive on such-and-such a date should stay standing. As they got closer and closer to Laurie's birthday, the intervals between dates became smaller and smaller, to humiliate her. She was not amused.

After class on Friday, we had our first skydecks, in which the students who sat in the back row of class, known as the skydeck, gave their humorous take on the week in class. This was an HBS tradition and was supposed to lighten the mood of the section and defuse brewing conflicts. Five students from the skydeck row gathered around the overhead projector. First came awards. The Arctic Winter Survivor Award went to a student who had survived two cold calls in the same day. The Lifesaver, the student with a knack for intervening in class when others were floundering, was Brian, a Canadian. The Great Strides Award went to Victoria, a shy Austrian, who had just made her first comment. The Statue of Liberty Award was given to two students who held their hands up throughout every class, begging to speak. The Jedi Mind Trick Award, for those who were called on by the professor whenever they wanted, went to a Palestinian student. Sexy Beast was the prank victim who had confessed that he'd had sex in a car at Exit 14 on I-95 in Connecticut. The Days of Our Lives Award for Drama went to Emma, whose life seemed ripped from a daytime soap opera. She dressed more fashionably than most students, and during a marketing case about the customer buying process, she told of a friend who had bought a BMW 7-Series because it was "fast and strong," a "big cat." The Wave Maker was a student who talked, then paused, then talked, prompting everyone to put their hands up and down. Gordon Gekko was Chad, a hot-shot financier, whose every contribution included the phrase "basically, case closed." Jun, a fabulously unengaged Chinese woman who came in late and left her cell phone on, was dubbed the Smooth Operator.

The final slide read, "And lastly it's all about fun and Section A love!!!!"

Section love remained outside my emotional range, but I had at least made a new friend, a seven-foot man from Augusta, Georgia, called Bo. He alone was worth the price of the HBS education. We became friends once we discovered we both lived on the same street in West Cambridge. There were few other MBA students in the area, and soon we were bumping into each other in the local grocery store and sharing rides to and from school. Bo was also married and had two dogs, so we would often walk our dogs together in a local park. He was five years younger than I and had studied engineering at college before working at a medical services company in Kansas City. His father had owned his own medical device business, which he had sold for a good amount of money, and retired quite young. Unlike me, Bo had come to Harvard with a very specific mission. He knew that he was going back to the South or the Midwest where, he said, the opportunities to become rich were more abundant than in places where thousands of MBAs jostled for attention.

"No point going to New York or Los Angeles," he said one day, leaning back in the driver's seat of his colossal SUV. "You'll just be a commodity. In Nebraska, Missouri, Georgia, people kill for Harvard MBAs. Maybe not you, because you're this weird English dude, but most Harvard MBAs." Bo wanted to make a very large fortune in health care or biotechnology and then buy an NBA team. He even had his dream house sketched out in his mind, a place with high ceilings so he would not have to stoop and a full-size indoor basketball court where he could play with friends and host tournaments for the local community. I was envious of his certainty, but his sunny disposition made him impossible not to like. He took the academic work seriously but never freaked out about it and always seemed to have time to watch hours of basketball on ESPN. He was an antidote to the HBS bubble and seemed less interested in the section and more in the welfare of his wife, a trainee doctor going through her grueling residency, which included spending night after night in a local emergency room. One autumn day, on the dog walk, as I complained about yet another torturous accounting case, he stopped me and made an excellent point: "Everything we do is squat compared to what my wife's going through."

Chapter Five

WHO AM I?

Before arriving at Harvard, we were required to take two personality tests. The first was the Myers-Briggs Type Indicator, the second was called CareerLeader.

The Myers-Briggs Type Indicator is intended to help one think about one's own psychological type and consequently how to use that understanding in everyday life. It is used on the employees of most of the Fortune 100 companies and some 2.5 million Americans each year, and is the closest business gets to issuing bar codes to personalities.

Myers-Briggs is based on an interpretation of the work of the Swiss psychiatrist Carl Jung by a turn-of-the-twentieth-century Washington, D.C., housewife and her daughter. Jung believed that healthy people use their minds in different ways, which accounts for different forms of behavior. For Katharine Briggs, Jung's theory explained why her creative, bold, beloved daughter Isabel had married a boring, pragmatic stiff named Clarence Myers. Jung wrote that people's active minds are always perceiving, taking in information, or judging, processing that information. He further identified two different ways of perceiving, sensation and intuition. Sensing is about practicalities, the immediate, the facts staring one in the face. Intuition is about imagination, inspiration, the wild blue yonder. Judging could also come in two forms, thinking, a rational approach, and feeling, acting on hunches. Jung then went on to state that people also tend to be energized either by the external world of people and experience, or the internal world of thought, memory, and emotion. He labeled these two ten-dencies extraversion and introversion. Each person, he argued, was either extroverted or introverted and was characterized by one of the perception or judging functions, one of which would be dominant, the other auxiliary. This led him to conclude that there are sixteen basic personality types.

Jung, however, added a crucial caveat. "Every individual is an exception to the rule," and to "stick labels on people at first sight" was "nothing but a childish parlor game." The handbook that explains the Myers-Briggs Type Indicator offers a diluted version of Jung's caveat: "Type does not explain everything. Human personality is much more complex." So why then do so many organizations insist people take the test?

The answer, I think, is that to most companies, the idea of people as individuals is terrifying. Of course they talk a great deal about allowing individual expression and letting creativity flower. But what could be more frightening than trying to get thousands of different personalities through each working day without revolts, strikes, criminal subterfuge, and assault, let alone corralling their energies toward a money-making enterprise? What makes this even harder is that every other aspect of business is so sus-ceptible to measurement. You can measure the efficiency of your machines, the accuracy of your accounting, and the returns on your investment. But then along comes your work force. Who among them, you wonder, grew up longing to be in product management or marketing research? Who lay in the summer grass aged ten staring up at the sky thinking how magical it would be one day to sit in a glass box beside a freeway running pivot tables? Or revising contracts? No one. Instead, you know that beneath their suits and khakis your employees are an army of militants. Lepidopterists, poets, chess wizards, baritones, fantasists, whittlers, spankers, and Sudoku nuts. Animal lovers, gamblers, knitters, Episcopalians, Satanists, gluttons, and cheats.

So you try to control them with the tools at your disposal: salaries, perks, promotions, sackings, ethical codes, mission statements, team-building exercises. And then someone comes along with a test that says every individual can be put into one of sixteen boxes and given a four-letter code that tells you what he is like, the kinds of tasks he will do well, and the kinds of people he will work best with. Well, Hallelujah!

The MBTI is owned and administered by a Californian company called CPP—formerly Consulting Psychologists Press—whose vision is "to be a positive agent for change by advancing the cause of individuals by enabling them to achieve their goals." In the brochure delivered to test-takers, CPP suggests that we think of a dominant personality function much in the same way we think about which hand we write with. Writing with one hand feels natural and easy. The moment we switch hands, we can probably still write, but it is far more of a struggle. Likewise, if we happen to be extroverted sensing types, it can be a shock to work with an introverted thinker.

The directions to the six-page test say, "There are no 'right' or 'wrong' answers to these questions. Your answers will help show how you like to look at things and how you like to go about deciding things. Knowing your own preferences and learning about other people's can help you understand where your special strengths are, what kinds of work you might enjoy and be successful doing, and how people with different preferences can relate to each other and be valuable to society." The test-taker is advised not to think too long about the questions and to skip difficult ones.

The first question is "When you go somewhere for the day, would you rather A) plan what you will do and when, or B) just go?" The penultimate question is "Which mistake would be more natural for you, A) to drift from one thing to another all your life, or B) to stay in a rut that didn't suit you?" The final question is "Would you have liked to argue the meaning of A) a lot of these questions, or B) only a few?" The truth, of course, is that to most of the questions, the right answer would be "well, it depends." Regarding new fashions and trends, the test asks, are you usually "one of the first to try it or not much interested?" It depends what the trend involves. Is it worse to be unsympathetic or unreasonable? Am I dealing with my four-year-old son or Idi Amin? Is it more important to be able to "see the possibilities in a situation or to adjust to the facts as they are?" How about both? It is only by forcing the test-taker to make these false choices that Myers-Briggs can reduce human character to its sixteen brackets. If you let people tell you what they honestly feel about choosing between a kind boss and a fair boss, that tidy matrix would end up looking like a Jackson Pollock painting.

Before we showed up at the HBS campus, we were given a long to-do list, from taking an online accounting course to buying a laptop computer. Myers-Briggs was on there, and I zealously followed the directions not to linger over my answers. I was diagnosed as an ENTJ. The characteristics of an ENTJ were: "Frank, decisive, assume leadership readily. Quickly see illogical and inefficient procedures and policies, develop and implement comprehensive systems to solve organizational problems. Enjoy long-term planning and goal-setting. Usually well informed, well read, enjoy expanding their knowledge and passing it on to others. Forceful in presenting their ideas."

It sounded pretty good, validating even, as though I had actually performed well on the thing. Until I read the characteristics of other types. ENTP—"quick, ingenious, stimulating, alert and outspoken." ISFJ—"quiet, friendly, responsible and conscientious." It was like reading horoscopes beside my own. I could just as easily have been Sagittarius or Cancer as Leo.

Critics of the test say it is an example of the Forer principle. In 1948, the psychologist Bertram Forer created a personality test for a group of students and then gave them an analysis based on its results. He asked the students to rate the accuracy of the analysis on a scale of zero to five, with five being a first-rate description of their personality. The average rating was 4.26. But Forer had played a trick on the students. He had given each one exactly the same analysis, one he had cobbled together from various horoscopes. It read:

You have a need for other people to like and admire you, and yet you tend to be critical of yourself. While you have some personality weaknesses you are generally able to compensate for them. You have considerable unused capacity that you have not turned to your advantage. Disciplined and self-controlled on the outside, you tend to be worrisome and insecure on the inside. At times you have serious doubts as to whether you have made the right decision or done the right thing. You prefer a certain amount of change and variety and become dissatisfied when hemmed in by restrictions and limitations. You also pride yourself as an independent thinker; and do not accept others' statements without satisfactory proof. But you have found it unwise to be too frank in revealing yourself to others. At times you are extroverted, affable and sociable, while at other times you are introverted, wary and reserved. Some of your aspirations tend to be rather unrealistic.

His test demonstrated the truth that people are more likely to accept positive things said about them than negative things. Is someone likely to pay more attention when you say "I love the way you work" or "Hey, asshole, stop that"?

My own pitfalls, Myers-Briggs advised me, would be overlooking other people's needs, ignoring practical considerations and constraints, and suppressing my feelings. I wished they had just said, "Dear Philip Delves Broughton: when you're not busy taking an action-oriented, energetic approach, taking charge and forcing your ideas on others, you can be a selfish, thoughtless, uptight fantasist. Just try to be nicer sometimes, would you? Please?"

The other test, CareerLeader, promised a "unique profile of interests, abilities and motivations." I would learn about my "core interests and what they mean for your career and happiness," the organizational structure I would most enjoy, the rewards that motivated me, my strengths and weaknesses, and the characteristics likely to limit my success. Consequently, I would be able to "find the careers that are most likely to bring you success and satisfaction, along with suggested actions to take to work toward your career goals." The test asks a series of very similar questions that iteratively home in on these actions, goals, and interests. Do you value financial rewards more highly than interesting work? Do you value financial rewards more highly than having more time to yourself? Do you value having time to yourself more highly than interesting work? On and on until the test can conclude how exactly your motivations are prioritized. The questions are so repetitive and niggling that the temptation is to blitz through them without much thought. To let your instincts take control.

My interests, it turned out, were "creative production, theory development and conceptual thinking." I would probably enjoy activities such as "designing new products, developing marketing concepts, creating visual and verbal advertising ideas, planning events, creating innovative approaches to business-service delivery and managing public relations." I would also be happiest in a "work culture marked by a spirit of cooperation, interpersonal sensitivity, a tendency to assume the best of people, and perhaps a degree of altruism in the organization's mission." I could certainly imagine being unhappy in the opposite kind of environment, one marked by a spirit of dictatorial behavior, thoughtlessness, suspicion, and selfishness.

My assessment indicated that I tended to be "agreeable, trusting, generous, sincere, open to other people and sympathetic," and hence I should avoid work environments that called for "less sympathy and more toughness, shrewdness and assertiveness." I should "steer clear of organizations in which a high level of toughness and political savvy are essential for success." And in interviews, I should beware of my "modesty and genuineness" getting in the way of my selling myself. "To get comfortable with being a little bit immodest, go over your key 'selling points' before every interview."

My initial reaction to these tests was suspicion. I felt that their animating spirit was conformist. Unless there were some broad standard for selling yourself in interviews, why should I worry about being too modest? I could not help wondering what failure of imagination and human understanding must have occurred for these tests even to exist. What insecurity and mistrust lurked at the heart of the companies that implemented them? Of course, I didn't have responsibility for making sure billions of credit card transactions were properly executed or toilet paper rolled off the production line. I was not in a position where I had to persuade feuding employees to work together or prevent a star manager from jumping ship. I thought that these tests took the rich tapestry of human character and reduced it to a sterile batch of letters. More fundamentally, I did not trust what I thought was an attempt to quantify the unquantifiable. But given what I was about to go through, I should have given the tests more credit. They were closer to the mark than my ego was allowing me to believe.

A few weeks into the semester, this process of self-examination continued with a personal development exercise called "My Reflected Best-Self." The instructions read,

> The Reflected Best-Self Feedback Exercise differs from other performance feedback mechanisms in its explicit focus on understanding how key constituents experience individuals when they leverage their strengths constructively . . . [It] encourages people to create a developmental agenda for leveraging their reflected best-self and expanding their capacity to add value in work organizations. This exercise also enables people to reflect on how leaders might create an environment where others can engage their best-self and work maximally from positions of strength.

Aside from being written in the densest management-speak, the exercise required us to contact ten to twenty friends and former colleagues and ask them to share moments when we were our best selves. The grumbling within the section was immediate and intense. "There's no way I'm sending this to my old friends at work," said Graham, a phlegmatic Minnesotan. "They already think Harvard MBAs are arrogant without being asked to tell me how great I am."

The exercise also demanded we paint our own best-self portrait, offering the following example:

> When I am at my best, I tend to be creative. I am enthusiastic about ideas
> and I craft bold visions. I am an innovative builder who perseveres in the
> pursuit of the new. I do not waste energy thinking about missed opportuni-
> ties or past failures, nor do I take on the negative energy of the insecure or
> worry about critics. I stay centered and focus on what is possible and impor-
> tant. I use frameworks to help me make sense of complex issues. I can see
> disparate ideas and integrate them through "yes and" thinking. So I make
> points others do not readily see. In doing so, I frame experiences in com-
> pelling and engaging ways. I paint visions and provide new ways for people
> to see. I use metaphors and stories to do this. I find the stories in everyday
> experiences, and people find it easy to understand them. The new images
> that follow help people to take action. . . . I help people and groups surface
> the darkest realities and the most painful conflicts . . . I liberate people
> from their fears and help them embrace new paths. In all of this I try to
> model the message of integrity, growth and transformation.

Reading this, I badly wanted to know what this person had read growing up. And at what point did he decide to abandon the limpid expressions
of childhood for this strange new tongue? When did the phrase "model the
message of integrity" first make sense to him?

We were expected to craft our own best-self portraits by answering the
following questions: How does your best-self profile correspond with the
sorts of things you spend the bulk of your time doing? What situations or
contexts encourage your best-self to emerge? What keeps you from operating at your best more of the time? How can you prioritize your life so that
you maximize the potential for your best-self every day? What can you do
differently? What might you consider not doing anymore? Are there certain contexts you can put yourself in to maximize your potential?

I could see the point of all this. It was not enough for me to think about what I was best at or in what situations I thought I thrived. It was also useful to know what others thought were my strengths. So late one evening after a drink or two, I sat down with a pencil and joined battle:

My best self emerges in new and challenging environments where I can satisfy my curiosity about people, cultures, and situations. I enjoy making the best of difficult situations. I like opportunities to be creative and to make connections with people on a human level. I dislike excessively professional or rule-driven environments. I do not like authoritarian business structures. I dislike situations where I am obliged to conform to too strict a standard. I am not very good at following orders. [I am actually not too bad at following orders, but this ordeal was bringing out the anarchist in me.]

I try to prioritize my life so that I do not find myself trapped in the tentacles of an organization. I am disinterested in large-scale management challenges and more interested in working in a small, upbeat environment where both I and the people around me can pursue their own interests. My potential will likely be maximized in contexts where I can express myself. I have little interest in developing myself as an authority figure. I'm best when I have plenty of sleep. Any job that requires me to work flat out, through nights, is not for me. I need time to spend with my family and pursuing whatever interests me. I will be dissatisfied with any career which denies me this.

I should consider spending less time imagining myself as a business person and more figuring out how to make a living by other means. [Not a good sign less than a quarter of my way through business school.] I should care more for my fellow man. I need to defer less to others when big decisions need to be made. I need to develop my decision-making abilities. I will do best if I can help create a good working environment for others.

Nine out of the ten people I asked for feedback replied, "This is ridiculous. Is it essential to your course?" I told them not to waste their time with it. But one friend just could not resist.

"Have had a wonderfully windy email inviting me to assist with a field exercise on behalf of you," wrote Quentin, a British journalist, my first boss on Fleet Street and an aficionado of the absurd. "Is this genuine, or the creation of Monty Python?" Genuine, I replied. A few minutes later he zinged back: "Have just sent the following. Thought I'd give it a spot of top spin, just to brighten their day!

From: Quentin Letts

Re: Philip Delves Broughton

Dear Professor,

Thank you for your email. You ask me to help my former colleague Philip Delves Broughton with his exercise for your course. I am naturally happy to do so, even though we emotionally restrained Englishmen are generally hopeless at self-examination—or, for that matter, dwelling on the nitty-gritty character strengths of our confreres.

I am not sure I can run to three examples of his best self but here are two:

When Philip worked for me at the *Daily Telegraph,* a million-circulation British broadsheet newspaper, I was one day unable to attend the morning news conferences of senior executives. This was the meeting where the day's news list would be prepared and where the paper's coverage was planned. To the untutored youngster it was a daunting event to attend, requiring, as it did, a high level of bluff and confected confidence in front of the editor in chief (a tall man with a military manner and a formidably short attention span). I asked my deputy to attend the conference in my place. He was having some sort of nervous breakdown and fled to the lavatory, there to drain a small flask of some alcoholic spirit. I invited another staff member to represent our column at the meeting. She whitened, clutched her throat and decided she, too, was unwell. With mounting dismay I turned to Philip. "Phil? Fancy going to conference for us?"

He replied at once: "Sure, why not?" And with that he straightened his tie, brushed the lint from his jacket, and strode off to do battle with the top brass—and, in the process, conquer any fears lurking in his breast. It was brave. It was immediate. It got me out of a jam. It was classic Philip, seizing the moment and an opportunity.

The second example concerned a time when Quentin had brought his family, including two young children, to Paris and I had put them up at the *Telegraph* apartment. I had no idea if any of this would ever help me leverage my reflected best self or work maximally from a position of strength. But it was good to wallow in the flattery for a moment after the insecurities of those first few weeks at HBS, to be reminded of one's qualities rather than one's inadequacies. And that, I believe, was the point.

Chapter Six

FORMIN', STORMIN', NORMIN', PERFORMIN'

The fifth and final course of the first semester was finance, which did not start until the fourth week. Despite my dunking in the subject during Analytics, I was still feeling woefully unprepared. I had gone over the cases from Analytics several times, drafting and redrafting summaries, but it had become apparent during Accounting and TOM how facile many in the class were with numbers, and of course Excel, and how far behind I was. I had overheard students sharing jokes about Excel shortcuts and "macros," a way of programming certain buttons on your computer to perform calculations that come up again and again. I was a million miles from macros, a Luddite still, with a stubby pencil and calluses forming on my index finger from pounding away at my calculator.

I was further unnerved by the fact that I had only the vaguest of ideas what exactly finance was. I knew it was about buying and selling and numbers, and that lots of people I knew claimed to be "in finance." I knew that there were financial services companies who gouged me every time I used an ATM, and financiers who wore well-cut suits and frameless spectacles and sat in places like the City of London and Geneva packaging debt and floating stock and taking a cut of everything they touched. These people were higher in the pecking order than accountants; there or thereabouts with corporate lawyers; as powerful, on occasion, as politicians; and regarded with suspicion, bordering on contempt, by the owners of businesses. It turned out that finance is really about one thing: valuation. How do you put a price on an asset? From that basic question flows everything else. How much should I pay for it? What will the owner accept? How should I pay for it? Cash or credit? How can I increase the value of an asset I already own? Would now be a good time to sell? What risks may jeopardize the value of my asset? What can I do to mitigate them? Only once you have a clear sense of something's value can you move on to everything else.

Teaching us finance, or FIN 1, was none other than Rick Ruback, the wisecracking head of the RC program. Our first case dealt with the Butler Lumber Company. The case was just three pages long, with two exhibits: a balance sheet and an income statement. Butler Lumber was a small business in the Pacific Northwest that sold lumber products. It was growing and making good profits but kept experiencing cash shortages. The first question Ruback asked was "do you like this business?" The cold call went to Shelly, a woman in her mid-twenties who had worked at Home Depot. She had been staring down into her notes, clearly hoping that she would not be dragged into this. But of course she was. Professors would scour the class cards to find a fitting student to cold-call for each case. If the case was about lumber, it was the Home Depot employee. If the case protagonist had graduated from Brown, the Brown alumnus would be called. If the case dealt with a newspaper company, I knew I would be picked on.

"Yes," Shelly said, gathering herself. "It seems like a good business. The bank says the owner has good judgment, and it seems the business is growing."

"So if you were its bank, would you let it borrow more money?"

"Ummmm, yes, I think so."

"Why?"

Shelly winced and rested her arms on her desk. "Looking at the income statement, its profits are growing. Its operating expenses seem to be under control. There seems to be a stable set of customers." She paused, and Ruback began asking for numbers and ratios. Shelly held her own for nearly ten minutes, and when she ran dry, Ruback called on others in the room. It turned out that Butler Lumber was making a mistake common to small businesses as they grow. It was mismanaging its cash. In order to grow, it was buying more and more wood from its suppliers. It would then store the wood in its warehouses until a customer bought it, giving its customers thirty days to pay their bills. In the meantime, of course, it had to pay its suppliers either in cash or on credit regardless of whether the wood was sold or the customer paid on time. In order to cover the time between buying the wood and selling it, it was borrowing from the bank and from its suppliers. And as the company grew, so did its dependence on credit. It was also losing out on discounts offered by suppliers for prompt cash payment.

It turned out that Butler Lumber was not such a good business after all. Its cash conversion cycle—the period between when it paid for goods and when it was paid for them—was a disgrace, which only grew as the company grew. It had, we learned, a "funding gap." Instead of borrowing yet more from the bank, it needed to stop being so generous to its customers and pay its suppliers in cash earlier.

I learned my own lesson about cash as an undergraduate, when I was perennially short of funds. In order to buy food once my bank account had run dry, I would cash checks at a local pub, which would charge me one pound for every check I cashed. Not only was I being charged a usurious fee, but I always ended up writing a check for more than I actually needed and then spent it. Eventually, the bank would call me in, and I would have to plead for a further line of credit. And so it went. The worst thing was that no matter how I tried to right the situation, it deteriorated. Each semester, the portion of my allowance that went toward paying off the previous semester's debt increased, until by my final year, my first act was to sign over my entire allowance to the bank and begin the year with absolutely no money. It required sackcloth, ashes, and prolonged groveling to Mr. Lester of the Midland Bank to salvage my university career. I had let my cash conversion cycle get away from me.

One company that had mastered the cash conversion cycle was Dell. In fact, in the period we studied, 1996, it had managed to turn its mastery of cash management into an advantage over its competitors. Whereas other computer makers built computers, warehoused them, and sent them into stores where customers might or might not buy them, Dell waited until it had an order and payment in hand before making a computer. While its rivals risked making computers that might be obsolete by the time they reached stores, Dell never made a computer no one had expressly ordered. To do this, it needed a far slicker production system than its competitors, which it built. It needed to have the parts and capacity at hand when the orders came through, which it did. It needed to have accurate forecasts of customer demands, which it obtained through its sales force. As Michael Dell himself explained, "what we're all about is shrinking the time and the resources it takes to meet customers' needs."

Inventory, as we would learn again and again, is a dirty word in business, and the less you have of it, the better. For a company that made computers, complicated-seeming products, and promised to deliver them within a day or two of receiving an order, Dell, staggeringly, had almost no inventory. If only Butler Lumber had been so lucky. The cash effect of this was that while Dell's competitors sank money into product they weren't sure people wanted, Dell earned interest on the money it was not spending on inventory. This added millions of dollars to its bottom line, increasing its value.

If finance, then, is really only about valuation, the only serious means to establishing an asset's value is understanding how much cash it generates. People will occasionally try to obscure the issue with all kinds of curious terms like *intangible value* and *synergy value,* but really all that matters is cash. Because without cash, you could find yourself like Butler Lumber, thinking you are growing but becoming a credit junkie for lack of short-term cash. With cash, you could become Dell, leapfrogging your opposition on a trampoline of greenbacks.

But just knowing how much cash your asset produced now was not enough. You wanted to know how much it would produce in the years to come. If I put in a hundred dollars today, how much cash would be returned to me in the next ten years? Would I be better off investing in something else? The rest of the semester's finance course would be devoted to this one task: forecasting cash flows. It was the root of valuation, and though it sounded simple enough, it turned out to be a beast.

The word *leadership* lurked in every corner of HBS. When the student clubs requested new candidates for "events organizer" or "speakers coordinator," they emphasized that these were more than mere jobs. They were "leadership opportunities." Every club position, no matter how menial, carried the title of vice president. One day we, too, might be part of corporate America's bulging vice-presidential class, so we may as well get used to the weightlessness of the title. Within our section, we held elections for posts ranging from president to sports rep, alumni rep to international rep, with ten or eleven more in between. It was part of what the school called "making the section our own." Everyone at HBS, it seemed, could be a leader of one sort or another.

In the run-up to our section elections, Ben Esty, our section chair, told us that we should run the section however we wanted. He then passed around a case concerning a section in which two members had taped up a poster of Britney Spears. Some in the section had found it offensive. Others said their right to put up the poster was a free speech issue. They ended up holding a vote in which more than half chose to leave the poster up. After a vigorous case discussion within our own section, we decided that our main duty was to create a positive learning environment.

Each candidate for the section's leadership posts had to make a stump speech to the class. These candidates varied wildly in quality, from the aspiring Martin Luther Kings to one poor man who was so nervous he stood behind the desk fumbling with his notes and lost his chance for the presidency there and then. One student composed his own rap song to tell us why he wanted to be admissions rep, a job that involved arranging for applicants and recently admitted students to sit in on classes. Of the two leading candidates for section president, one spoke of the section as a family. The eventual winner, Brian, promised to get to know each and every one of us and keep us together over our lifetimes.

Dean Clark came to speak to us one lunchtime, and it was immediately apparent where HBS had derived its present image. He was focused and talked repeatedly about the HBS mission to educate leaders who would make a difference in the world. He spoke of the "transformational experience" of HBS as if it were a form of religious conversion. He must have given this talk dozens of times a month, but he managed to make it sound fresh and important. Several other university officials had accompanied him, and they sat in their seats like Politburo members while the party chief spoke. The Mormons in the class came to know Clark better than most of us because of their shared faith. One of them told me that at a meeting of the Mormon Club, Clark explained the secret of his success. He had whittled his life down to just four things: work, family, faith, and golf. As an academic, he used to arrive at his office at dawn and work in silence until lunchtime. Only then would he engage with the world, returning telephone calls, answering letters. On Saturdays he played golf, and on Sundays he spent the day at church with his family. Such discipline had propelled him to the leadership of the school.

When he invited questions, several hands went up. The first question was about HBS's place in the media's ranking of business schools. A *Wall Street Journal* poll had just come out ranking Harvard number thirteen. Numbers one and two were the business schools at the University of Michigan and Carnegie Mellon, respectively. Harvard's low rank was in large part due to the negative opinions of recruiters, who had told the newspaper that HBS MBAs were "arrogant," with a "sense of entitlement" and "ego problems." Clark said he took these rankings seriously, but not too seriously. He said he didn't want to talk about them too much as he could go on forever, but then spoke about them for fifteen minutes. If you looked at all the polls over ten years or so and averaged them out, he said, HBS came out decisively on top. Of this particular poll, "you've got to ask yourself, what are the questions to which this list is the answer." The *Wall Street Journal* poll was taken among recruiters, many of whom find it hard to recruit HBS graduates. Harvard MBAs, he said, often chose between several job offers, so left many companies disappointed and complaining to newspapers.

Clark said that two of his biggest challenges were trying to change the image of HBS alumni as stuck-up jerks, though not quite in those terms, and encouraging a more diverse group of applicants by making clear to prospective students how nice and comfortable the HBS environment was. One of the most common reactions among students after their first month or so at HBS, Clark said, was how different the people were from how they had imagined they'd be. Once I had recovered from Crimson Greetings, I agreed with him. HBS was a civil place. Occasional horror stories would leak out from other sections—of sharks seeking to humiliate their class-mates and fights over section norms. I had taken a dislike to Misty, who now bellowed, "Hello troops!" when she arrived in class each morning. But she was the exception. The rest of our section could not have been nicer. If I did not understand a concept discussed in class, there was always someone there to explain it. But I was quite removed. My days consisted of nothing more than attending class, studying, returning home to see Margret and Augie, and then studying before going to bed.

Those who lived more intimately in the bosom of the section had noticed darker rumblings. The skydecks had quickly become quite vicious, targeting the same few people in class who either spoke too much or made fools of themselves at section events. It was hard for them to complain, given the peer pressure to see the funny side. One man, an Indian, who was mocked again and again for his rambling contributions to discussions, now packed up and left before the skydecks began. "I don't need to take that shit," he told me later, when we bumped into each other in the cafeteria. "I don't see why we have to be stuck with the same people day after day. One guy in the skydecks came up to me this week and told me if I talk again, they'd nail me in the skydecks. I don't need this."

Shortly afterward, the underlying disquiet about the turn the section had taken became explicit. Ted Fallows, a serious finance wizard from Louisiana who acted as our liaison with the professors, asked us all to stay back after class. He was perfect for his role as he displayed the same empathy and rigor whatever nonsense crossed his path. There had been several complaints, he said, about buzzword bingo. The game had been proposed during a skydecks session the previous week. The idea was to offer a prize to whoever could drop certain phrases into their classroom remarks. The phrases chosen were "as my father used to say" and "as future business leaders." The game was goofy but harmless. It was supposed to break up the monotony of classes a little. Sure enough, it did. In the days before Ted called his meeting, several students had managed to use the phrases. Every time someone did, all round the class, heads jerked up and grins had to be checked. Even the professors seemed to sense the flutter in the class. Unfortunately, a number of students had told Ted they were worried that we were risking academic sanction. He explained that since we had received so many warnings about our academic performance and the importance of respecting the learning environment, everyone was a little jumpy. If we were going to get into trouble at HBS and jeopardize our academic records, buzzword bingo hardly seemed worth it. He invited comments. The skydeck came thundering in.

Rodger, one of the older students, who was still running his own technology business between classes, said that we needed to be able to strike a balance between joking among ourselves and being responsible. Annette, an African American ex–investment banker from Chicago, exploded. "Why are we being treated like kids with all these rules and regulations?" she exclaimed. "I feel like I'm being treated like a teenager. Why do professors have to stop talking and stare at someone if they arrive late? And then just cold call them for the hell of it? We are grown people."

Eric, a former advertising executive, pointed out that evidently the classroom was not the safe environment we thought it was if we hadn't heard from whoever had complained about buzzword bingo. Finally a twenty-three-year-old Arkansan, one of the youngest in the class, spoke up.

He said he was not so much worried about an official sanction, but he found the game distracting. He often missed thirty seconds or so of what was said after the buzzword was used as conspiratorial smirks went round the room.

Since we were on the subject of rules, Misty had to raise her hand. She was unhappy with the number of people arriving late to class and getting up to go to the bathroom. Gurinder, an ornery Indian software engineer, said we were all adults and if people were late, that was their problem. Ted added that the professors had noticed the number of times people were going to the bathroom during class, and told Gurinder it was out of control. Misty beamed. Earlier in the year, Ben Esty had told us that every time someone went to the bathroom they took ninety minutes of classroom time away from their section. He had reached this number by adding the thirty seconds it took to leave the classroom and the thirty seconds it took to return and multiplying it by the number of students in the section. He assumed that none of us would be able to concentrate if one of us went for a pee. "If you've got to go, you've got to go," Gurinder growled. "We can't be setting up rules for this." Bob intervened: "We're all percolating. But where I come from, you show up on time and you go to the bathroom beforehand." Gurinder shot back, "We're not all in the army here." The military folk bridled, and an angry frown usurped Misty's smile.

Afterward, I bumped into Shelly, the former Home Depot employee cold-called by Ruback. She had been elected our Leadership and Values Initiative rep. Her job involved communicating news from the school's Leadership and Values Initiative and proposing ways in which leadership and values could be encouraged in the section. In her pre-MBA job, she said, groups went through four phases: "formin', stormin', normin', and performin'." "We're clearly still stormin'," she said. Riding home that day with Bo, we concluded that it must have been difficult to go from the military, with its unified chain of command—where every point of order and discipline was codified and, if challenged, could be referred to a higher authority—to this loosey-goosey world of business school, full of truculent Indian software engineers and sarcastic English journalists. Misty, for one, hated it.

. . .

Soon afterward, I opened my mailbox to find a single piece of paper. It was just after lunch, and there were lots of students in Spangler doing the same thing. We stood there along the basement corridor, engrossed by what we had found. The letter was from a member of the class of 2005, addressed to the entire student body. It began with some generalities about the transformational experience of HBS and how the author had learned the importance of responsibility. Before HBS, he wrote, most of us had not assumed much responsibility beyond taking care of ourselves and our immediate circle. (This was not the case with many of the people I had met so far, but I let that pass.) As business leaders, he wrote, the scope of our responsibility would be far wider. "No longer will we be the most junior person at XYZ investment bank or consulting firm," he wrote. "No longer will we assume a series of two-year jobs with business school to look forward to as a safe zone. Real life for HBS graduates entails power, leadership and success." HBS had given him "heightened self-awareness." Liberated from hundred-hour work weeks, he had been able to focus on the big questions, what mattered most to him and what he was going to do with his life. On he went, talking about how his moral compass had been reset by the school, until finally we got to the meat of the letter. Just before Christmas the previous year, he wrote, he had drunk too much at the end-of-semester party, Holidazzle, and been involved in a "regrettable property damage incident" in one of the campus apartment buildings. His moral compass had gone haywire that night and he was deeply sorry. The experience had forced him to reconsider the value of discussing moral situations at HBS. If he could fall off the rails so easily, perhaps he should not be so cynical about having to spend time discussing values. His behavior had made him realize he still had work to do figuring out who exactly he was.

The school had evidently required the author to write this letter and distribute it to the entire MBA class as a punishment. I felt bad for him. The letter reminded me of one of those videotaped statements made by kidnap victims. You know, the ones where the victims sit between a peeling radiator and a wilting potted plant, wearing an ugly sweat suit and read from a prepared statement. They thank their captors for treating them so well and say that fundamentalist terrorist organizations get an unfair rap, while all the while you can see a shadow of a Kalashnikov hovering against the wall above them. The author's crime, Bo later told me, was coming back drunk from Holidazzle and peeing on the door of his neighbor's apartment. Two months earlier I would have howled with laughter at this kind of thing. But now my cynical reflexes were in spasm. It didn't feel right to laugh at this stuff anymore. It was serious, right? Leadership. Core values. Transformation. Not peeing on other people's property. Being true to oneself.

I took the letter back to Margret, who read it standing at the kitchen counter. She didn't flinch until she got to the phrase "regrettable property damage incident."

"What did he do?"

"Bo says he peed on his neighbor's door."

She kept on reading. When she had finished, she set the letter down on the counter and looked me in the eye. "You know, these people are freaks. Why do they think they're all going to be leaders anyway? Who wants them leading anything?"

"I know, I know," I said. "I'm just worried that if I stop recognizing the freaks, I'll become one of them."

"That's something worth worrying about."

Our first midterms, in TOM and FRC, were fast upon us, and the challenge for HBS was to persuade nine hundred people incapable of *not* taking an exam *very* seriously not to take this one too seriously. It was almost impossible to fail out of Harvard Business School. If you showed up and said nothing, professors would eventually pick you out and make you talk so you could get some credit. If you kept coming in the bottom 10 percent in every subject, you would be given warnings, help, and every kind of support to keep you there. To fail out, you basically had to stop showing up to class. And be mean to everyone who tried to help you.

Yet as the midterms approached, the section swung into action, delegating students who understood the course content to help those who didn't. Our in-boxes were swamped with PowerPoint presentations of the "key takeaways," summaries, anything and everything to try to get us through the multiple-choice quizzes, which would represent 20 percent of our final grade. Zeynep tried telling us not to get too worked up, but to no avail. Eddie Riedl drew a bell curve to show the distribution of students at business schools. HBS students, he said, were at the far right of the curve, the very smartest and likeliest to succeed. Even if we came last in our HBS class, he said, we would still be way ahead of most other MBAs. But then again, he said with a resigned shrug, "these are exams, there's going to be pressure, what can you do?"

The night before our TOM midterm, I received via e-mail a six-page summary of the course from a student in another section. There were dozens of names in the recipient box, but almost none from Section A. Without even hesitating, I sent the summary to the entire section, receiving various messages of thanks or "I had this already." Within five minutes, however, an e-mail came back, addressed to us all, from Misty.

A-Team,

I realize everyone's trying to be fair sending out these study notes. It shows real section spirit. But are we risking breaching community standards? I reckon we're getting pretty close with this. Let's discuss.

Happy studying, y'all.

Misty

I hadn't even considered the possibility that my action had violated community standards. I was just trying to be fair. The next morning, before class, a man I had never spoken to in the section, a former hedge fund analyst, came over to my desk to reassure me: "Thanks for sending out the note. That woman is insane." As promised, there were no surprises in the midterms. There were twenty multiple-choice questions. I came in the top 20 percent in TOM and the middle 60 percent in FRC. It was satisfying to know that my struggles with the numbers were paying off.

To blow off the mid-semester blues, the Australia and New Zealand Club organized one of the biggest events on campus, the Priscilla Ball. The men were to dress as women and the women as sluts. The cost was $120 per person. Since we were living on loans and not that into cross-dressing, Margret and I decided to pass. But we took Augie along to the pre-ball party hosted by the section. One man looked like Virginia Woolf in a white boa and black wig. Another was dressed in Gothic black leather, nose rings, and studded bracelets, while another wore a skimpy Heidi outfit and women's underwear, which failed to contain his errant balls. A Frenchman, Vincent, had vowed to me that afternoon that he would be "the most beautiful woman" at the ball, and sure enough he arrived as an impeccable Marilyn Monroe.

Chapter Seven

TO BETA
AND
BEYOND

I am standing on the edge of the Efficient Frontier. Somewhere out in the darkness, I see the winking light of extreme risk and extreme reward. And beneath me lies a Milky Way of ill-judged investments. The Efficient Frontier drops away in an arc like Sagittarius's bow, but I am clinging to a sharply sloping tangent, my heels pressed deep into the ice. Far behind me lies the clean, breathable air of the risk-free investment. But I have chosen to don the oxygen mask and climb ever higher, my feet and lungs aching, my nerves fraying, driven by faith in a religion called diversification and a hope that I can bring my risks and rewards into perfect balance.

"We call this OCRA. It's my favorite vegetable." My reverie was snapped by Ruback's piercing voice. He was a nice man and an eminent professor. But for me, a financial *ingénu,* he was death. Death on a bad day, with a chill in his bones and an itch in his cape. He made me desperate for something other than the case method. There were elementary, practical things to learn in finance, and I wanted a simple lecture to help me understand them. For those in the section who had studied finance as undergraduates and then worked in the field, the subject matter in FIN 1 was elementary. For those of us new to the subject, it felt like learning physics starting at $E = mc^2$ while having to figure out the basic laws of motion on the fly.

Ruback spent several minutes at the beginning of each class eulogizing the Boston Red Sox, who were on their way to winning their first World Series in eighty-six years. This meant nothing to at least a third of the students, who did not come from the United States. But it made more sense than when we moved on to the numbers. For Ruback, the theories and squiggles of finance must have glimmered in a kind of crystalline state, pure, uncomplicated, and perfectly logical. How could anyone not get it? When he was asked a question, he stood in the middle of the room looking dumbstruck and disappointed. A few souls bold enough to venture an answer would raise their hands. But the discussions drifted. We groped around in the fog, searching for something recognizable, a tree stump, a boulder, something to give us a sense of place out here on the Efficient Frontier. Some notes, a problem set. No such luck.

It was barely 9:30 A.M. and I was lost again. In fact, since Butler Lumber, I was not sure I ever quite knew where I was. Six weeks into Harvard Business School, and Ruback was talking in dog whistles. Others heard him, but not me. I felt like a grizzly bear standing over a mountain stream watching a school of fish go by. I plunged my paw into the water to grab one but came up with nothing. I plunged and plunged again. Every so often, I managed to seize hold of something—discounted cash flow!—but missed ten others.

For the first twenty minutes of each class, I would know where we were. I could feel the outline of the problem we were trying to solve. But then the chalk began to scratch on the board and the ground vanished beneath my feet. It was late October, though you would never know it from our windowless classroom. The air was heavy with concentration, bafflement, and the faint stench of scrambled eggs, brought to class each day by a student who had recently gone on the Hay diet—no carbohydrates, lots of protein. He sat in the next-to-last row cheerily digging into his breakfast with a plastic fork, oblivious to the nauseating effect he was having on others.

Finally, a Scottish doctor in the front row put up his hand. "I'm sorry, but what is OCRA?"

"It's the optimal combination of risky assets."

"So it's not a vegetable, then."

Ruback screwed up his face. "No. I should have explained. It's the point where you get the maximum benefit from diversification. You have diversified enough to minimize risk for this level of reward, but not diversified so much that you are actually getting less than you should."

Before studying finance, I had thought about investments almost solely in terms of reward. I had some idea that the index funds I owned at Vanguard were tied pretty closely to the fortunes of the broader U.S. economy. If the United States did well, I did well; if not, I suffered. But as long as I remained roughly in place, I was getting all I wanted for very little investment of my time. What I did not realize was that serious investors think as much about risk as they do reward. Whereas reward can be expressed in a simple percentage, risk is a far more slippery creature, making it the preserve of specialists.

During the first few finance classes, we had been working our way toward predicting the future cash flows of a business. Like any kind of prediction, this was a process of educated guesswork. You began with a company's historical revenues and tried to project them forward. If they had been growing at 10 percent a year for five years, perhaps they would have a couple of years of this kind of growth before settling down to grow along with the rest of the economy. If the company planned to acquire a rival, however, or launch a revolutionary new product, those revenues could be much higher. The key was to make reasonable assumptions for a reasonable period into the future, normally five to ten years. The next step was to predict costs. Would they rise in lockstep with revenue? Perhaps they might fall as a percentage of revenue if the company became more efficient. Would revenue growth require some additional investment, a new factory, perhaps, in five years' time? Would tax rates change or stay the same? Once again, the most important thing was to make sound assumptions based on all the available evidence. Then it was simply a question of putting the numbers into a spreadsheet—"plug and chug" as the bankers called it.

At this point you had, say, ten years of predicted profits or losses for your company. But these values applied to the future. What was all that cash worth now? We started with the idea that a dollar today is worth more than a dollar in a year's time. If I had a dollar today, I could buy a one-year Treasury bill promising 5 percent interest, and have a dollar plus five cents in one year. Whereas the dollar in a year is just a dollar. And if I wanted a dollar in a year, I could buy 95.2 cents' worth of T-bills and earn 5 percent while having those 4.8 cents to spend. A similar logic applies to figuring out the present value of a firm's future cash flows.

In the case of the T-bill, we could simply take the promised cash flows in future years and discount them back by 5 percent. The dollar in a year's time is worth 95.2 cents today. We can do this because a T-bill is considered a risk-free investment, since your counter-party is the U.S. government. That 5 percent is the rate at which people are happy to lend money to the government, and it tends to be the lowest lending rate around because no one expects the government to default. A company, however, can expect investors to demand higher returns to compensate for the risk of their business. And the riskier the business, the higher those expected returns will be. General Electric, with its long history and portfolio of diverse businesses, will be able to attract investors with the promise of lower returns than a single business start-up, say, a wallpaper company. The next stage in valuation was to figure out what kind of return was expected by investors in a firm, lenders and equity holders combined. If you were an investor, you would call this your opportunity cost of capital, the return on the best alternative to this investment, which you were forgoing to make this one. If you were management, it would be your hurdle rate, the minimum return you would expect on any investment you made. If you were an investment banker valuing the company, it would be the discount rate, the number you used to discount the company's future cash flows to see how much they were worth today. Whatever you called it, it would be the same number. And calculating it forced us to think seriously about risk, asking the questions for company after company: What are the risks to its future cash flows and how does this affect how I value it and the decisions management should take?

Each of us has an intuitive sense of risk and of the nature of the risks we are likely to take for a given reward. Someone placing ten dollars on an outsider in the Kentucky Derby is probably doing so on the off chance of winning, but is reaping additional rewards from the excitement of having a stake in the race. Others are comfortable with the odds of throwing themselves off a bridge attached to a bungee cord. People in dire straits are inclined to take bigger risks for bigger rewards than those in comfortable situations, whose main goal tends to be preserving what they have.

When I bought my first apartment in London, with a friend who had recently graduated with an MBA from INSEAD, he drew up this elaborate spreadsheet showing the opportunity cost of investing in an apartment rather than stocks.

"What," I said, jabbing at his laptop screen, "is an opportunity cost?"

He explained how illiquid an apartment was and how much easier it would be to trade in and out of other investments. He told me that part of the reason ordinary savings accounts offered such minuscule returns was that they were highly liquid. If you tied up your money for a long period, you should expect higher returns. The downside, of course, was that you could not get to it so easily if you needed it. Part of the difference in returns could be explained by the fact that a long-term, illiquid investment denied you certain other investment opportunities. And you should expect to be rewarded for that. I listened patiently, but couldn't help but feel that all of this was make-believe. Intuitively, I could not grasp the idea of an opportunity cost. It seemed that you made decisions in life, some worked, some didn't, but the idea that you would ever try to put a sum on the price of making one decision rather than another seemed fantastical. I told him that all I wanted was a place of my own that I could afford and that no bank was offering to lend me a hundred thousand pounds to buy stocks.

He tried to put it another way. Say you had a choice of two parties to go to on a Saturday night. You chose the wrong one and missed out on meeting the person who could have changed your life. The opportunity cost of not going to the other party was enormous. Risk, he said, was not just the possibility of something bad happening, but also the chance of something good not happening. First understanding and then pricing this kind of risk did not come easily.

Fortunately, we have a wonderful window into humans' appetite for financial risk: the stock market. The market provides decades' worth of data showing how the prices of companies in every field of business move in relation to one another. We can see, for example, not just how a single telecom company has performed but also how the broader telecom sector has performed. We can track the market, the entire portfolio of listed stocks, and then see how companies and sectors performed in relation to it. If the market was up, for example, were telecoms up at the same rate, or at a higher rate? Or were they down? Some companies tend to outpace a rising market, such as luxury goods, and some perform poorly in good times but soar when the rest of the economy sours, such as debt collection. Divining the patterns in all this data gives us a pretty good idea of people's perception of risk.

By this winding route, I found myself face to face with beta. Beta is a nifty way of describing the risk of a stock. A beta of 1 implies that the stock, on average, tracks the market perfectly. If the market goes up 8 percent, the stock goes up 8 percent. A high-beta stock is one that exaggerates the market's movements. Say the market goes up 10 percent; a stock with a beta of 1.5 goes up 15 percent. If the market falls by 10 percent, that stock falls by 15 percent. A low-beta stock is less volatile than the market. If the market goes up 10 percent, a stock with a beta of 0.5 goes up only 5 percent. If the market goes down 10 percent, the stock goes down 5 percent. It is less risky, and consequently less rewarding. Calculating a company's discount rate became a process of using historical data to figure out a company's beta—if it was not a listed company, you could draw on the data from similar companies—and then multiplying it by the risk of investing in the stock market as a whole. You then combined this risk to the equity holders in a company with the risk to debt holders to reach a discount rate.

Once we had discovered beta, people began bandying it around in every context. They referred to themselves as high or low beta, risk-takers or risk-avoiders. Presented with a new and dubious choice in the cafeteria, they might say "that grouper is a high-beta fish dish." Or if they saw someone driving a boring secondhand Toyota, as I did, they observed that my car was a low-beta automobile. Low risk and definitely low reward. Once my class found itself looking for work, jobs were defined as low-beta (consulting) or high-beta (your own start-up).

The problem with such a handy little way of assigning risk and reward is that some of the greatest investors in the world consider it trivial. Warren Buffett, for example, is the anti-beta. Buffett's argument goes something like this: Imagine a perfectly good company with strong revenues, low costs, and a sustainable competitive advantage. Its stock trades at an earnings multiple just above its peers. Then, one day, the chief executive is found in bed with a sheep. It turns out he has been using company money to amuse both himself and his sheep. The chief executive is humiliated, and the company becomes a nationwide joke. The stock price plummets in relation to the market. For reasons that have nothing to do with the company's fundamental performance, it suddenly looks like a high-beta stock—volatile and risky. But for the value investor like Buffett, an investment in the company just became dramatically less risky. The stock is now cheap and will more than likely recover ground, as the company is still appreciated by its customers, giving the investor a higher return for pretty much the same company-specific risk as existed before the sheep incident. The key is to keep your focus on the price of the stock in relation to the future cash flows it will generate. How that price has moved historically, either in absolute or relative terms, is all but irrelevant. Focusing on beta is a near-certain way of denying yourself alpha, the true measure of greatness.

Alpha is the white whale of the investment community—coveted, precious, sought with a maniacal fury, and yet rarely captured. It reflects the extent to which you make nonsense of standard risk/reward measures. To understand alpha, imagine a situation in which you take the risk of having your foot stamped on for the high-probability return of an apple. Everyone in the market knows that if you risk having your foot stamped on, you should get an apple, and they can decide whether or not to take the risk. But imagine if someone in this market is taking exactly the same risk of having his foot stamped on, but receiving both an apple and a five-dollar bill. That five-dollar bill is alpha and it is what the very best investors are measured by.

If an investor can look at ten car companies that have all historically returned 6 percent, and pick the one that will return 15 percent for the same degree of risk as the others, that 9 percent is his alpha. If he can find weird alternative assets—say, aluminum futures or documentary films—that have the same risk profile as the car companies but return 20 percent, even better. Like beta, alpha also cropped up regularly in conversation at HBS. "Matt's alpha is his quantitative skills, whereas Ben's is his ability to shoot from outside the three-point line." You can achieve alpha in all kinds of ways, but there are two basic ones: picking the right investment and picking the right mix of investments, which, bundled together, provide higher reward for lower risk than any of the individual investments would. Serious investors will always insist on talking not about returns but about risk-adjusted returns. This was one of the most important lessons I took from Finance.

Between classes a group would form at the back of the room to track the portfolio of Chad, the finance stud, in his search for alpha. Some days would be headily alpha, a successful exit from a short position on a biotech firm. Others would be gloomily beta, just moving along with the market. Very occasionally, a pencil would snap between Chad's meaty paws as a negative return showed up on his Yahoo! Finance page.

Benjamin Graham, the intellectual godfather of value investing, spoke about risk in yet another way. He liked companies that had a "margin of safety," some cash in the bank, perhaps, or a very manageable amount of debt. A good product needed or loved by customers was another good sign. You basically want to look at companies much as you would people. Do they work hard? Are they honest? Likeable? Creative? Entrepreneurial? Do they spend more than they earn? Are they mortgaged to the hilt? What if they lost their job tomorrow, what would happen? Would they find another one quickly?

There seemed to come a point in every class involving the use of numbers when the professor would say, "This is an art not a science." And there always seemed to be a note of regret in his voice. Valuing companies, for all the sweat and effort people put into it, always ran into immeasurable uncertainties. The bankers in the class told us that they would frequently produce proposals to companies, with elaborate valuation spreadsheets, knowing they were nonsense. They bore the appearance of competence and intelligence but meant desperately little. These deal books were simply churned out by overworked analysts in their early twenties, using hoary valuation tricks, to make the banks look as if they had done their work. The cost of capital used was normally 10 percent and then adjusted up or down if necessary. In many cases, the bankers simply took a book created for one firm and adjusted it a little for another. It was not even art, it seemed to me, but downright deception.

I asked Annette about this. I had admired her since her angry intervention in our section discussion of bathroom breaks. She had grown up in Chicago and spent five years at a major Wall Street investment bank before coming to HBS. She did not speak often in class but had a real presence in the section. She was committed to the African American community at HBS and to encouraging more African Americans to apply to the school. She had been an accomplished college athlete and a dancer before going into banking. She admitted that her life up to now, from college to Wall Street to HBS, had been modeled on that of African American women she admired. But there was going to come a time, very soon, she felt, when she would have to find her own path. She had intervened in the discussion of bathroom breaks, she said, because she felt it was an affront to her as an adult. She seemed to take the right things seriously. "You can't get upset about these valuations' not being right," she told me after one of Ruback's classes. "They make no claim to be exactly right. They are negotiating tools. If you spent any time at a bank you would see that all these techniques and models just serve the political needs of the bankers and their clients. If the bankers come up with one valuation and the client says, can't we make that a little higher or lower, the bankers will go back to their model and adjust it to get it where the client wants it. And the more complex-seeming the model, the more tricks there are to pull. You should never mistake what they do for objective science. All that matters is the assumptions, and anyone can have a discussion about them, regardless of how much finance they know. The main thing is understanding the business in question."

The only necessary tool in the chaos of finance, then, was not a computer or a set of formulae—which were incapable of grasping the complexity of risk—but old-fashioned judgment, honed by experience. In fact, experience is really the only backward-looking metric worth trusting. The rest are the products of idle mathematical minds. Once I reached this conclusion, I saw that all these weeks battling to build even the simplest financial models had not been in vain. They had forced me to understand how the pieces fit together. I was starting to see the structure, the plumbing and wiring of finance, where before all I had seen was the façade. I recalled Mihir Desai saying in Analytics that if we could not explain finance to our mothers, then we did not properly understand it ourselves. My mother was due a telephone call.

Accounting, to my great relief, had undergone a similar transition, from the numerical to the philosophical. I could crunch the numbers more easily, though, still, I was repeatedly surprised in class by how far ahead others were in this regard.

During our study group sessions, Alan consoled me: "Number games are what consultants play all day long," he said. "They reach big conclusions from a handful of numbers. You know, they get the aspirin sales for one store and the number of people who use the store, then they figure out that number as a percentage of the people who live in the area, then they apply the percentage to the entire population of the United States, and now they gross up the sales at that one store and they've got a pretty good estimate of national aspirin sales. It's like a party trick. It sounds great at first, but it gets old fast."

In an FRC case about a medical products company that was selling products through television commercials, we had to decide if their advertisements were assets or expenses. These were not any old commercials, but direct-to-consumer ads, the kind that drag on forever on late-night television and include a specific toll-free number to call to buy your product. Each number in each ad was different, so the company knew exactly how much revenue each ad generated, unlike with more generic television advertising, where you never really know who is watching or whether they are responding to what you're selling. In the latter case, where the benefit of the ad is uncertain, you would expense it. In the former case, where the revenue from the ad is measurable, you could treat it like an asset and depreciate the cost over time.

This led to a discussion about the nature of an asset. It was an economic resource, we decided, which produced measurable and reliable cash benefits. So what was an expense? It was more like throwing your money away in the hope of getting it back. Everything accountants called an asset had a degree of uncertainty to it. Even a chemical plant could collapse or its chemicals could cease to be used. But the more uncertainty surrounding an asset, the more like an expense it became. The founder of modern accounting, Luca Pacioli, a fifteenth-century Venetian monk, was also the first man to describe card tricks, and accounting, I found, was more impressionistic than I had ever imagined. There could be rigorous accounts that stuck to every accounting standard yet that somehow made no sense at all. And then there were accounts that broke every rule and yet seemed to reflect the truth about a company. It was the difference between a formal studio photograph that failed to capture a sitter's character and a portrait in thick, crude oils that summed up a person in a few brushstrokes. As Eddie kept repeating, it was economic truth we sought, and accounts, properly kept and interpreted, helped us find it. They themselves were not the truth.

I once heard a church sermon in which the priest said you could tell most of what you needed to know about a person from looking at their bank and credit card statements. How they prioritize their spending will tell you how they prioritize their life. So it was with companies. You looked through the numbers for very human traits such as character, resilience, or imagination. Then you could apply versions of the old high-school yearbook tag "most likely to . . . go bust, produce steady returns, make me a billionaire."

In one case, we looked at Microsoft's financial reporting strategy. It had often baffled investors why Microsoft kept so much cash on its books. Investors tend to like to see cash either invested in improving the business or returned to them as dividends. Accountants and financiers and corporate strategists who looked at that cash number had come up with all kinds of explanations. Software was an intensively competitive business. Microsoft needed a cash cushion to carry it through the dark times. Others said it was a typical Microsoft trick. They persistently created this aura of doom and gloom around their prospects to minimize earnings expectations so that, quarter after quarter, they could beat Wall Street's predictions and keep their stock price on a steady upward curve. But Bill Gates gave a very different reason in a panel discussion at the University of Washington with his friend Warren Buffett: "The thing that was scary to me was when I started hiring my friends and they expected to be paid. And then we had customers that went bankrupt—customers that I counted on to come through. And so I soon came up with this incredibly conservative approach that I wanted to have enough money in the bank to pay a year's worth of payroll, even if we didn't get any payments coming in. I've been almost true to that the whole time."

I knew many people thought of Bill Gates as the devil. And they would rather believe that everything he did was the product of some fiendish strategy dreamed up while he hung upside down in his dank cellar beside the Pacific Ocean. But when he said he simply wanted enough money to pay his friends, I believed him. Imagine starting a business, getting all your friends to leave their jobs to come work with you, and then not being able to pay them. It would be a betrayal. The cash number on Microsoft's balance sheet was not some accounting gimmick. It was a direct reflection of Bill Gates's start-up mentality. Whatever happened, if his little rinky-dink software company was ever going to have a chance, he could not let down his friends. And if it worked then, why stop when the company had grown to be worth billions? Was it not still worth knowing that whatever happened, he could pay all the people who depended on him for their livelihoods? Perhaps, I began to wonder, accounting firms should hire psychoanalysts as well as accountants. The accountants could work on the numbers, and the shrinks could explain those numbers as indicators of ordinary human behavior.

One day Eddie brought in a newspaper article in which the CFO of an airline explained why he had accounted for his aircraft in a particular way, saying, "all I do is follow the rules as they are written." Eddie tossed the newspaper to his desk in disgust. "If I ever, ever hear any one of you saying something as stupid as that, I promise I will personally come around to your house and noogie you." The rules are the messy by-product of corporate and technological change, lawyers, lobbyists, politicians, and companies all scrapping for some advantage. Sometimes the rules make sense; other times they don't. But economic truth remains constant. If accounting ceases to reflect what is actually going on but becomes some game in itself, it becomes worthless and possibly dangerous.

It was dispiriting, then, to discover the extent to which companies exploited the murk around accounting. For example, there was the "earnings game." Wall Street, it was claimed, liked companies that showed smooth, frictionless growth, quarter by quarter. To achieve this, chief financial officers deployed all their tricks, deferring losses with one hand while booking unearned income with another, accruing expenses one year so as to stash profits from the tax collector the next. This may have produced a smooth curve, but to what real purpose, beyond the aesthetic? Could investors not accept that companies might have good and bad years? What was so wonderful about smoothness? Didn't it seem in the least bit sinister or suspect to find all this orderly perfection amid the jungly chaos of business? A company with a seamless upward curve of earnings seemed no more credible to me than a man whose brow never furrowed or whose eyes never blinked.

From the accounts companies showed to the world, we then turned to the internal accounts companies could use to track their business, the Control half of Financial Reporting and Control. These internal accounts were less like a self-portrait and more like the control room of an ocean liner. A wall covered with dials and gauges told you how fast you were going and how much fuel you had left. Each day a different set of charts arrived detailing how much lobster salad your passengers consumed, how much they spent in the casino and spa, how much time they spent in their cabins watching movies instead of shopping in the designer stores. You might also want to know how well your staff was doing. Were the chefs churning out meals fast enough and the waiters waiting charmingly enough? Were the personal trainers standing around the water cooler all day or actually training people? Was it even worth having such a lavish gym when all anyone wanted to do was eat? Perhaps you could ditch the gym and use the space for another restaurant. Who spent more? Young families or retirees? Was anyone stealing from the cash registers? Your ship, or business, was a vast organism whose health you were constantly monitoring and hoping to improve.

At some point, the cost of monitoring every little thing that went on would exceed the benefit from any improvements. Trying to find that point was just another damn thing to think about. But, still, it's worth doing. We studied the case of a small grocery store, like a 7-Eleven, and Chad took a break from tracking his investment portfolio and summed up the challenge with a salty question: "How long will it take for a dead rat on the floor to show up in the financial metrics?"

Robert Kaplan, an HBS accounting professor, took on the challenge of how to monitor the myriad aspects of a business and came up with the balanced scorecard, which has since been adopted by hundreds of small and large companies. It incorporates financial metrics with customer feedback, assessments of managerial and employee behavior, and opportunities for learning and growth. Done right, a balanced scorecard should tell the story of a business, incorporating all the strands that matter. It will tell you what a good, trustworthy manager would tell you. Done poorly, it is just a lot of money wasted generating a lot more useless numbers.

During some classes, you could tell from the buzz in the room that the case under discussion would stick in everyone's mind. One such case, discussed in a LEAD class, dealt with Meg Whitman's work as CEO of eBay. The case described her rise from Procter and Gamble to HBS to Bain consulting to Disney, on to Stride Rite, FTD, and finally, in 1998, to the online auction company, where she became a billionaire and a business world celebrity. During the class, we watched film of a speech Whitman gave at HBS soon after the dot-com crash of 2001. She reminded me of Katharine Hepburn, tall, a little galumphing, but resolutely jolly, as if at any minute she was going to let rip with a wolf whistle and a "C'mon fellas!" and have us all swimming in a freezing lake or singing around a piano. She spoke of the importance of hewing to classic management principles, even in supposedly new businesses. Returns on assets and investment, she said, would never go out of fashion. Fundamental analysis of things such as costs, customers, and competitors still yields rewards. Experience builds intuition, which is invaluable. Disney, she said, was a great company to work for, something she did not fully appreciate until she worked for a bad company. Culture and mission were not to be sneezed at. Employees are motivated by the feeling that they are on a mission.

But it was when Whitman turned to career advice that I could see everyone in the room perking up, waiting for "the secret." "You're never as good as you think you are. But you're probably never as bad as you think you are," she said, before going on to elaborate her nine-point personal philosophy. The first point is to do something you enjoy, because if you don't enjoy it you're unlikely to be any good at it. Second, deliver the results, whatever you're doing. Third, codify the lessons learned. Since HBS, she said, she had experienced 1.5 successes, 1.5 failures, and 1 gigantic home run. Fourth, be patient and stick around good people and good things. Fifth, build a team and share credit. Sixth, be fun to work with. Seventh, ask what you don't know or understand. Eighth, don't take yourself too seriously. Ninth, never, ever compromise your integrity.

She said she had long ago given up trying to be perfect in every facet of her life—the perfect wife, mother, and hostess and the perfect CEO. There was no balance, no wisdom, just an unremitting set of personal choices about what would work for her. Every day, every weekend, every living moment, she asked herself what was most important at that time. "Remember this. And this is something that I have not been particularly good at," she said. "You probably won't look back and wish that you'd worked harder . . . In the end your family and your friends are the most important thing. And just remember that as you think about what you're going to do." As I listened to her speak, I wanted to know if she actually regretted her choices. Would she have given up any of her business success to recoup what she had lost in her personal life? I imagined her being more explicit: "You know, all this money, all this praise, frankly I could do without it if I could have back those years when I spent more time working than with my family and friends. In fact, I would give up my fortune in return for those years." What then? Almost everyone in the room was contemplating a future of ninety-hour work weeks, personal sacrifice in return for professional success. Could Whitman have done more to change their minds?

. . .

The day before the 2004 presidential election, I spoke to a woman in our section who I thought might care about the result. She had earned a political science degree and worked for a senator before spending four years in investment banking and private equity. Would she be watching the results come in? "No," she told me emphatically. "I've given up thinking about politics and elections. I can't change them, and they don't impact me directly. So they're not worth my time." A poll in the student newspaper showed that among the American students at HBS, 8.3 percent described themselves as "politically indifferent" (a high number, I thought, for a graduate school focused on leadership), 49.4 percent claimed to be Democrats (15.4 percent strong Democrats, 34.0 percent moderate), 34.8 percent Republicans (9.5 percent strong, 25.3 percent moderate), and 7.5 percent Other. A week after the election, *The Harbus*, the student newspaper, carried a grudging report of the result: "HBS alumnus prevails in second cliff-hanger election. George W. Bush, arguably HBS' most famous alumnus (HBS '75) eked out a victory earlier this month over Democratic challenger John F. Kerry."

The first half of the TOM course had been heavy on numbers. We learned to calculate the cycle times and output rate of complicated manufacturing processes and studied the benefits of job shops versus assembly lines. The mind-bending climax was the National Cranberry Corporation case, in which we had to calculate the rates at which cranberries were delivered to a plant and then sorted, cleaned, and packaged. Thankfully, after the midterms we broke into clear water with a class about the Toyota Production System. Early in its history, Toyota had established a goal of delivering an affordable range of cars in as efficient a way as possible. The Toyota Production System was designed to eliminate waste of every kind, be it overproduction, mistakes by employees, or an excess inventory of parts. One aspect of this was Just-In-Time production, a method of producing what was needed, when it was needed, and nothing more. Another was called *jidoka*, a means of making any problems immediately obvious and stopping production to resolve them. Anything that deviated from the correct process, including a mistake by a worker, was considered waste.

To implement *jidoka*, Toyota had to eliminate any sense of stigma for an employee who halted the production process. Above each station along the production line, the company installed a pull, an *andon*, which the worker was encouraged to pull whenever he spotted a problem. Lights would flash and loud music would blare and the team leader on the assembly line would rush over. After diagnosing the problem, the leader would then lead his team in the Five Whys, a means of getting to the root of any problem. If you just asked why, you would get the immediate cause of a problem. If you asked it four more times, you would get to the bottom of the problem. The company encouraged workers never to assume any process was set in stone and to seek constant improvement. This was known as *kaizen*, change for the better. It was the power of process, Zeynep said. Toyota was such a success because it considered nothing too small. The company was constantly seeking to improve even the minutest details of its operation, and every employee was involved. Coming from the world of factory floors and production, these lessons resonated more loudly than if they had come from a organizational behavior course. I owned a Toyota. It was ten years old and drove beautifully. *Kaizen* worked. That evening, I saw Bo running across the street to the local grocery store to pick up dinner. "PDB," he shouted, raising one enormous hand in the air. "I'm never going to buy in bulk again. It's going to be Just-In-Time all the way. *Kaizen, kaizen.* I love it!"

Shortly before the Thanksgiving break, the school organized Thanksgiving dinners for all the sections and their professors. I arrived late and found a seat next to Ruback. We steered clear of finance and spoke instead about his role as head of the RC. Most of his time, he said, was spent trying to improve the experience. He wished there was less fear of missing out (FOMO) and that students felt less obligation to conform. Married students, he said, tended to have a much better time at the school than unmarried ones. "Maybe they're just more ready to commit." He was worried that the younger students went out drinking too much. "We had one of those section lunches recently with Kim Clark, and he was standing there giving his talk about the learning experience and humility and the mission of the school, and I looked up and written on the board behind him in huge letters was 'Happy Hour at 9:00 P.M.' It was a Wednesday." To better understand and improve the student experience, Ruback said, the school had started a longitudinal survey in which around fifty students were chosen to come in every couple of weeks and spend two hours describing their lives at the school. They would do this throughout their two years at HBS and continue on a less frequent basis once they had graduated. However frustrated I was at times with the school, I could not fault it for taking its methods and aims seriously.

A weird moment occurred in LEAD during a discussion of Martin Luther King, Jr.'s, "I have a dream" speech. After we had read it and watched a video of King speaking on the steps of the Lincoln Memorial, Podolny asked the class for comments. What was there to say? It seemed an outrageous leap to apply our observations of office politics and corporate leadership to King. There was a long silence. Salvation came from an unexpected quarter, the front row on the right. There sat Benny, the heir to a large African oil fortune. Up until then, Benny had never said a word until called upon. He spent most of the classes hiding beneath the brim of a baseball cap, sleeping off the night before. But here he was at this sensitive moment to break the silence.

"I was thinking that in presenting his facts, King might have used a few more numbers." No one put up their hand.

"What kind of numbers do you have in mind, Benny?" Podolny said, straining not to smile.

"You know, the scale of suffering of African Americans. The number of lynchings, for example."

"Does anyone else think King's speech could have been improved with more numbers and less rhetoric?" Podolny asked. The laughter started in the skydeck with Annette, and soon billowed across the room.

Later in the semester, Podolny gave us the profiles of six members of the class of 1976, written for their tenth and twentieth reunions. Just before each five-year reunion, the members of each class were asked to write a few paragraphs about what had happened in their lives since HBS. These were collected in a book and distributed only to members of that class. Among the six profiles there was a man who had devoted himself to the restaurant business only to have his daughter chase him down the street crying because he was working for the forty-second day in a row; a woman who had divorced her husband and rarely saw their daughter, who had a chromosomal defect; and a self-described "entrepreneurial maverick" who moved tirelessly around the country setting up businesses and who had remained single by avoiding "several near Mrs." By far the most contented person was a man who went to Wall Street right after graduation and stayed with the same firm. He had a home in New York, a country house in Connecticut, and a private life that revolved around family and community. He considered his main career objective as "making it through the day" and defined a good place to work as a "place to have fun and make money."

These were our futures. A mixture of success and failure. Work stress and family struggles. The ceaseless tussle between wanting to make money and following your heart.

Podolny made the point that HBS never fêtes those alumni who have gone out into the world and just made it work, those who achieved happiness in their lives, a balance between family and work and friendships. The ones invited to speak at Burden to audiences of nine hundred were those who ran huge companies or who made colossal fortunes. The very ones who told us "you have to get the balance right in your lives" often admitted, as Meg Whitman had, that they had not done so themselves.

One of the Mormons in the class, a man in his mid-twenties with three children, spoke emotionally about the pressure to succeed according to the HBS template: "Why has it taken until now for us to read about this guy who takes a banking job and likes it? We never hear about the HBS grads who say, 'I'm not in this for the money. I'm going to open a small firm in my hometown, be home every day at five P.M. to see my children, and take four weeks of vacation each year.'" I agreed. We patted these people on the head and said, "Bravo," but seemed not to take their success as seriously as that of hyperactive wing nuts like Jack Welch. In order to live the life of quiet, personal fulfillment, Podolny said, you could expect thanks or admiration from only a very limited audience. And for many people, especially Harvard MBAs who had spent their entire lives being applauded and coming first and winning contests and being praised for everything they did— whether it was mathematics or community service or gymnastics—the idea of private, discreet fulfillment being of equal worth to public success was nearly impossible to grasp.

Or perhaps it was just impossible to value, said Cedric, a West African and former banker. "I think MBAs struggle to make these comparisons," he said. "We're so into putting values or numbers on things, that if we can't value something, we just sweep it away. How do you compare the value of a healthy relationship with one's child when the alternative has a distinct value, say, a million-dollar bonus." For those in the market for the $1-million bonus, he was saying, the notion of "priceless" did not imply "beyond price and therefore the most important thing in the world" but rather "impossible to price and therefore not worth arguing about when the alternative is so tangible."

In the last fifteen minutes of the class, we were all asked to write down what we imagined we would submit for our tenth-year HBS anniversary book. I wrote that I was now living in a comfortable house outside New York, working from an office in my garden. I was still married to Margret, and our children were growing up in a clean, healthy place. I owned a handful of media properties and had a small group of like-minded and enthusiastic employees. I set my own schedule, took vacations when I liked, and yet loved my work. In fact, there was no division between my life and my work. Podolny instructed us to swap what we had written with a neighbor, and he then called on a Japanese woman to read the one she had been given. It had been written by a Chinese American man who had been a management consultant before HBS. "I am still struggling," his profile began. "I'm working far more than I'd like, often ninety hours a week, and not finding enough time to see my wife. I enjoy the work while I'm doing it, but I can't see ever getting the work-life balance thing right. We have a decent house and are making decent money, but we'd like to have kids someday and can't see how that's going to happen. One of us is going to have to step back, but we don't know who. It is a burden carrying the expectations of an immigrant family, but one I am proud of."

At the end of each course, each professor gave a brief personal speech. Eddie Riedl put up a slide on which he had written, "Why I do what I do. My motivation for this course is the thought that during your careers, you will collectively make decisions that will affect the flow of billions of dollars worth of resources and the lives of countless individuals, and that the quality of these decisions can be improved, in part, by what you learn in this course." He was immediately challenged by a man in the skydeck. "You need to change that word *billions*," the man said. Riedl looked nonplussed. "It should say *trillions*." "You're right," Riedl replied. "It's ridiculous how much financial muscle Harvard MBAs wield." Podolny wrote the word *serendipity* on the blackboard. You start looking for one thing, he said, and you find another. He spoke about the twists his career had taken to land him here with Section A for the past four months. He told us he had found teaching us meaningful and satisfying.

Steenburgh told us the story of his father, a paunchy man who was underestimated on the softball field. Opposing teams would always bring in their fielders when he came to bat, and he would smack the ball over their heads and round the bases chuckling. When Steenburgh had left his job at Xerox to return to academia, many of his friends wondered what he was doing. But he said he found a joy in teaching he had not found elsewhere.

Zeynep said she was too young to have any great wisdom to impart. So she gave us another case to read instead. It was about an HBS professor called Jai Jaikumar. He was an Indian who loved climbing in the Himalayas. But as an undergraduate in India he had suffered a terrible fall, tumbling thousands of feet over rocks and trees, snow and ice. He was badly injured and lost his climbing companion. After walking for twenty-four hours in acute pain, he stumbled across a small hut in a clearing. A shepherdess took him in, fed him, and tended to his wounds. Then she carried him on her back for three days to the nearest village, from where he traveled for two more days on a donkey to the nearest hospital. When he recovered, he resumed his academic career, which brought him to America and eventually Harvard, where he specialized in manufacturing science. But he never forgot the shepherdess, and when he could afford to, he built a school in her village and raised money to pay for teachers and supplies. He always encouraged his students to enjoy and celebrate their lives instead of becoming stressed out. Success, he taught them, was the result of good fortune, and this brought obligations to others. He died at the age of fifty-three while mountain climbing in Ecuador.

In between these classes and final exams, I had lunch with Luis, a half-French, half-Argentine entrepreneur and the striker on the HBS soccer team. He was one of the older members of the section and a Pied Piper for many of the international students. You could find him on campus chattering away in English, Spanish, French, or German or leading a gaggle of Latin American students to a bar in Boston. Before HBS, he had worked in consulting in Madrid and then cofounded an online shopping company. He had opened offices all around Europe in the late 1990s, before being forced to close them again when the Internet bubble collapsed in 2001. I often wondered why people like him, with so much business experience already, came to HBS.

"I'd gone through the whole process of starting a company, but I had a feeling that I needed to go back to the basics," he told me, speaking quickly and intensely. "I'd learned by a trial of fire. In consulting, I'd learned a lot at the beginning, but then you start to repeat things again and again. At the start-up it had been crazy; I'd been on a steep learning curve, but there were a lot of things I felt I needed to sit back and learn properly."

Once he had decided to go to business school, he knew it had to be a top school, because the network was vital for him. His brother-in-law had been to HBS and loved it. After what he thought was a poor interview with a "typical Spanish investment banker with cement in his hair," Luis was elated to be accepted. Arriving on campus, he was surprised by the diversity of people but also by how young they seemed. "There are lots of people who are young. They are analytically and technically very sharp, but I can recognize the skills people have, and it was surprising to me that there was so little experience in the class. People spoke like they had experience, but often I'd be sitting in class thinking 'practically, what you're saying would never work.'" This had happened most often in LEAD. "People would often say, just fire the guy. But if you've never fired someone, you don't know what it's like and you can't just imagine it. We should have a course on just that, hiring and firing. We all took the Myers-Briggs, but we're not being taught how to use it in hiring people. I think there are some very pragmatic things missing from the course."

I also met up with Vera, a Chinese woman who had emigrated with her husband to Silicon Valley and had worked for a large technology firm. During the semester, Bob had organized a "section buddy" system, whereby each of us monitored a classmate's in-class comments and told that person how he or she was doing. Vera was my buddy. She spoke excellent English but with a heavy Chinese accent, and had to force herself to speak in class. It had been exasperating. "I hate all this stuff about the network and relationships and being able to bullshit in front of other people," she said. "That's what we're being trained to do. That's not what Chinese immigrants think business is. We think it's about good ideas and hard work." It was hard for her to accept that 50 percent of her grade was based on what she said in class, not just because she found public speaking so awkward but also because much of what she heard seemed so mediocre. She had resigned herself to taking what she could from the classes and filtering out the rest.

The term ended with written exams in each of the five subjects we had studied. The exams were open-book, but I spent a couple of days going over my notes from each course, trying to boil them down to just a few pages so I could work more quickly. The professors told us that if you showed up to class and prepared the cases, the exams held few surprises. They were simply reviews of the concepts we had encountered so far. Doing well in them, of course, was no proof you might be good at business, only that you were good at business school.

We were split into two classrooms for the exams, so we could each have a couple of desks' worth of space. Some students wore headphones to block out the noise. Others arrived with piles of gum and candy as if about to go on a hike. Some came bleary-eyed, wearing their sweats, looking as if they had been studying all night. We all plugged in our laptops and waited until our exam supervisor said go. I felt the greatest trepidation with Finance, but when I turned over the exam sheet, I suddenly felt very calm. I began systematically working through the problem.

A cinema owner was trying to figure out whether or not to acquire new digital projectors. Was it worth it? I forecast the free cash flows and calculated the cost of capital. I found a present value for the investment. I made a recommendation and finally, after four and a half hours, printed out my spreadsheets and write-up and turned them in. It felt deeply satisfying. In FRC, TOM, Marketing, and LEAD, this sense of achievement was the same. After so much work, I felt I was finally speaking this new language. I was still far from fluent, but at least I was communicating. My grades were better than I had hoped that first night of Analytics: ones in TOM and LEAD, and twos in FIN 1, Marketing, and FRC. Academically, at least, I knew I could cut it.

Finishing the exams, I realized how much I had learned about business and myself during those first five months. It was strange no longer to have a professional identity. I had become used to thinking of myself as a journalist, and abandoning that had been harder than I had imagined. It also felt odd always to be one of the older people in the room. I worried when people said HBS was all about the network, and I spent so little time socializing. But then I had gotten to know people in the classroom, or over lunches or coffee, instead of standing in a room watching someone frozen to the booze luge, and this, overall, had led to some richer relationships.

Chapter Eight

THE RISK
MASTER

During the vacations, HBS students set off around the world on treks to glamorous destinations such as India, China, Turkey, or Brazil, and more humdrum ones such as Chicago or Washington, D.C. Besides sightseeing, they met CEOs of companies, presidents, and prime ministers. At HBS you felt you were never more than two degrees of separation from the most powerful people in the world. There was always a classmate who knew the prime minister of India or who worked for the president of Mexico or whose father ran the largest construction business in Latin America. No one was out of reach. But the reports that came back from these treks tended to focus on other things. In India, there were murmurs of displeasure at students who wore dispensers of hand cleanser on their belts. Every time they boarded the buses ferrying them around, they would purify their hands, disinfecting themselves and antagonizing their hosts. The China trek was oversubscribed and ended up taking more than two hundred MBAs. The following account appeared in the the student newspaper, *The Harbus:*

"Drunken shrimp, midnight karaoke, rows of empty glasses of Chivas & green tea and venture capitalists—what do these all have in common? These were just a few of the highlights of this year's China Trek." The party had started in Beijing and moved on to Hong Kong and Shanghai.

The trekkers were "treated like imperial royalty" and given access to the "hottest nightspots" and "senior corporate executives." In Beijing, they ate drunken shrimp—"you thought MBAs were the only drunk ones on this trip!"—observed preparations for the 2008 Olympics, toured Lenovo's manufacturing plant, and were courted by "executives from Motorola, real estate developers and local investment banks." Finally they reached Hong Kong, "the land of Louis Vuitton stores and bright psychedelic neon lights."

Reading stories like this, I felt two things. The first was how privileged we were to see the world as Harvard MBAs. The brand was stronger than I had ever imagined. The second was how weird this perspective was. To go to China and focus entirely on the clubs, booze, shops, and corporate entertainment seemed inane. The trekkers need not have spent all their time hearing tales of woe from displaced peasant farmers or women wrenched from their families to work in garment factories supplying Western clothing, or human rights activists harassed for posting their thoughts on Yahoo! But it did feel like the pursuit of business goals allowed, or even required, a self-imposed ignorance. Instead of being part of society, the MBA überclass seemed to exist apart from the rest of the world, with its own set of standards. You needed to yank hard to get its attention.

Ben Esty, our section chair, had told us that when it came to these treks, we should take on more loans and seize the opportunities. The costs, running into thousands of dollars per trek, would be nothing but a "rounding error" on our future net worth. Bob and I, who were both supporting families on financial aid, agreed that while this might be true, it was also obnoxious.

The one exception I made was the Westrek to Silicon Valley at the end of the Christmas vacation. As a newspaper reporter, I had felt the gusts of change brought on by the Internet and had witnessed my colleagues and management flailing in the face of them. I knew the media would always be a part of my professional life, and I wanted to become literate in the language and business models of the technology companies now looming over the industry. Westrek promised access to the very biggest names in the valley: Google, eBay, Yahoo!, and the fabled venture capitalists at Kleiner Perkins Caufield Byers (KPCB).

About eighty of us, two thirds of whom were Chinese or Indian, checked into a hotel in the middle of a business park next to the headquarters of Oracle. I took a drive around the surrounding streets, past the glass-fronted buildings and rows of one-story homes stacked up against each other behind high wooden fences. I wondered why people at HBS kept harping on about the Silicon Valley lifestyle and the beauty of the Bay Area. Around here, it looked dreadful, like an engineering school campus squashed flat over several square miles. I turned onto Route 101, the drain of Silicon Valley, full of cheap restaurants, car repair shops, strip malls, and laundries. Up in the hills were towns such as Palo Alto, Woodside, and Atherton, where those with the real money lived and worked and rose early to go bicycling with one another.

At eight thirty the following morning, one of the most famous venture capitalists in Silicon Valley loped into the hotel's conference room to open Westrek. He was a tall, athletic man with dark floppy hair, a craggy face offset by a goofy grin, and the sloping shoulders of an aging prep school sports star. His hair was still wet, suggesting he may already have played a couple of sets of tennis. Tim Draper was a third-generation venture capitalist who graduated from Stanford with a degree in electrical engineering and from Harvard with his MBA. He had boosted the family fortune with investments in technology start-ups such as Hotmail and Skype. We were eager to hear from him how we could horn in on the next multibillion-dollar technology business.

Venture capital, said Draper, was much easier than trying to climb the corporate ladder. All you needed to be set for life was one success. After that, you just had to sit there while hundreds of people pitched you their ideas and you picked the best of them. It was a no-brainer! He grinned, and we sat there dumbstruck. Beside me was Gurinder, from my section. He had graduated from the finest engineering school in India and had already earned the Indian version of an MBA. Before coming to HBS, he had been an executive at one of India's top technology firms. All he wanted from Harvard was the opportunity to become a West Coast venture capitalist. On snowbound days in Boston, you could find him in the corner of Spangler rhapsodizing about the beauty of the Bay Area and bemoaning the stupidity of his HBS classmates. He regarded the academic content of the HBS MBA and many of the professors with bare contempt. He always had heavy bags under his eyes from spending his nights on Skype talking to India, where he was setting up an online travel company.

As people asked Draper questions, I could feel Gurinder growing uneasy. When someone asked Draper how they could be in his shoes one day, he flicked off his large penny loafers and invited his questioner to step into them. No one laughed. Gurinder began rubbing his temples. Impatient at the best of times, he now felt he was being taunted by this big white fraternity boy.

Draper then told us he had written a song that had been set to music and performed by a famous rock star whom he could not name. The song was called "The Risk Master." He passed around CDs on which he had printed a photograph of himself in a white floppy-brimmed hat sitting astride an elephant holding up his right hand in triumph. Then he popped a copy into a player and asked us to listen closely. The song began with a long, low strum of a guitar, a bass joined in and a steady rhythmic beat. The lyrics then appeared on a screen behind Draper, who cleared his throat. His song told the story of a man who had spent fifteen years struggling to bring his company to an initial public offering on the stock market, the dream of every venture capitalist. He had invested everything he had. His wife had lost patience and divorced him. He had been abused by his investors and bankers, but he remained convinced the big payday would come. When the song reached the chorus, Draper began waving his arms and shouting, "All together. Come on. Sing!" Gurinder had now dropped his notebook and thrust his head down deep between his knees.

He is the Risk Master
Lives fast and drives faster
Skates on the edge of disaster
He is the risk master

We went quiet again, leaving Draper to sing the verses. The hero of his song was fearless, with the soul of an artist. He had weathered a recession, flirted with bankruptcy, and fired his best friend. But then, with one dramatic sale, everything had turned around. The sky, Draper sang, "opened astronautic."

"Come on, you guys, you're so quiet!" Draper shouted, reveling in the awkwardness. "Come *on!*" We mumbled through the chorus. "Again, again," he urged. Again we mumbled. Finally, the song's hero was deluged with money, but instead of being happy, he found he was hounded by the press and the courts as everyone assumed "anyone this rich must have lied." Finally, after two more renditions of the chorus, the song wound down. We sat there in silence. Draper wrapped up his remarks and we wandered out into the lobby.

A large group of us then drove over to see Yahoo! in Sunnyvale. The company's headquarters was a complex of boxy glass buildings fitted out with yellow-and-purple furnishings, as if Barney the Dinosaur had moonlit as the decorator. There were playrooms with table football, free coffee, and mini basketball hoops in the corridors, telltale signs of a company that would rather its employees not go home. Despite the infantile décor, ten years after its founding, Yahoo! was part of corporate America. We were addressed by a senior vice president at the firm, in charge of mergers and acquisitions. He described his rapid ascent. After university in Britain, he went to work for Goldman Sachs, then earned his MBA at HBS. After graduation, he worked at Allen and Company, a media-focused investment bank in New York, then at an Internet venture fund run by Terry Semel, a former

Hollywood studio chief who was appointed CEO of Yahoo! The senior VP rattled through his presentation in a whisper and seemed horribly pleased with himself. Perhaps he had a right to be. He was exactly the same age as I.

The following morning I woke up with a start at eight thirty. It had taken me hours to fall asleep, stewing over that precocious Yahoo! VP, and I was supposed to be at Kleiner Perkins by 8:45. I washed and shaved as fast as I could, pulled on my clothes, and ran to the elevator holding my jacket and the directions. I sprinted over to the parking lot and launched my rented Impala out onto Route 101. It was 8:40. The receptionist had told me it would take half an hour to get to KPCB's offices on Sand Hill Road. I burned down 101, climbed west to the Junípero Serra freeway, past Stanford University, and then from there onto Sand Hill Road. By the time I pulled into the KPCB lot, in between a Mercedes two-seater and a Toyota Prius, it was shortly before nine.

The main office building resembled a large Swiss chalet. Two dark wooden beams, soaked with rain, pitched steeply over the glass entrance hall. A towering orchid display greeted visitors. I breathlessly announced myself to the receptionist.

"They've already started," she said, sourly. "In the conference room to your right."

I opened the door, and the speaker paused while I pushed my way to the only available chair, tucked away in a far corner of the room. Those of my classmates who had snagged one of the high-back black leather swivel chairs around the conference table moved gently from side to side, looking thoughtful yet inquiring, as if auditioning for a future there. The table was a single cross-section of what must have been a colossal tree, at least six feet across. It had been polished, but you could still appreciate the knots and the grain of the wood. I wondered how many great businesses had been plotted out at this table. Kleiner Perkins, after all, had funded so many of the great technology firms, from Sun Microsystems to Amazon to Google. Our speaker was Russell Siegelman, an engaging man who had graduated from

HBS and spent several very successful years at Microsoft before becoming a venture capitalist. He said that he was amazed by how many people wanted to be in venture capital these days, seeing it as a straight shot to vast wealth. It wasn't, he said. Of course there were people who did astoundingly well. And being at a top firm with access to the most brilliant technical and commercial minds in Silicon Valley made the odds of success that much better. But he had been at Kleiner Perkins for four years and he was still two years away from knowing if any of his investments would work out. Compared to working in operations at Microsoft, this was lonelier, less involved, less exciting work. Your main role was to find the right people and the right venture and make the right investment. After that, providing you had done your job well, you should get out of the way and wait. You were not there to meddle daily or weekly. You were there to help when required. I looked through the glass wall of the conference room to the offices, laid out along another glass wall facing trees. It was raining outside and there didn't seem to be anyone here besides us. VCs do not need to come to their offices to get things done. I understood Siegelman's point about the detached nature of his role. If you were really into business and good at it, this was no life. It would be like being Michelangelo and suddenly finding yourself a patron, no longer painting or sculpting but merely issuing checks for other painters and sculptors. You either had to want to be a patron to start with or else had gotten to a point in life where you preferred investing to building, and your advice was actually worth something. Lots of Harvard MBAs wanted to become VCs straight out of school because it seemed to offer large rewards for basically opining and playing with other people's money. But they were really not ripe for the job yet.

Google, which we visited later in the day, was how I imagined Yahoo! must have been five or six years earlier. Same glass campus, same childlike atmosphere, but somehow more authentic given the age of the company, its founders and employees. You did not sense that the toys and free coffee

were there for show, while the grown-up executives were actually chomp-
ing cigars in a wood-paneled suite. There were Segways in the lobby, people
could bring their dogs to work, and a line snaked past the cubicles of
employees waiting for free massages. The company threw a reception for us
and a group from MIT. Sadly only five of the eighty or so Westrekkers
showed up. Most had chosen to go to happy hours thrown by banks and consulting firms in San Francisco. We were saved by the MIT students, who
arrived in force and excited.

I was standing eating a chicken satay and wondering whom to talk to
when a young-looking guy in a blue "Blogger.com" T-shirt tucked neatly
into his jeans shambled up, scarfing everything he could grab from the buf-
fet. It was Sergey Brin, the cofounder of Google. All six billion dollars'
worth of him (at the time). He looked about fifteen, his skin glowing, his
thick black hair brushed back from his high brow. I pointed at his T-shirt
and asked him which blogs he read. Technology ones mostly, he said, but he
doesn't even read too many of them. There was too much else to do besides
reading blogs. Quickly, we were surrounded by eager MIT students who all
stood there, bouncing on their toes, staring at him like hungry cannibals.

Google's cofounder Larry Page arrived wearing jeans and a tracksuit
top. He and Sergey gave a droll presentation, exchanging remarks and
asides like an old Vegas double act. They were happy we were there, they
said, because Google was at the beginning of a grand adventure and there
was plenty of work to be done, especially if we were ready to start up their
operations overseas. It was funny to think that just five years before, these
two men were getting to know each other in Stanford's computer science
doctoral program, and now here they were, the objects of such intense fascination. "But we're not here to give a talk," Page said. "What we'd really
like to know is what you think of Google. So what is your least favorite
Google product?" Lots of hands shot up. The MIT students were intense,
steeped in Google and its technology. They had queries about algorithms
and functionality and business models. I imagined what a similar group of

HBS students might ask. "How do we get to be in your shoes?" "What do you think of India and China?" "Do you think it's a good idea to go into consulting first to get some more experience before bolting together some servers in a computer science lab and setting up a world-changing technology?" I asked Page what he saw as the future for Google News. He rambled around the subject as if he weren't that interested before concluding that he'd like it to be a way of making reporters more accountable.

Google felt like an incredible place. The energy was palpable and the institutional weight that had smothered Yahoo! had yet to impose itself. As I was leaving, I saw a woman clearly very upset sitting on a low wall beside one of the buildings. She was staring at the ground and holding a tissue to her nose. Sergey Brin was crossing the lawn in front of her and he sat down beside her and put his arm around her. It was still that kind of company.

At eBay, meanwhile, the zombies had taken over. Twenty HBS alumni, roughly the same number as those of us attending the presentation, were lined up to talk about their work. They stood in a long row, like police suspects, and explained what they did. By the end, I couldn't figure out who was a product manager, who a product marketing manager, and who was in charge of marketing jewelry products. Maybe it was the lighting and the thin gray drizzle falling on the floor-to-ceiling windows, but no one looked well here. Suddenly a door opened in the back of the room and in marched Meg Whitman, the CEO. She spoke of the great career opportunities at eBay, but I looked at her and kept thinking back to the video in LEAD where she said, "you probably won't look back and wish that you'd worked harder . . . In the end your families and friends are the most important thing." By those criteria, and given her own experience, why would I ever move to San Jose and work here?

That evening, I found myself lost in Palo Alto with Nico, a Romanian student. I had first noticed him during Analytics when several of the military veterans who had served in Iraq decided to give a talk about their experiences after class. One man who had worked for the Coalition Provisional Authority described the conditions on arriving in Baghdad in 2003 as "the worst imaginable." The administrative hit squad flown in from Washington to establish a postwar Iraq found themselves huddled around a single light in a vast, empty palace. Their computers had been left on the airport runway and had melted into the asphalt. They had no means of communication. While most of the room gasped at these tales from the front, Nico put up his hand and asked if the former CPA guy thought the invasion was the inspiration of American oil companies. He was given a very cold shoulder for this, but he didn't seem to mind and stayed for the rest of the talk, leaning against a column at the front of the classroom. I thought his question was poorly timed, but I quite admired his cool.

We were trying to find a bar where the trek organizers had arranged a mixer for HBS and Stanford MBAs, but we had become hopelessly lost in the suburban twilight, driving back and forth between the elegant streets surrounding Stanford and the Hispanic edge of Palo Alto, searching for our destination amid the taco stands, gas stations, and sprawling bungalows. Nico told me he had left his friends and family in Romania to give himself a few years in America to earn his MBA and work for a big American firm, either in technology or finance. Then he would go back home. He had found HBS to be a mostly ludicrous experience. "The Americans just talk even when they have nothing to say," he said. "I feel like I'm paying all this money just so that these American kids can have an audience and say they know this Romanian guy."

Like many of the foreigners, Nico had found HBS's claim to be an international school bogus. Many of the purported international students had spent so much of their lives in the United States that they brought very little international flavor. There were Japanese students who had lived in the United States since they were ten, Nigerians who had moved to Texas in their teens, Princeton-educated Indians. These students may have dressed up for International Week, but they were culturally close enough to the Americans as to be indistinguishable from them.

By the time we found the mixer, it was almost over. There were three forlorn-looking HBS-ers perched around a small table. None of the Stanford students had shown up. Nico and I thought about buying a beer, but it was too sad. We got back in our car, drove away, and got lost again.

Chapter Nine

INSECURE
OVERACHIEVERS

You thought we were going to be the intellectual elite. Well, we're not. We're not the hereditary elite, and we're certainly not the artistic or creative elite. What we're being groomed as is the competent elite. Get used to it . . . we're being trained to be the guys who stay sober at the party. We're being handed the tools to get out there and run things.

—*THE BIG TIME: THE HARVARD
BUSINESS SCHOOL'S MOST
SUCCESSFUL CLASS AND HOW
IT SHAPED AMERICA,*
BY LAURENCE SHAMES

Just before returning for the second half of the RC, I met Justin, my friend from Analytics, for breakfast in New York. We went to a Cuban café on the Upper West Side. Soon we would have to find jobs for the summer, and he was trying to figure out how deep into business he wanted to go. The same people who had encouraged him to go to business school were now advising him to spend a couple of years in investment banking. People in New York took you seriously if you had spent a couple of years on Wall Street, they said. If nothing else, it showed you could work hard and survive. Justin was not so sure.

"I don't know if I can do it," he told me, sipping his Cuban coffee. "You've seen me doing finance. It's just not my core competence. Listen to me. I never said 'core competence' before HBS."

"Do you want to make a career in finance?"

"Not really."

"Then why do it?"

"Because it might be useful. I feel like everyone else at that friggin' HBS has done two years in banking or consulting, and if you haven't, companies just won't take you seriously."

"Fine, then go ahead. Climb into the belly of the beast."

"Don't just say that. Why don't you climb into the belly, too?"

"Sometimes I want to. I think it would do me good. But then I hear about what it involves and I just know that I can't. What's the point in hearing everyone say 'put your family first,' 'be around for your kids while they're growing up,' and then taking a job when you know you'll be working nonstop? I'd like to do it for my career, and I think it might be interesting, but I know I'd hate the demands." Whenever I was tempted to try for a well-paid but punishing job, I recalled how I felt as a journalist being sent on a fatuous assignment, how I loathed sitting in a hotel room or on a plane, doing my employer's bidding and missing being at home. Could I tolerate the life of a junior banker? Hours staring at a screen, drinking stomach-rotting coffee, building model after financial model that no one would read and then listening to a senior partner bitch about his disintegrating marriage. Even for all that money, why would I ever do that to myself? But then again, having bothered to come to HBS, what did I think business was about? Greek islands and poetry?

"I know what you mean," said Justin. "I met a guy the other day who spent his summer internship last year at Goldman Sachs. He said he spent sixty-seven straight days in the office. Basically he arrived on day one and never left."

The race for summer jobs began the moment we returned to campus. Ruback's stress curve, I recalled, had hit its peak during the recruiting season. A good summer internship was regarded as essential for a good post-HBS job. For some companies, especially the top-tier banks, private equity firms, and hedge funds, if you did not spend the summer with them you had no chance of working for them later. At others, a good performance over the summer meant a guaranteed job afterward and a stress-free second year. For many in the class, the coming weeks would determine not just their summer but also their post-HBS career. It was an opportune moment for *The Harbus* to republish an article headlined "Being Depressed at HBS." It had been written by a student who had battled with depression and was intended to help others who felt unable to admit to their condition in this competitive environment. The author wrote that she almost killed herself three times during her first year at HBS. Everything had been fine at first, but then one day she started to feel different. Soon this feeling morphed into an unrelenting sadness. She could not fathom why everyone else seemed happy. She was simultaneously battling with the great question—what do I want to do with the rest of my life?—while fending off calls from recruiters. Seeing the same faces every day in her section was wearing her down. She began crying herself to sleep and staying in her room. She stopped exercising and began second-guessing every comment she made in class. The cases dragged on. "I started hating myself for ever applying to HBS," she wrote, "and then one day I just didn't get out of bed. I stayed in bed all day and just cried and cried. Then a strange calmness came over me. 'Everything would be alright if I just killed myself,' I thought. 'Then it would all go away.' So I made my way to the bridge and stood there for nearly an hour. But I couldn't jump off."

Thankfully, the author of the piece recovered, but HBS knew that her experience was not unique. We were a class full of insecure overachievers, a term I heard again and again. None of us was facing unemployment or working for the minimum wage. Instead, we were searching for identity and meaning in all the fine grades and career achievements that filled our résumés. The school had taken measures to calm us down. They gave us pep talks before the first-year midterms, telling us that however we did on them, we were still high up the MBA totem pole. There was Podolny's lecture on serendipity. Even the magnificent gym was there to help us relax. A mental health counselor kept an office in Spangler, and her help was sought by eighty or ninety students in each class.

Through Cedric, the West African in our section, I had gotten to know Hasan, an Arab student from another section. His family had come to America but found it hard to assimilate and had returned to live in the Middle East. Hasan had attended international schools and eventually won a place at Dartmouth. He was captivated by America and decided to stay, taking a job as a technology consultant. He loved the academic work at HBS but found the social atmosphere stifling. "I'm used to having two personalities, work Hasan and social Hasan, and they're very different," he told me. "At work I'm very serious and professional, but socially I like to be really relaxed. Here I feel people are so obsessed with their place in the network, with their own personal brand, they never let go. You are expected to be the same person in every setting. I can't really blur my personalities." He complained that he was ridiculed for being so serious in class. "People use very passive-aggressive methods, like the skydecks, to control behavior. They don't confront you, they're really politically correct about that, but their attitude is closed-minded. It's supposed to be an open environment, but I feel like everything you say or do is being scrutinized so they know where to put you on the curve."

I had not had the same experience as Hasan, but I was beginning to feel the pressure to conform, to pick one of the paths floodlit by HBS. When I first arrived at the school, I was halfway to convincing myself I could be an investment banker. There was the money, of course, and the status. But there was also the sense that it would be an exciting kind of life—in the thick of things, forever transacting, dealing with different people and companies at a pace I had never experienced. Some of my cleverest and nicest friends had become bankers and had done very well. But none of them seemed to love it. Whenever I suggested I might try to join their ranks they insisted, "Don't!" They told me that I would never survive, that I was too impatient. I would find it tedious and repetitive and the people humorless. But what about the money? It palls, they told me. They all had a figure in their heads and once they had made it, they would retire. Still, I didn't believe them.

During the first semester, the section hosted lunches in which the ex-consultants talked about consulting and the ex–investment bankers about investment banking. The overwhelming lesson from both was, don't go into either. They pay you well but leave you with no life. During the consulting session, Max, a brainy ex–management consultant, said that at his firm, and at most of the other big consultancies, if you arrived single you would stay single, and if you arrived married you would end up divorced. "They pretend to support people with families, but the moment hard times hit, it's the people with families who get fired first," he said. Other consultants talked about the unending round of meetings, the way their bosses knowingly ripped off clients by offering useless advice wrapped up in fancy presentations. It was a culture, they said, of intellectual arrogance and extreme cynicism. They described the four days of travel every week, starting on a Sunday night, ending on Thursday, if you were lucky, and the prison of the hotel conference rooms where they spent their time. They spoke of their bosses' wrecked personal lives. The best thing, they all said, was that their companions in this purgatory tended to be intelligent and like-minded.

In the session on Wall Street, Stuart, the hunk who had described the psychological contract regarding taxis and Chinese food at his firm, said that whenever he told his family back in Nevada how much he was earning, they whooped and slapped him on the back, congratulating him for milking the system. "There was only one person getting milked, though," he said, "and that was me." It was not unusual for him to leave the office at four in the morning, sleep in the car home, have the car wait while he went inside and showered, and then get back in and return to work. He recalled working after 9/11 to help reestablish his bank's operations and being in a meeting with a senior woman banker. Her phone rang. It was her daughter's school. There had been a bomb alert and the school was being evacuated. "And what do you expect me to do about it?" the woman screamed. "You're meant to be looking after her." She slammed down the phone and continued the meeting. Stuart said he tried to be as discouraging to us as possible about Wall Street, because if people still wanted to do it, they must really want it. If you accepted the money offered by these firms, then you had to accept that your life was theirs. They had no respect for your time.

Another sign of how draining consulting and banking could be was the effort the industries had to put into recruiting. It felt as though the consulting firms and the Wall Street banks had buried encampments on campus from which they deployed their fresh-faced recruiters. They made unsolicited calls to our homes offering to describe their work. It was like being badgered by the Church of Scientology. Barely a day went by without the firms offering free drinks in the campus bar or dinners in Harvard Square to try to lure people down their chute. They referred to their former employees in each class as their "alumni" and used them as moles to glean information about potential hires.

A story went around about one investment bank that liked to humiliate MBA students working there over the summer by greeting each on arrival with a small folding stool. The student was told to set it up each day in a certain department, rotating every couple of weeks, and simply observe. Sometimes the student would be given a task to do, in which case he would take his stool to whatever desk space he could find and set to it. The work would be time-consuming and trivial, involving the extensive manipulation of spreadsheets to no apparent end. The poor MBA would be ignored, jostled, and occasionally abused before finally being graded on his performance in consideration for a full-time position. The ordeal of "the stool" summed up the indignity and absurdity of the summer internship.

Nevertheless, when the banks and consulting firms came recruiting, there was a stampede. The first time this happened was during a week in February called "hell week," when classes were suspended for the full-time pursuit of summer jobs. During the days leading up to hell week, Spangler was filled with students hunched over the blue void of their screens, completing applications and scouring the alumni database for contacts. One woman in our section applied for sixteen jobs, all in banking and consulting. She quickly found that there was no way she could schedule the interviews. She drifted through the cafeteria like a wraith, muttering to anyone who would listen: "If I get a second round at Lehman Brothers, it will clash with the second round with Bain, New York, so what do I do?"

Even Stephen, my study group friend, was swept up in the hunt. I thought he would be more sanguine. "You have to do this, Philip. You can't be cynical about it," he told me. "For people like us, who don't have business experience, it's even more important. You have to show you can do this." I struggled to take it all so seriously. Could my future really depend on whether or not I went to this consulting firm or that bank for a ten-week summer placement? It was as if no other jobs existed. My peers wanted these jobs in the way that contestants on television game shows want the jackpot prize, and they were ready to submit to any kind of humiliation to win it.

My range of summer job choices had shrunk by early February when we discovered Margret was pregnant and due to give birth in September. She now also had a part-time job in Boston that she enjoyed. If I was going to work over the summer, it had to be in Boston, and my sights had settled on investment management. Two executives from one of Boston's largest fund managers had come to campus a few weeks before and painted a rosy picture of their work: you looked around the world and the companies in it and tried to deduce which were worth investing in and which not. The size of the funds the company managed meant that the managers could meet almost anyone in business they liked, while their investors did not expect them to do anything too radical. Most days, the managers were home by 6:00 P.M. Several people told me that my background as a journalist would serve me well in such an environment because much of the work involved sizing up people and situations and truffling for useful facts. I also hoped that since large mutual fund companies were not sexy at the time, I would not be competing with the finance propeller heads who would be pitching their wares to the Greenwich and New York–based hedge funds.

The more I read about investment management at one of these big mutual funds, the easier the work seemed to be. All most of them did was track the market and if possible beat it by a few basis points. Even when they failed, the inertia of their investors was so great that they rarely suffered. The fund managers talked about having great investment ideas and theses about the direction of the world—buy alternative energy/social networking sites/coal/barges!—but most of their work seemed to involve computer-driven weighting of large holdings in blue-chip companies that lumbered along with the market. For further inspiration, I read Peter Lynch's books about running the Magellan Fund, one of the largest pots of money at Fidelity. Lynch's approach seemed simple. He took notice of the most ordinary marketplace signals. If his wife started buying a new detergent, he found out which company made it and bought its stock, preferably cheap. He looked for stocks he thought could multiply three, four, or even tenfold—"three-baggers," "four-baggers," and "ten-baggers," he called them. This was in a time before CNBC and the other stock-picking guides on television and magazine shelves. As far as I could tell, Lynch was remarkable for his energy and open-mindedness in an industry whose dominating culture lacked both.

I also read Roger Lowenstein's biography of Warren Buffett, *The Making of an American Capitalist.* Buffett had come to campus in the first semester to talk to the Democrats Club five days before the presidential election. When he stepped onstage, the entire auditorium of nine hundred gave him a standing ovation. He had been rejected by HBS as a young man and had gone to Columbia. Thirty-five billion dollars later, he had the last laugh. He was as charming as a seventy-four-year-old could be. His clothes fit awkwardly around his paunch, and he held a bottle of Coke throughout his talk, while taking barely a sip. "We own eight percent of the company, so you should drink lots of it," he said. "Or at least, open lots of it, even if you don't drink it."

He did not have a prepared speech but said we could ask him about anything we wanted. I thought my classmates would ask for investment advice or stock tips. But instead they asked big political questions. What can U.S. business do about Iraq? What can U.S. business do about global warming? Buffett's answers were bland and predictable. Then Marnie, my section neighbor during the second semester, came to the microphone. She was tiny and hated speaking in class, so it was surprising to see her so exposed. But speaking in a strong voice, she asked Buffett how he would resolve the inequity created by America's inheritance tax policy. He came to life with a long riff about what he called the Ovarian Lottery. Imagine you're in the womb the night before you're born and a genie comes to you and says you can design the world however you like. You can lay out the rules of society. But you must also know this: Before you enter the world, you will have to grab a ticket from a barrel and that ticket will say man or woman, United States or Bangladesh, crippled or athlete. How does that change how you design the world? He said it was ridiculous that a $3-trillion economy like that of the United States, with an average GDP of $40,000, couldn't afford health care for seniors. He said good fortune in life and success was basically good luck. "If my friend Gates had been born two hundred years ago," he said of the founder of Microsoft, "he would have been some wild animal's lunch."

The best advice on choosing a career, Buffett said, was to find something you loved. After that, the money would seem unimportant. He said he drank the same sodas as us and ate the same fast food, though he got a discount at Dairy Queen because he owned it. He slept on the same kind of mattress, which meant for at least seven hours in the day we were no less comfortable than he. The only real difference, he said, was that "I fly differently."

Reading Lowenstein's book, I saw behind Buffett's avuncular demeanor to the extraordinary diligence and prescience, the almost mystical feel for companies, prices, and markets, a refusal to use anything but his own judgment, a pencil, and stacks of printed company reports to make decisions. Since childhood, when he had begun with a single paper route and consolidated the paper routes of all the children in his neighborhood into a cartel, Buffett had been obsessed with the idea of building, conserving, and growing his capital. Every cent spent now he viewed as ten cents lost in the future. I found myself admiring Buffett in the way I admired those flinty old American pioneers who appear in nineteenth-century paintings— gaunt, bespectacled, and oozing Protestant virtue. If he had not been an investor, I thought, he might have been a small-town grocer, wearing his brown, ankle-length smock, counting every penny, and squinting through the evening gloom rather than turning a light on. He was never happier, I read, than when hunkered down in his favorite nook off the landing of his home in Omaha, a Cherry Coke in one hand and a company report in the other, scouring for the next opportunity in razor blades, local newspapers, or insurance.

I could not envisage being either Lynch or Buffett, but when I applied for these summer jobs, I envisaged being a well-paid stooge, comfortably off, doing some interesting work and having time for myself and my family. With a second child on the way, a large part of me wanted to take care of the financial side of life as easily as possible. The balance of low risk and high reward in mutual fund management seemed ideal. In fact, the only real risk in this work seemed to be boring yourself to death. When I told Justin all of this, he said I had to change my attitude.

"You just don't realize how seriously everyone else is taking this, do you? You're going to be competing against people who have been plotting their route into investment management from the moment they stepped on campus." He was right. Many students had compiled elaborate color-coded spreadsheets to plan their job searches, relentlessly calling alumni and pressing them for help and contacts. I had read a few books and thought about them a bit.

I was invited to interview at two companies: one in California, which I had applied to before finding out that Margret was pregnant; the other in Boston. The evening before my first interview, the California firm held a get-to-know-you dinner at an Alsatian restaurant off Harvard Square. Thirty of us crowded into a basement room, tricked out like a German *Stube*. You could spot the executives by their gleaming white shirts and the fact that they were throwing back red wine while the rest of us sipped delicately at soda water. I was seated opposite a fund manager who had bristling silver hair and a burning red shaving rash all over the lower half of his skeletal face. He was a caricature of dissatisfaction. His breath, which worsened with every gulp of Merlot and slice of roast duck, was paint stripper and his humor barbed.

He told us he was a technology consultant for years before achieving his dream of stock-picking for a living. "I lived and breathed stocks," he said, staring at me goggle-eyed. "That's the only way to do this. I read every book I could. I learned about every company I could. I didn't go to business school. There were no short-cuts for me. I ran my own portfolio while I was working and kept on applying for these jobs until finally I got this one." He asked us how many of the cases we read in preparation for class. All of them, I told him. Two Indian men at the table said they read only one in three or one in five at the most. I could not tell if they were joking, but they said that they had better things to do with their time at HBS than read sloppy marketing and LEAD cases. For example, they liked to play poker five nights a week. The fund manager seemed to like this. With dessert came a shuffling of places and another of the executives came and sat at our table. He and his colleague began to trade war stories while sloshing back more wine. "Did you see Howie just played Pebble Beach? Howie runs our media fund. He's the guy who bumped off the CEO of AOL. Brilliant guy. Legend. Beats the market every year. Never misses. Twenty years straight. Rupert Murdoch calls him for advice. I mean, the guy's a legend. He bought Viacom at ten!"

Away from home with nothing to do but interview students, they were wallowing in their fully expensed trip, ordering more wine, more chocolate ganache with raspberry sauce, swapping more war stories. "So Bill was reading the financial statements—Bill's our head retail analyst, guys—and he noticed that inventory had just gone through the roof and same-store sales were lagging. They were just piling up crap in the stores and no one was buying, but it was still seen as this hot company, right? So he started unloading the thing. No one else had seen it and he got out before the stock tanked thirty percent. Unbelievable."

I left as soon as I could. The freezing air in Harvard Square was sharp and refreshing. I was happy to be out of there.

I arrived in Spangler at 8:30 A.M. to find my two interviewers, an older man and a woman who had graduated from HBS just a couple of years earlier, gingerly peeling back the plastic tabs on their Styrofoam coffee cups. They had had a long night. The first question they put to me was this: In fifteen minutes, you have to make a realistic bid to purchase Harvard Business School. How much do you bid?

They were trying to see how I went about the process of valuation.

"Who's buying?" I asked.

"You are," said the man.

"But am I a private company planning to turn HBS into an executive retreat or an educational business or a real estate developer or what?" They shrugged. I began building a balance sheet for HBS, listing its assets, liabilities, and equity. First there was the real estate on the banks of the Charles River, close to Boston, populated by office buildings, apartment blocks, classrooms, a gym, an auditorium, and a library. I took a wild stab. I had read that the new Spangler building, by far the largest building on campus, had cost around $100 million to build. I reckoned Spangler made up perhaps one tenth of all the real estate on campus. I also assumed that if the campus was forty-four acres in size and that each acre in this area of Boston cost around $1 million, then you had at least $44 million of raw land underneath all of these buildings. So how about a billion dollars for the real estate?

Then there was the endowment, $1.5 billion or so sitting in various accounts. I did not think this could be considered in any purchase, since the money would be tied to the specific mission of Harvard Business School and not be available to some new acquirer. It would probably have to be returned to the donors or credited to the general university endowment. The school had no debt to speak of, and its sole equity holder was itself. As to revenue and costs, our section had recently had a visit from the school's management department and I seemed to recall that tuition from MBA students made up around one third of HBS's total income. The rest came from executive education and publishing books and cases. So, if there were 1,800 students each paying $38,000 per year for tuition, that came to around $68 million; multiply that by three, comes to just over $200 million in total revenue. Since the school does not run for profit, all of that is spent each year in various ways, from paying professors to manicuring the grounds. If you wanted to run HBS for profit, you could probably do so handsomely at first, though over time, I wondered, the loss of not-for-profit tax advantages and the official links to Harvard University might shrink your margins. But assuming you could make 20 percent before interest and tax, and a valuation multiple of fifteen times earnings, HBS might be valued at $600 million.

Time was running out, so I tried to ask some more questions. Could the school still call itself HBS? Would it retain its links to Harvard? If not, what would this mean for one of the school's key assets, its professors? Would they decamp to a more traditional university? If there was no way to retain them, this would drastically lower the value of the asset. My interviewers refused to give me any hard answers. There seemed to be so many variables, and by now the piece of paper in front of me was a mess of numbers, squiggles, and arrows leading nowhere.

"So what number are you going to write on the check?" the woman asked.

"I read recently that the New York Yankees were worth around six hundred million," I said. "So given the unique uses for the real estate, and stripping out the endowment, and with all the uncertainty about this new institution's ability to use the Harvard name, how about a little more than the Yankees, around seven hundred million." It was a deranged muddle, and they gave me this strange stare before jotting something down on their notepads. They were probably writing "half-wit."

The next morning, I interviewed with a Boston-based mutual fund firm. True to its thrifty reputation, there was no dinner beforehand, just a conference room, two white men in white shirts and dark ties, and me.

"You have an interesting résumé," the older of the two began. "But what makes you think you could evaluate and pick companies to invest in?" I had developed a spiel about how journalism and investment research required similar skills, principally the ability to discover and weigh up many different kinds of information, from quantifiable facts to softer judgments about the character of individuals. I told them how I had been through a number of very tough situations, from earthquakes to terrorist attacks, where I had to gather information quickly and write clearly under strict deadlines. They nodded and noted and asked me what I thought about buying Apple stock.

This was February 2005. The iPod was already a runaway hit, and Apple was hoping its PC business would be able to piggyback on its success. So I said that I thought Apple was a great company but that its historic difficulty in achieving sustained success made me hesitant. It had always been an innovator but it was inconsistent. I wondered how long the iPod would continue to make money and whether consumers would really choose Apple computers simply because of their experience with the iPod. As an investor, I might wait to see what else Apple had in its pipeline and also wait for some heat to come out of the stock. And I would also like to find out who beside Steve Jobs could run the company. Having such a dominant CEO had advantages, but the great risk was succession. My interviewers nodded to each other and jotted something down.

Next, they asked, what makes a stock price move? This was one of those questions where you think you have an answer, until you have to give it. All kinds of things, I said. Fundamentally, the price moves according to changing expectations of future earnings, but what influences those changing expectations remains a mystery. Some say the markets are so well informed that all changes are rational, based on accurate forecasts of future earnings. Others believe a herd mentality can set in and that prices end up being set by the most basic human emotions: greed, fear, envy, lust. I do remember my hand seeming to take on a life of its own as I offered my explanation, moving up and down and round and round as if on an invisible roller-coaster. I tried to read my interviewers' reaction. But their faces were expressionless.

That evening I learned that neither company wanted me for a second interview. I thought I wouldn't care, but I did. I wanted to adhere to the HBS culture because it seemed to promise so much, but then again I didn't, because it seemed so formulaic. I wanted to be a part of this thing, but did I really? It was turning out to be more of a struggle than I had ever imagined.

Fortunately, I was not alone. Luis cornered me one day to ask about my plans for the summer. He was carrying his soccer boots and heading off for a game.

"This pressure, man, it's insane," he said. "When I got here, I knew I wanted to pursue the entrepreneurial path. But now, with this interview thing—and you see all these big famous companies coming to campus like Google and Skype—I'm thinking maybe I should go and work for one of them."

"I know," I told him. "I nearly convinced myself I could be an investment banker. I realize I'm comparing myself to the other people here and it's killing me. I've got to stop."

"You've got to have a super strong conviction about what you want to do here," he said, resting one soccer boot on my shoulder. "You know what finally stopped me chasing these things? It was hearing about the grilling people were getting for these stupid summer jobs. For people like you and me, the old guys, it's too undignified." Luis had decided he would go home to Madrid and spend the summer helping an American online travel company that was seeking to crack the European market. "I'll be able to do it on my own time," he said. "No boss."

Justin applied to the investment banks and got a job. "It's going to be great," he told me, waving his offer letter at me.

"No it isn't."

"I can't listen to you anymore," he said, plugging his ears. "You're a corrupting influence. La, la, la, la, I love investment banking, investment banking's what I love."

Annette, also from the section, had performed the most stunning volte-face. She had arrived at HBS with a scholarship from a top investment bank, which was paying for her tuition and had guaranteed her a summer job and a job when she graduated. But the prospect of returning to Wall Street tortured her.

"I knew that if I went back, that was it," she told me. "I would be there for the rest of my career. The money and status are very addictive." Instead, she wanted to get out of financial services and into a company with a real, physical product to sell. She had received an offer from a fashion house to work in their marketing department over the summer. The money was half of what the bank was offering. And if she took the fashion job, she would forfeit her scholarship and more than sixty thousand dollars in tuition grants. "I did what I always do when I face a dilemma," she said. "I locked myself away and just forced myself to make a decision. I had to leave finance."

All her life up to then, she said, she had been following a formula for success, and doing so very effectively. What was unnerving about choosing the fashion house was the reaction of those closest to her. They were baffled, and their bafflement stoked her insecurity. It was as though she had dropped the veil on a hitherto secret part of her soul. Was she crazy? Or self-indulgent? How many people would kill for the opportunity she had to succeed on Wall Street? Why would she have made all these decisions to get to this point and then make this one? It was exactly what I had felt when I left my job in Paris. People asked what was wrong with me. How could I leave such a great job? Why had I even bothered getting to that point in my career only to walk away and start afresh? But as Annette had just found out, when you know, you know.

Chapter Ten

ETHICAL
JIHADISTS

Business is the activity of making
things to sell at a profit—decently.
—EDWIN GAY,
SECOND DEAN OF
HARVARD BUSINESS SCHOOL

Despite the onslaught of recruitment, there was still a course of academic
study to pursue. Besides more finance, the second semester would introduce
us to strategy, negotiations, entrepreneurship macroeconomics, and business ethics. Strategy was taught by a Swiss professor, Felix Oberholzer-Gee.
He looked like the quintessential academic, with round glasses, hair
brushed forward, and an absentminded gaze when he walked across campus. But he had spent five years in the injection-molding business in
Switzerland and then another five in the economics department of an
investment bank. He brought a wry worldliness to the classroom and
quickly became a favorite of the section.

Harvard prided itself on its strategy department, not least because it
was the core of the general management program. Establishing and executing a strategy was precisely what a general manager did. We were not

being trained to be excellent financiers or operations managers but rather good generals. We were learning how to marshal disparate forces and resources to pursue the goals of creating and capturing as much value as possible. Strategy was not about filing the right accounts or making sure the machinery worked. It dealt with the big picture: building and managing a business to make superior returns over the long term.

The first thing to understand about strategy, we learned, is that it is not operational efficiency. You could run the best laundry in the world, but if what you were doing was quite simple and thousands of others could do it, you were not going to make any money. You lacked, as Felix liked to say, "a great strategy." A beautifully run restaurant with the greatest chef in the world could be an economic disaster, while owning a few grubby fast-food franchises could make you a millionaire. Being very good at doing something was absolutely no guarantee of financial success. I recalled Steenburgh in marketing telling us, "A good product alone won't get you there." So the first challenge for the strategist was picking the right thing to do.

Felix showed us a graph of the distribution of returns on equity of major American companies over the past twenty years. Most returned between 10 and 15 percent a year. But a few had returns on equity over 20 percent. What were they doing that enabled them to do this? The most profitable companies year after year tended to be in a few sectors: pharmaceuticals, high-technology, financial services, discount department stores, and oil. The worst major industry to be in was airlines. There were exceptions, such as Southwest, which had done phenomenally well. But even Southwest, we had to assume, would eventually struggle to escape the broader trends of its industry. Picking the right industry, one with a sound structure, where your chances of making a profit were highest, was where good strategy began.

In 1980, a Harvard Business School professor called Michael Porter published an article, "What Is Strategy?," that laid out the five forces he believed determined a company's ability to capture value. They are: barriers to entry, supplier power, customer power, substitutes, and rivalry.

Understanding the five forces allowed you to see why the well-run laundry or the wonderful restaurant floundered, while a shoddily run muffler store flourished. The five forces are the cornerstone of modern strategic thinking.

Take the laundry. The barriers to entry are relatively low. It does not require highly skilled labor, and almost anyone could buy a small Laundromat with a bank loan. This is why so many immigrants run laundries. When you are new to the country, laundries are simple businesses to acquire and run. If you speak little English, have a little money, and are prepared to work hard, laundries make sense as a first entrepreneurial endeavor. But you must expect a lot of competition from people with the same idea and the same access to the opportunity.

The suppliers to the laundry are the companies that make laundry machines and cleaning products. There are plenty of both, which keeps down prices and provides you with options should you decide to change. The bad news is your customers. In big cities, there tend to be laundries on almost every street corner, offering identical services and prices. If one laundry wrecks your shirts, you can easily go to another. The only cost of switching from one to the other might be a slightly longer walk. The main substitute for a laundry service is the washer-dryer at home. In Manhattan, many apartment buildings do not allow people to have washer-dryers in their homes, which forces them out to laundries. If that rule were to change and everyone were permitted a washer-dryer, the laundries would be in deep trouble. The degree of competitive rivalry among laundries is stoked by all of these forces—low barriers to entry, weak suppliers, powerful customers, and substitutes in the market where the business is located.

Since Porter came up with his five forces, a couple more have been added. Complements are those products that might enhance your own. In the computer business, complements to a PC include software and printers. Better software or printers make the PC more desirable. Beautiful shirts and ties are the complement to well-made suits. Nurturing these complementary businesses can have a positive effect on your own business. For some businesses, especially those that are highly regulated, government is the seventh force. No major media company, for example, can ignore the workings of the Federal Communications Commission.

The five-forces analysis provides a good idea of a firm's competitive advantage over its rivals, and hence its chances of relative success. But first we had to understand the notion of competitive advantage. It came in two flavors: either you had a cost advantage, whereby you made things cheaper and sold them cheaper, or you differentiated your product somehow, either by making it better than your rivals or by designing it differently to appeal to a different group of people. These two forms of differentiation were known as vertical or horizontal: vertical meant better or worse; horizontal meant different. If you had two cars and one had a better engine, brakes, and interior than the other, they were vertically differentiated; one was simply better than the other. But if you had two identical cars, but one was pink and one black, they were horizontally differentiated, appealing to different kinds of customer. One nightmare for a business is to have no advantage, to be neither the cheapest to produce nor clearly differentiated. This was to be "stuck in the middle."

A competitive advantage exists in the gap between a company's costs and what consumers are willing to pay for its product. If your gap is wider than that of your competitors, you have the advantage. If you can keep that advantage over time, despite all the usual competitive pressures, the advantage is sustainable. Building sustainability is the strategist's next challenge. If you are profitable, rivals will come after you. Success tends to breed complacency, which is why Bill Gates keeps a photograph of Henry Ford in his office. It reminds him that however pioneering and successful you are, you have to keep innovating and protecting your competitive advantage or else a rival will defeat you, as General Motors eventually defeated Ford. The pace of technological change has also shrunk the life cycle of successful business models. When you think you own the very latest cell phone, a new one comes out to trump it, offering entirely new services and features. This is why so many companies, however well they start out, eventually revert to the mean. Very few maintain outstanding returns for any decent length of time, and these are the jewels. Building a durable competitive advantage is the goal of any manager. Finding the companies that achieve it is an investor's dream.

Having established the goal of sustainable competitive advantage, the strategist's next task is to develop and integrate a consistent set of mutually reinforcing activities. The aim is not to have the greatest marketing department in the world but, rather, the best marketing department for your company. You want to build a system in which every activity, including marketing, supports the others. It is the difference between having great individual players and a great team. Wal-Mart's magic is not just in its low costs and low prices. It also has a frugal corporate culture, low store-construction costs in rural and suburban locations, limited advertising, a stellar logistics operation, no unions, a stranglehold on suppliers, who depend on it to sell colossal volumes of their product, and top-notch technology and inventory tracking. It is the integration of all of this that makes Wal-Mart successful and so hard to replicate. And the more it does what it does, the better it gets, making life for its rivals all but impossible.

To make their advantage sustainable, all companies should try to develop a pattern of causes and effects that over time becomes an irresistible flywheel blowing away competitors. Procter and Gamble, for example, sells a lot of toothpaste. This means it produces a lot of toothpaste. Producing a lot of toothpaste makes Procter and Gamble a better toothpaste maker and allows it to use its toothpaste factory, employees, and marketing more efficiently. It can then set a lower price, without reducing its profit margin, and sell even more toothpaste. Its rivals may be able to make toothpaste, but because they do not have the scale advantages or marketing muscle of Procter and Gamble, they struggle to compete. The notion of "the more you practice the better you get" is known as the learning curve and was first observed by business academics during the Second World War. The more factories produced military aircraft, the faster the planes came off the production line and the better they were.

Companies that move up the learning curve fastest tend to do better than their rivals.

A similar flywheel effect can be set in motion for willingness to pay. The more people bought Apple's iPods, the more people wanted them. To reach this audience, music companies made their entire catalogues available on iTunes. Consumers downloaded more and more music, making their iPods even more precious. When rival device makers tried to enter the market, they found they were not just competing on the quality of their device but also taking on the entire ecosystem that Apple had created. Cheaper devices of equal quality failed in the market because people were ready to pay more for an iPod for its familiarity, the cool brand association, and its compatibility with iTunes and other Apple products. Apple had built a sustainable competitive advantage.

After integration, the strategist must next consider the reactions of his company's competitors. If I do this, what will my rival do? At HBS we were introduced to game theory as a means of analyzing the consequences of a competitive situation. In its simplest form, game theory involved understanding the financial consequences of a decision for two parties. If Bill opens a new store to compete with Bob, what should Bob do? Should he close his store or compete with Bill? What will be the costs to Bob of competing versus closing? What will be the costs to Bob if Bill decides to stick around? Mapping out these options and applying values to their consequences offers an aid to decision making rather than a specific answer. It is another means of making the best decision with incomplete information, the main goal of our two-year course.

Finally, we moved to issues of scope. What should our business do? What should it own? Where should it operate? The value test, we learned, should be applied when considering whether you or someone else is better off owning a particular business. General Electric demands that its separate businesses be ranked one or two in whatever sector they operate. If they are ranked lower and cannot be improved, GE assumes it is not the best owner for that company and sells. The ownership test asks whether your business needs to own a certain asset to create value. McDonald's decided long ago that it was far better off selling franchises and then servicing them than owning millions of parcels of real estate. A fashion designer does not need to own the factories that produce her clothes, provided she can be sure the clothes will be made to her specifications. Sound contracts and long-term relationships, Felix explained, could be far less hassle than ownership.

With so much fevered discussion of globalization, the ownership and value tests were more relevant than ever. Could an American company with global ambitions adapt to new countries and cultures and run businesses better than local firms? If a product or service worked well in one country was there any reason to believe it would work well in another? Did global growth allow you to reduce your costs? What were the realities of doing business overseas—developing manufacturing capacity, training employees in uncertain political environments, and risking your intellectual property in markets that might not respect it?

One of the most remarkable companies we studied was called Li and Fung, which was founded in 1906 in Canton as a trading company, helping English and American merchants get access to Chinese factories. Based in Hong Kong, it now managed the supply chains for many of the world's largest retailers and manufacturers. In 1976, Victor Fung, the grandson of the founder and a professor at HBS, returned to Hong Kong to take over the firm. He and his younger brother, William, a Harvard MBA, decided to expand the scope of the company's operations. Instead of being an intermediary between foreign companies and Hong Kong suppliers, Li and Fung built relationships throughout Taiwan, Korea, Singapore, and eventually deeper into China. It went from simply fulfilling customer requests to developing unique production programs that allowed manufacturers to create products of a quality and cost they never thought possible. If you wanted shirts made in Asia, Li and Fung would know separate places for cotton, buttons, and stitching and be able to move the unfinished product from one place to another and still deliver it cheaper than if you had picked a single factory. They called what they did "dispersed manufacturing," and their staff, "little John Waynes," because they spent their days "standing in the middle of the wagon train, shooting at all the bad guys." By the time we studied Li and Fung, the firm was working with 7,500 suppliers in twenty-six countries and owned none of them. It organized design, engineering, and production planning, material sourcing, physical production, quality control, and global shipping for hundreds of well-known clients and yet it owned almost no physical assets. Unless you were in the industry you would never have known its name. At the end of our class discussion of the firm, the projector screen dropped down and Victor Fung appeared via satellite linkup from Hainan Island in China to take questions. He talked about the fragmentation of the global supply chain, how even the tiniest step was becoming the preserve of specialists, and how Li and Fung helped customers find their way through the maze. Margret had decided she wanted to see a class and this happened to be the one she sat in on. Afterward, I asked her what she thought. I had found it riveting but worried she might have been bored.

"Are you kidding?" she said. "This is what you get to do every day? You get chief executives beamed in from China to take your questions? It was amazing." Sometimes I needed to be reminded how lucky we were.

One morning in January I decided to spring for parking on campus. After five months of taking the bus or driving and then spending fifteen minutes cruising around Allston looking for a spot, I thought it was time to treat myself. The previous night, Margret and I had finally cracked and ordered takeout from a very fancy Chinese restaurant on Massachusetts Avenue. We needed a break from the hairshirt life. However good it was for our souls to step off the bourgeois ladder we were on in Paris and return to the stringencies of student life, it was equally good to say to hell with it once in a while. Sesame chicken and dan-dan noodles had never tasted so good.

So there I was cruising onto campus in my $2,000 used Toyota, unfolding a five-dollar bill and handing it to the attendant, feeling for all the world like a big-spending Russian oligarch. The roads were covered in ice and slush, and I was looking forward to a briefer-than-usual exposure to the Boston winter, a quick dash from the car park to Spangler and perhaps one of those croissants stuffed with bacon and eggs that Cedric scarfed down every day between classes.

Once I got to the garage, I found a space on the third story—but not before passing the most extraordinary assemblage of student transport I had ever seen. Ascending the ramp of the car park, they went, roughly, BMW, Lexus, BMW, BMW, Mini Cooper, Lexus SUV, BMW, Porsche, Lincoln Navigator, BMW, and on and on. Finally I found the lower-rent district. There was Betsy, Bob's ten-year-old Saturn, which he'd told me on a ride home, stroking the plastic dashboard with pride, had done more than 130,000 miles. I also spied an olive-green Chevy Lumina, which belonged to a former submarine captain in the section. "No one likes to buy these cars secondhand because they are only driven by old people," he told me. "But that means you get a lot of car for a lower price. And old people tend to look after their cars much better." I was developing a soft spot for the ex-military guys. They were refreshingly sane.

In the Spangler cafeteria, I found one of my section mates, Vivek, lingering as usual by the coffee station. He couldn't decide whether to go for a latte today. Aside from knowing everything a man should know about finance, Vivek also happened to know everything about cars. Everything. He knew torque ratios on a Honda Accord as well as the interior specs of a McLaren super car. He knew prices, speeds, RPMs, detailing history. You almost felt bad asking him for advice on buying a car—it was like asking Einstein to help you with long division—but he loved any opportunity to talk cars. He went about your problem like a clinician, diagnosing your situation, personality, and budget and then delivering his answer. "You should take a look at the Acura range" or "The Korean cars aren't quite there yet. But give them a couple of years."

"Have you seen the cars in the garage?" I asked him that morning.

"Yes." Vivek only ever answered the specific question you asked him.

"Well, how come I'm driving a two-thousand-dollar Toyota and everyone else has a BMW?"

"Lots of people buy them when they get into HBS and want to get financial aid."

"What?"

"Once you get accepted by HBS, you want to clear out your bank account so that you get more financial aid."

"I'm sorry, I'm not getting this. You buy a BMW to get financial aid?"

"When you list your assets in the financial aid application, you don't have to mention your car, but you do have to list any savings or property. So you buy a car for twenty thousand dollars, maybe you get an extra twenty thousand dollars in financial aid, so basically HBS buys you a BMW. If you hadn't bought the car, you'd have to pay the twenty thousand dollars out of your savings."

"But don't they check this kind of thing? I thought that if you were caught lying on your financial aid form, you could risk losing your place."

"But this isn't lying. Nor is taking all your money and parking it with your parents while you apply for financial aid."

"So your personal accounts look empty."

"Right."

"This is unbelievable. How many people do this?"

"Everyone coming from Wall Street knows about this. And the consulting firms. It doesn't always work. But lots of people try it." In its brochure, HBS said that roughly half the class received financial aid and that the average financial aid package was worth $10,000 per year. I knew that some, like Bob, had received much more, but the man had four children and had flown the Stealth bomber. He deserved it. I had received $3,000 in my first year. Probably what I deserved. But the idea of these twenty-five-year-old Wall Street jerks fiddling with their financial aid forms, with the connivance of their parents and the local BMW dealerships, ruined my morning.

. . .

No matter how hard it tries, business can never escape the fact that it is the practice of potentially thieving, treacherous, lying human beings. Its challenge is in reining in the thieving, treachery, and deceit sufficiently that the entire edifice of business and society does not dissolve into a medieval vision of hell. Harvard Business School has produced its fair share of ne'er-do-wells. Their involvement in Well Street's insider trading scandals of the 1980s prompted the then head of the SEC, John Shad, to fund an ethics chair at the business school. The most recent, and spectacular, HBS blowup was Jeff Skilling, the CEO of Enron. In the late 1990s, a job at Enron was one of the most coveted gigs for a graduating MBA. When Skilling visited HBS, he was greeted as a hero, given standing ovations and hotly pursued by professors wanting to write fawning cases about him and his marvelous money-making machine. Beneath him, inside Enron, were scores of other Harvard MBAs built in his mold. When everything was going well, they were geniuses. When it all collapsed and Skilling went to jail, the reputation of the school and its graduates suffered.

In 2003, a class called Leadership and Corporate Accountability was introduced into the required curriculum to allow students to discuss the perils of chasing dollars down ethical sewers. Here was the time to access the moral compass I had read about all those months ago and which had been going haywire with so much talk of money and power. Our guide was an owlish professor called Joseph Badaracco. He had been a Rhodes Scholar at Oxford, had obtained both his MBA and doctorate at the business school, and had carved out a well-padded niche for himself as a business ethicist. For a couple of weeks each year, he taught in Japan, which provided him with that extra layer of financial comfort all academics crave. He was certainly a change from all the hard-charging, weight-lifting, marathon-running types at the school. His shoulders sloped, he wore rubber soled shoes, and he looked as if he would much rather be dozing in a library or fishing on some quiet New England lake. He prided himself on the leisurely life of the tenured Harvard academic. If our last class of the week with him took place on a Thursday morning, he'd smile and rub his hands together and make a point of telling us that his weekend began the moment class ended. He gave the impression that teaching ethics at a business school was one of the cushiest jobs in the world.

Before LCA began, it was the subject of considerable scorn. For the hard-core financiers, it was precious time taken away from studying derivative structures. For the aspiring entrepreneurs, it had nothing to do with creativity or cash flow. The only ones who looked forward to it were the wafflers, the isolated individuals who loved to just talk and talk about nothing in particular and who one day soon will be coming to destroy a company near you. Bo loved the course for his own particular reason. It required very little work. The cases tended to be short, with no numbers to run. They could easily be dealt with lying in bed or in front of a basketball game.

Harvard's response to skeptics who did not believe that ethics had a place at business school was expressed by an HBS professor, Tom Piper, in a book called *Can Ethics Be Taught?* "We reject this assertion emphatically," he wrote. "These students are at a critical stage in the development of their perceptions about capitalism, business practice, leadership, and the appropriate resolution of ethical dilemmas in business. This is a period for inquiry and reflection . . . Extended time is necessary to develop sufficient strength and sophistication to acknowledge the presence of ethical dilemmas, to imagine what could be, to recognize explicitly avoidable and unavoidable harms. It takes time to develop tough-minded individuals with the courage to act." Badaracco had written his own book on business ethics, called *Defining Moments: When Managers Must Choose Between Right and Right.* The title was intended to describe the twilight zone in which most ethical decisions exist. "Life-defining moments," he warned us, "do not come labeled." Consequently, we had to be girded for these moments at every turn, forging our characters and morality in everything we did.

The key framework for LCA divided the responsibilities of corporate leaders into three categories: economic, legal, and ethical. We had to meet criteria in all three categories if we were to satisfy our short- and long-term financial responsibilities without breaking the law or hating ourselves. We began by learning that the U.S. courts take the idea of fiduciary responsibility very seriously indeed. Even the slightest breach of trust with an investor or financial partner would be stamped on. We were given the equation $M \times F = D$. This means that a decision by a court (D) is the product of the legal model (M) and the pertinent facts (F).

The first real dispute in class flared up during a discussion of bluffing in business. In 1968, the *Harvard Business Review* published an article by Albert Z. Carr titled "Is Business Bluffing Ethical?" It generated a slew of critical letters. Carr compared business to poker, in which bluffing, short of outright cheating, was a perfectly legitimate activity. He said that many successful businesspeople lived by one set of ethical standards in their private lives and a quite different set in their professional lives. The explanation, he said, was that they perceived business not as an arena for peacock-like displays of high ethical standards, but as a game with specific rules. Knowing that you could win the game of business playing all manner of tricks that you would never inflict on your spouse, children, or friends made for a calm, unstressed, uncomplicated life. But to some, it seemed to be an acknowledgment that business was fundamentally unethical.

Behind me, Joe, a keen poker player and ex–potato chip salesman, harrumphed his approval of Carr. Across the room, Lisa was seething. She had spent her entire life in Louisville, Kentucky, from school all the way into a job marketing household detergent. Whenever an ethical dilemma came up, she was always the first to raise her hand to say that what was most important was "doing the right thing," whatever the cost. If you were in rural China trying to get a factory built, you should under no circumstances whatsoever offer a bribe, whatever the local norms, because bribery was just wrong. No excuse for it. If you were in Nigeria drilling for oil, there was no excuse for not turning over all of your profits to the locals who accused you of capitalist exploitation. There was no argument to be had about the cost of economic development. You had to do what was right. If you found out hackers had broken into your credit card system but had stolen nothing, you must tell all your customers *immediately*. There was no excuse for sitting on the information. You had to be honest, and the market would reward you. And even if the market didn't reward you, you could sleep well at night knowing you had done the right thing. Nurtured in the bosom of a vast American corporation, she had descended upon us a full-blown ethical jihadist.

"If you employ people, and their jobs depend on you, you can't treat your business like it's poker," she said, drilling her finger into her desk. "If people find out what you're doing they'll never trust you again."

Joe shot back: "But if you're a good poker player, you don't explain your bluffs. You play them in order to win over the long term. In business, you'd be insane to be completely open about everything you're doing. You have to keep some secrets, and the way you keep them secret sometimes is by bluffing. You're not lying or breaking the law or cheating people out of money. You're protecting what's yours from other people who are playing the game the same way. If you didn't bluff you'd just lose again and again."

Eric, a former advertising executive, chimed in: "I think it's about what you're comfortable with. I mean if you're happy to bluff, lie, whatever you want to call it, in one area of your life, you're probably going to do it in other areas, too. If you're happy with that, then fine, you have to live with the consequences. But surely you can find aspects of business where people aren't playing these kinds of games."

"Where?" said Joe.

"I don't know," said Eric. "Nonprofits, maybe."

Badaracco was clearly enjoying this. He said that the executives who come for courses at HBS love debating this question. It goes to the heart of everything they do. Every advertisement their companies put out slightly exaggerating the quality of their product, every machine they build that is specifically designed to break down one day after the warranty

expires, every sales pledge they make knowing they will have to
scramble to find the spare capacity to fulfill it—everyone in business is
basically bullshitting his way through, finding a way, saying yes before he
is ready, overpromising, underhyping, anything just to get by. Call it
bluffing or anything else you like, but the environment is not kind to the
honest man.

When I was a journalist, I often had·to deal with public relations firms.
I wondered if they existed because the media had become so diverse, complicated, and malicious, or because companies were populated by individuals who had lost the capacity to talk in plain English. Each side, of course,
blames the other, while the PR pros reap the fees. One of my editors used to
compare PR professionals to the kind of adaptor plugs you buy at the airport so you can use your electric razor overseas. The corporate titan these
days, so competent and brilliant in so many ways, can relate to the great
unwashed who watch television or read the press only when plugged into a
mediating flack. This discussion of bluffing cut to the heart of it. The business class had become so used to the rules and language of its own particular game—the bluffing, the subterfuge—that it seemed to have lost sight
of the honesty, plain speaking, and plain dealing that non-businesspeople
expected in human transactions. When a business leader spoke of "off balance sheet accounting," was he aware that most non-businesspeople immediately thought "fraud"? Or was it such a given in the business world that
you did not call your fellow business-class citizens out on their
euphemisms? Weren't we all bluffing, after all?

After a few months at HBS, I was torn between the conviction that business had become its own freak show and my deepening understanding of
and sympathy for what businesspeople did, stimulated by the cases. HBS
endured the same struggle. Its reputation meant it would always shoulder
some of the blame for the very worst in business, the jargon and aspects of
the culture. But no one who spent any time there could doubt the serious
approach the school took to very real problems. When the school sought to
regiment and quantify, to create frameworks and equations for subjects that

might better be dealt with by a good novel or film, it could look ridiculous. But occasionally the approach yielded powerful results. However trivial it might seem to grade employees' leadership talents on a scale of one to five, businesses did so because it helped them to build a better business. I realized that before lambasting any attempts to quantify the unquantifiable, I needed to reassess what I considered "unquantifiable."

My friend Gregor, who taught at a business school in Europe, explained to me that MBAs are rather like scientists. They learn things about the world that they are not expected to abuse. Biologists are taught biology with the expectation that they will not assist in germ warfare. Likewise, MBAs are taught accounting on the condition that they do not then manipulate their company's earnings or minimize taxes to such an extent that it amounts to evasion. "But the hallmark of ethically bad businesspeople," Gregor said, "is that generally they don't break the law, because more often than not they had a hand in drafting the law. They write laws, through their lobbyists, so they don't have to break them. But you still wouldn't want them as godparents to your children." He mentioned an ethical failure I had not really considered: lavish executive compensation. It was one thing for a good CEO to pay himself well for a job well done. But increasingly, in the United States and Europe, mediocre CEOs paid themselves as if they were sports superstars or technology entrepreneurs, essentially robbing shareholders to do so. His remark made me think about the range of subjects that could be considered under the heading "business ethics."

We grappled with this in another rambunctious LCA discussion of the limits of a business's responsibilities, reading a piece by the economist Milton Friedman in which he argued that the only social responsibility of a business is to increase its profits. If it did that, it would pay taxes and reward its employees, and it was then up to the government and individuals to fulfill their responsibilities to society as they saw fit. Friedman loathed the idea of companies donating to museums or sending employees out to work in homeless shelters. To him that was robbing shareholders. A counterargument to this was presented by the British business writer Charles Handy. He wrote that companies were, in a crucial way, the sum of the people who worked for them. This meant that they had all the responsibilities of responsible people. It was not enough for them to make a profit. It was also vital that they served their communities, provided decent salaries and benefits. Companies had a moral as well as an economic purpose. The best employees wanted to work for good companies with good cultures, not just those that maximized profits. And given the interplay between business and government, it was disingenuous for business leaders to suggest that government set the rules and business just obeyed. Business had a duty to help government develop the best laws, not just those that benefited one company or sector.

We went back and forth in the section, with half the class championing the interests of shareholders and the duties of individuals over companies, and the other half advocating the importance of corporate social responsibility in a capitalist system where companies are social as well as economic actors. Badaracco seemed to love it, and when he wrapped up, he said of course the answer lay somewhere in between.

Right in the middle of our ethics course, the school found itself in its own ethical bind. When you apply to HBS, most of your communication with the school is electronic. You are summoned to interview via e-mail. You are accepted via e-mail. Consequently, the wait to find out where you are in the process involves a lot of nervous e-mail checking. This year, someone had figured out how to get inside the website that stored the application information and peek at his status—presumably so he could then get on with his life knowing whether he was going to HBS, and whether a financial aid BMW lay in his future. But rather than keeping this to himself, the hacker posted the simple four-step process for penetrating the site on the MBA message board hosted by *BusinessWeek* magazine. Unsurprisingly, scores of applicants followed the instructions, but as they came and went, they left an electronic trail. Once they were discovered, HBS had to decide what to do with them. For those not admitted, nothing changed. But those who had been admitted, a small handful, were told that their admission offers had been retracted.

Badaracco took a poll in class to see where we stood. Around three quarters of the class thought the school's decision was wrong. Only the ethical jihadists stood foursquare behind the administration. Everywhere, discussion of the matter raged until, on March 14, Dean Clark issued a proclamation in *The Harbus*.

> I would like to have the last word on Harvard Business School's policy regarding applicants who hacked into the ApplyYourself Inc. web site containing confidential admissions information. This behavior is unethical at best—a serious breach of trust that cannot be countered by rationalization. Any applicant found to have done so will not be admitted to this school. Our mission is to educate principled leaders who make a difference in the world. To achieve that, a person must have many skills and qualities, including the highest standards of integrity, sound judgment, and a strong moral compass—an intuitive sense of what is right and wrong. Those who have hacked into the web site have failed to pass that test.

In the next issue of the newspaper Aaron Bigbee, one of the class of '06, fired back, expressing what most people I knew felt. Was it really "hacking," as Clark had called it, to cut and paste a few instructions from a public message board into a URL? No one had been harmed by the applicants' actions. They had not violated any specific prohibition, certainly none specified by HBS. And how could the dean call this "intuitively" wrong when so many of those currently at the school did not share his intuition?

"To claim that a relatively minor ethical misstep disqualifies someone from a Harvard education is to indict me, along with most people I know

ETHICAL JIHADISTS 165

here," Bigbee wrote. "I realize that HBS needs to prove its commitment to promoting ethical behavior. Punishing rather harmless behavior using arbitrary standards is not the way to do this. We should apologize for our mistake, set a clear standard for the future, and cease to blame people who act in the same way many of us would have. That would be setting an admirable ethical example to follow." Nothing came of Bigbee's letter. Future applicants were warned to await their results rather than trying to obtain them in any way that might be interpreted as hacking. But as the vote in our LCA class showed, the MBA students thought the school's reaction excessive and self-righteous.

Negotiations, despite their importance in business life, were the subject of a short course shoehorned into the second semester. Our professor, James Sebenius, had been part of the founding team at the Blackstone private equity group, a fact he frequently brought up. He would feed our curiosity with asides like "back then, the Concorde was my bus and the Four Seasons my canteen." Unlike other professors, he loved to dominate the class. His justification was that since the course was so short, he had a lot to cram in and there was less time for rambling discussion. He needed to be directive.

The course was broken up into two parts. The first, negotiation fundamentals, began with a discussion of ethics followed by the basic analytical tools of negotiation. The negotiator's role was often to mislead his opponent, passively at least, while remaining ethical. The risk of unethical negotiation was a bad reputation, which would hurt you in future negotiations. Under U.S. law, negotiators had no duty of good faith, but fraud carried heavy consequences. Bluffing was fine. Knowingly misrepresenting facts to damage another party was not. The sophistication of the parties was also relevant. Selling a complicated financial product to an economic illiterate and then blaming the illiterate for not understanding the contract would hurt you in court.

There were basically three schools of negotiators: the poker player, who regards it all as a game; the idealist, who insists on doing the right thing every time; and the pragmatist, who knows that what goes around comes around. We were introduced to two concepts every good negotiator should know (whether or not they use these terms): BATNA and ZOPA. BATNA is the "best alternative to a negotiated agreement." Knowing your BATNA prevents you from making a bad deal. If the negotiation is going poorly, you know what your options are if it collapses or you decide to walk away. ZOPA is the "zone of possible agreement," the range of scenarios you and your opponent are likely to agree upon. You should have a pretty clear idea of both your BATNA and ZOPA even before your negotiation begins.

In every class, Sebenius emphasized the importance of mapping the interests of all parties in a negotiation and trying to figure out their BATNAs and ZOPAs. All too often, he said, people went into negotiations having labored to craft their own position but having ignored the other side's. The gifted negotiator adopts a three-dimensional perspective, working both at the table and away from it, understanding the personalities involved, investigating relentlessly to grasp the complete range of interests, and then crafting a strategy, including everything from the venue and the timing all the way through to the financial calculations. If the negotiations stall, the negotiator should "go to the balcony" to gain perspective and then try to reframe the issues, moving from defensive positions to shared interests, from hostility to problem-solving. Then he can set about "building a golden bridge" from his position to his goal. Power, we were told, was a tool to be used to educate the other party rather than to escalate the intensity.

All these phrases were incorporated into our swelling lexicon. As I stood before the noodle bar one day, trying to decide between the stir-fry and the ramen soup, I felt a long arm flopping onto my shoulder.

"Mon ami," said Cedric. "Let us go to the balcony to see the full range of choices. Then perhaps we can cross the golden bridge to reach your nutritional goals."

Chapter Eleven

EXTREME
LEVERAGE

Anybody who thinks money will
make you happy hasn't got money.
—DAVID GEFFEN

Private equity and hedge funds were the hottest topic on campus, for the simple reason that they were awash in cash. New MBAs joining a top private equity firm such as Blackstone, KKR, Texas Pacific Group, or Bain Capital, could expect to earn $400,000 in their first year. First-year investment bankers, by contrast, could expect maybe half of that, provided everything went well. To exacerbate the bankers' inferiority, they knew they would probably have to spend most of their time raising money and pitching ideas for their friends in private equity. Investment banking was considered a second-tier career. You could earn $200,000 a year straight out of school, and your peers would still think you had failed.

But what exactly was the magic of private equity? Students would talk about how much more interesting it was to acquire and run companies than simply to provide banking services. Private equity gave you an ownership stake that investment banking did not. The principle/agent problem of how to align the interests of managers and employees with shareholders to maximize performance came closer to being solved by the private equity model in which managers and owners were more tightly linked. But, as usual, the money was the main attraction, and the money came courtesy of debt. It took me several months at HBS to disabuse myself of the notion that debt was a bad thing. Hasan shared my problem. "I come from a culture where borrowing is shameful. You want to die debt-free," he told me. "But here I keep learning about the power of leverage, how to raise money and structure your financing deal. Suddenly everything is possible." Debt, we found, is the fuel of modern finance. It provides the opportunity of astonishing returns. It allows you to seize control of assets you could otherwise not afford and then slap them around for cash. Debt focuses the mind and forces people to concentrate on the only thing that matters: the cash flowing out of the business. If Gordon Gekko were speaking today, he might have to reword his classic boast about greed. These days debt, for want of a better word, is good. Debt works. It had become a running joke in our section that if we ever discussed a company struggling to increase its value, members of the skydeck would start pumping their arms up and down as if jacking up a car. It was the sign to "lever up," to load up the balance sheet with debt.

Whereas ordinary mortals talk about debt as a burden that requires relief, bankers talk about the discipline of debt and the wonder of "juicing the returns" through borrowing. The idea of debt as discipline is straightforward enough. Anyone with a student loan or mortgage payment knows how it hangs over them each month, forcing them to cut back on other expenses. Obligations to others in the form of debt create a kind of straitjacketed, focused behavior in which the ability to generate enough cash to meet one's payments becomes paramount.

But "juicing the returns"? Take two different companies. Each one has assets worth $1,000. The first has funded its assets with $800 in borrowed money and $200 in equity from investors. Let's say the interest rate on the borrowed money is 10 percent and the tax rate is 50 percent. Each year the $1,000 worth of assets produce $200 in operating profits. Eighty dollars goes to pay interest on the debt, which the government allows you to charge as an expense. Of the remaining $120, $60 goes to pay taxes and the remaining $60 goes to the equity holders. For their investment of $200, the equity holders receive an annual return of 30 percent. Now imagine the same company in which all the assets were funded with equity. They produce the same $200 in operating profits. There is no interest payment. A hundred dollars goes to pay taxes, leaving the equity holders with $100, a 10 percent return. Which would you rather have? A 30 percent return or a 10 percent return? Juiced or not juiced?

And the juicing opportunities just keep on coming. Now you have bought your company, which up until recently was quietly going about its business making lots of cash and avoiding taking on debt. You take the debt you incurred and dump it onto your acquisition. If possible, you then take even more debt and pay yourself a large management fee. If at all possible, this will equal or exceed the amount of cash you yourself put into the deal. Already you have recouped your investment. Piling debt onto some poor company carries the innocuous term "leveraging the balance sheet."

For the acquired company, the horror show is just beginning. Your sole focus now is to generate cash to keep up those interest payments. Such discipline, your investors will keep telling you from their lavish offices in New York, is vital to success. It will result in a better-run, more profitable company that two or three years down the line can be sold at a huge profit. First, you strip your headquarters down to its bare essentials, removing any perks or visible signs of comfort. You gut your health plan and sack loyal employees so as to keep up with those crushing interest payments. Then along comes a team of consultants from your private equity investor, sharp-suited number crunchers booked into the local Four Seasons, who tell you to keep turning the ratchet. Those who do so, they promise, will be handsomely rewarded—this is known as "aligning the interests of management and investors." But all it really means is forcing management to be loyal first and foremost to its equity holders—no matter that those equity holders plan to be in and out of their investment within a few years.

The humiliation is compounded when your company receives a bill from the private equity firm charging you for its consulting services. If you don't have the money to pay, they might suggest, how about taking on some more debt? It's cheap, after all. The government pays for a chunk of it by allowing you to charge interest as an expense. And it will enhance the returns on equity.

"But I've fired everyone I can fire!" the manager screams. "I've moved from our lovely old offices to this soul-wrecking office park. No one in my town talks to me anymore. I've outsourced everything humanly possible to China. There is nothing left but the trickle of cash, no life, no humanity, no higher purpose."

"Mission accomplished. Time to sell," says the man in rimless spectacles in his office overlooking Central Park.

Now the "improved" company is floated on the stock exchange. The private equity investor recouped his original investment months ago, perhaps even doubled it in fees and financial chicanery. And now he gets another bite. The market now regards the company as "turned around"— more efficient, trimmed of fat and waste, and ready to grow again. If the investor bought it for $1 billion and can sell it for $3 billion, the $2 billion is all his, plus, of course, his original equity investment. Even better, the tax rate on returns from private equity investment is lower than the standard corporate tax rate. Is it any wonder so many want to be in this business?

Private equity had created a form of accelerated capitalism that brings us back to the problem laid out by Milton Friedman and Charles Handy. The private equity model can serve investors very well, and in the best cases it can make companies much more efficient and valuable. But the drift of so much power into the hands of those who control the large private equity investment funds leaves companies and the communities where they exist prey to individuals who care for them only as economic machines. The social role of companies is diminished. The private equity investors can retire to their apartments in Manhattan trusting in the capitalist machine to make everything right but without having to deal with the day-to-day consequences of their actions. It is very different from when a factory owner has to face his workers every day. The fact that so many Harvard MBAs have succeeded in private equity and so many more want to go into it makes the issue pertinent. Where are the leaders and difference-makers in private equity? What conscience do they bring to their work? What balance do they see in their roles as economic and social actors?

Two giants of private equity came to campus to speak within a few days of each other and were rapturously received. The first was David Rubenstein, who cofounded the Carlyle Group in 1987. Since then, Carlyle had invested more than $50 billion of its investors' money in companies around the world. The second speaker was Steve Schwarzman, founder and CEO of the Blackstone Group and probably the man most of my class would one day like to be.

Rubenstein looked like any other Wall Street elder statesman, in a blue pinstriped suit and owlish tortoiseshell glasses. But the moment he spoke, he revealed a droll, self-deprecating wit. The difference between corporate leaders and those who start their own businesses, I had observed, was startling. The latter come across as so much smarter and independent-minded, so much less prone to platitudes, so much more comfortable in their own skins. There seems to be an anarchic streak in anyone who has taken a real risk in his life. And even when it has to burn its way through a pinstriped suit, it shows.

The entrepreneurs who came to campus—from hedge fund pioneers such as Richard Perry; to Barry Diller, the media baron and founder of IAC; to Paul Orfalea, the founder of Kinko's—seemed to be both enamored of their own skills and hard work and appreciative of the luck it had taken for them to succeed. Despite being dogged, competitive Darwinian types, they were more understanding of the world and its insanity, somehow more forgiving. They reminded me of generals who had experienced war, while all the corporate stiffs and consultants and lawyers and bankers were like the politicians who sent men into battle, with no grasp of the consequences.

I mention all this in the context of Rubenstein because he was so unexpected. It was easy to spot the entrepreneur when he arrived wearing a fleece pullover and jeans, and drinking coffee from a recyclable cup. But Rubenstein had never shaken the sartorial habits and manner of the Washington lawyer he once was. Within a few years of leaving law school, Rubenstein was working for candidate, and then president, Jimmy Carter. "When I started working for him in the 1976 campaign, he had a thirty-three-point advantage in the polls. By the time of the election, I'd turned the vote into a cliffhanger." Once in the White House, Rubenstein said he would stay later than everyone else to make sure his memos were at the top of Carter's in-box when he arrived in the Oval Office the next morning. His diligence, however, couldn't do anything to save the Carter administration as it battled a deep economic slump. After leaving politics, Rubenstein practiced law for a while until he spied a far greater financial opportunity.

Most industries have their creation myths, from Alexander Graham Bell and the telephone to Larry Page and Sergey Brin building the prototype for Google in the Stanford computer department. The private equity industry was fathered by an intemperate old banker and former Treasury secretary, William Simon. In 1982, Simon and a partner, Raymond Chambers, purchased the Gibson Greetings Card Company from RCA. The price was $81 million. Simon and Chambers put in $1 million in cash, borrowed $53 million, and paid for the rest through a scheme whereby Gibson sold much of its property and then leased it back. This was a case of extreme leverage, but Simon knew what he was doing. RCA was keen to unload the company in order to concentrate on its other businesses. The stock market was about to emerge from a prolonged slump. And there were efficiencies to be wrung out of Gibson. A mere eighteen months later, Simon and Chambers floated Gibson on the stock market with an IPO (initial public offering), raising $290 million. Simon had turned his personal investment of $330,000 into a holding worth $70 million.

Returns like that never go unnoticed. Rubenstein was soon scrambling to raise money and, more important, to find companies to buy. Carlyle's specialty has been finding value in difficult situations, often using high-ranking political connections to lubricate deals. When he spoke to us everyone was obsessed with India and China, but Carlyle was already scouting out virgin territory in Africa.

The reason Rubenstein had come to Harvard, however, was not to titillate business school students with talk of extraordinary returns. He had funded a building at the Kennedy School of Government and had crossed the river to offer us some advice on building careers that straddled business and government. When it comes to business and government, he believed "you can have your cake and eat it." There were two ways to do this. Either you started in government very young and then moved into business, or you made lots of money and then went into government. The useful thing about private equity, Rubenstein said, is "that you are highly compensated if you are reasonably successful. And even if you're not that good, you'll probably still make a fair amount of money, and with money comes freedom." And with freedom, he added, came the opportunity to do interesting things.

To his credit Rubenstein seemed generally unfazed by the industry that had made him so rich. Government, he said, had a far greater impact on the lives of others. "I had way too much of an impact at the age of twenty-seven." In answer to the inevitable question about what qualities he sought in a job candidate, he said, "a reasonable degree of intelligence, a strong work ethic, the ability to get along with others, a desire to build something important, the ability to keep one's ego in check." His most important piece of career advice, though, was even simpler: "be a principal or a decision maker, not a service provider." Principals make all the money. They can turn the cell phones off on weekends. They are the ones for whom everyone else runs around. They possess the grail: control over their time.

Steve Schwarzman grew up in the suburbs of Philadelphia, where his father ran a dry goods store. He attended Yale as an undergraduate, where he was elected to the Skull and Bones society the year after George W. Bush. Both men later attended Harvard Business School. After obtaining his MBA, Schwarzman headed to Wall Street, where he rose to be head of the mergers department at Lehman Brothers. In the mid-1980s, the firm was ripped apart by competing factions, and Schwarzman left with his fellow banker, Pete Peterson, to set up Blackstone. While many financiers shy away from publicity, Schwarzman courted it. He lived in a palatial apartment on Park Avenue, attended society events, and reveled in his status.

He came back to HBS to be interviewed by Charlie Rose for PBS. Sitting in his pinstriped suit—his shoulders hunched, his head poking out of the white collar of his striped shirt like a turtle's, looking as if it might disappear down into his torso at any minute—he clasped his hands in front of him. His features conveyed a sneaky playfulness, as if he had planted a whoopee cushion somewhere and was waiting for it to go off.

As a young man, he said, he went to visit his fellow Skull and Bones man Averell Harriman, a railroad heir who became a prominent diplomat. "I came from a normal, middle-class sort of upbringing," he said, speaking softly, making his points with slight, tidy hand gestures. "I was looking for role models. It was a political time, and Harriman was handling the Paris peace talks. He asked me, 'Young man, are you independently wealthy?' I said no. 'Well, that will make a great difference in your life. If my father weren't E. H. Harriman, chairman of the U.S. Pacific Railroad, you wouldn't be sitting here talking to me.' He basically said you really ought to go and make some money." It was a version of Rubenstein's claim that with money came freedom and the opportunity to do more interesting things. If you wanted to have footmen and beautiful paintings and smart people to lunch, you needed money. If you wanted to cruise down Park Avenue in a limousine surrounded by the chatter of deal-making and the thunder of power crashing in great waves around you, only money would get you there. Once cushioned by your great fortune, you could then devote yourself to pursuits such as politics and diplomacy, the work of statesmen.

When Schwarzman started Blackstone, he suffered the agonies of anyone going their own way in business. "You have to really like pain and suffering," he said. "Just because you start and make an announcement and assume they'll come, they don't come. Even if you sell, they don't buy. Nine out of ten businesses that are started fail. If that's the statistic, you know it's not working for you. So to get from zero to some element of significant success, defined by yourself, you have to be exceptionally resilient."

It took him until his nineteenth meeting to find anyone who would invest money in Blackstone. It was the head of an insurance company's investment fund, who pledged him $100 million over a tuna sandwich. Since then, Blackstone had invested more than $80 billion of investors' money. "When you do things in life that have a good feeling," Schwarzman says, "they tend to work out well, rather than having a great strategic plan." The trick, of course, is actually trusting that good feeling in the face of a barrage of artfully constructed PowerPoint slides explaining why you're crazy.

Asked to explain his business, Schwarzman said, "We raise large amounts of money . . . and then we buy companies. Then we borrow three dollars for every dollar of equity in the deal." He compared the search for companies to buy to dating. A lot of different factors lead to success. Part of it is figuring out how fast a company can grow and what can be done to assist that growth. And then there is the financing. How much debt could be loaded onto the company? How far could the operations be squeezed? To understand all of this, Schwarzman said, you need a combination of sharp analytical skills and a keen instinct for what will and won't work, where you are in an economic cycle and, as he put it, "what's gonna get you into trouble." He compared his business to basketball, where the skill is not just repeatedly putting the ball in the hoop from one point on the court but, rather, being able to score from all over the court, being guarded by different people of different sizes and skills. Then, of course, there's hard work, empathy, and "having a sense of where the world is going next."

But then even after all of this, he believed in a curious genetic predisposition to success. "There are some people who are constant winners in the game of life; from junior high school to high school and college, there are certain people who just have a knack for making things work in good times and bad times." It was a version of Napoleon's preference for a lucky general over a good one. They were the "talented tenth" who made the world run. For them, life's challenges just toppled at the slightest touch. For others, it was one damn thing after another. Sitting atop his pile, with his wood sprite's grin, Schwarzman left no doubt about what he saw in the mirror each morning. Life was a game of winners and losers. And there, staring back, was one humongous winner. Why wouldn't we all want to be like Steve?

A few weeks into the second semester, Bo and I decided we had had enough of talking about businesses. It was time to set one up. We were studying entrepreneurship in a class called The Entrepreneurial Manager, taught by Paul Gompers, a career academic, expert on venture capital, and former world-class marathon runner. He burst into our classroom on the first day wearing a striped shirt and black velvet jacket, a break from the corporate uniforms worn by the rest of the faculty. His eyes bulged and his voice exploded off the walls of Aldrich 7 as if to say, "Enough theory. Let's get down to the real stuff: starting your own business."

The HBS definition of entrepreneurship was "the relentless pursuit of opportunity beyond resources currently controlled." Our first case was a zinger. It was about an HBS alumnus called Bob Reiss who had made a small fortune from a Trivial Pursuit–style game based on *TV Guide*. Reiss had spotted the growing popularity of Trivial Pursuit and in less than a year had struck a deal with *TV Guide* to create a game using television questions. He designed, packaged, and manufactured his game and put it onto shelves in time for Christmas, when it sold extremely well. His story was one of seizing an opportunity, gathering resources, and deploying them. He knew the right people to finance him and help create and sell the game. It was breathtaking stuff and a change from all the stodgy corporations. By the end of the class, the entire section felt high on entrepreneurship.

As the course evolved, however, it became bogged down in frameworks and decision matrices. We were taught ways to analyze an opportunity and the different financing possibilities. We were taught to organize our thinking according to POCD, people, opportunity, context, deal. We examined the different skills necessary for starting a business and then managing it for growth. The importance of always having enough cash was beaten into us using the mantra of William Sahlman, HBS's venture financing guru: "More cash preferred to less cash. Cash sooner preferred to cash later. Certain cash preferred to risky cash. Never run out of cash." At the end of the course, Gompers presented us with two quotations, the first from Einstein: "One should guard against preaching to young people success in the customary form as the main aim in life. The most important motive for work in school and in life is pleasure in work, pleasure in its result, and the knowledge of the value to the rest of the community." The second was from Gandhi: "Live as if you were to die tomorrow. Learn as if you were to live forever."

This was all well and good, but what the course lacked was a discussion of what seemed to be the most important question for anyone undertaking his own venture: Do you have the stomach for it? It was easy to start something, but were you ready for that wet Wednesday afternoon eighteen months into the plan when customers were still scarce, your investors were losing faith, and you were running up credit card debt to pay your staff? Max, a German student, was one of the few in the class who had raw experience like this, having set up a successful financial data firm in Germany.

He complained that sitting through each session of The Entrepreneurial Manager was "like hearing virgins talking about sex." He received the lowest possible grade for the course, which told you all you needed to know about the futility of HBS grading.

Bo and I decided we should try setting up a media business. We envisioned a monster, a vast, world-spanning empire to make Rupert Murdoch feel like a pipsqueak. Disney, Viacom, even Microsoft would slither like blind, formless amoeba in the gloom cast by our shadow. If it went really well, Bo would be able to record an album of big ol' Georgia boy rap, and we would release it around the world. Japanese teenagers would spend their nights doing the Bo, in which you lean backward as if you were seven feet tall and rest your hand on the steering wheel of an imaginary Chevy Tahoe. My role in this project would be that of muse and occasional Svengali.

But first things first. What would our offices look like? Bo wanted something like an airport hangar. He would sit at a desk surrounded by computer screens, a sort of mission control. There would have to be a basketball court nearby. A personal chef would cook whatever Bo wanted, whenever he wanted. And he would spend a great deal of time on the company jet following his basketball team around the country and cutting deals.

I wanted something more like a Persian rug dealer's lair. A small, quiet room with a window overlooking a leafy courtyard. The sound of water in a fountain. A wooden desk with an old-fashioned black telephone and no computer. The only other item allowed on this desk would be the single sheet of paper listing my activities for the day. There would be two leather armchairs for guests. Outside, an extraordinarily competent secretary would control access to my inner sanctum and produce the most delicious coffee. "I do apologize, Monsieur le President, but Mr. Delves Broughton is busy. He would, however, be delighted if you could join him for lunch two weeks from tomorrow. Would that be acceptable? Wonderful. We shall have the *tête de veau* prepared just how you like it."

On a side table by the window, there might be a bowl of quinces to scent the air. Behind a hidden panel in one wall would be a television set, so that

I could watch European soccer matches with my lawyer, an old and trusted friend, whose modest and affable manner meant he was always fatally underestimated by our rivals. In a series of outer offices encircling the courtyard, a team of brilliant and loyal minions would manage the minutiae of my affairs.

Bo and I would sketch out the outlines of our peculiar senior management structure each morning over breakfast in Spangler. Neither of our study groups had survived into the second semester, so we had the time. Most mornings at the table beside us, three elegant Asian women who looked like they had stepped straight from a Shanghai luxury boutique fired up their laptops and prepared for class. They spoke in Chinese at what sounded like a ferocious pace and their palpable ambition goaded us on.

Now all we needed was an idea. It came bubbling up from the frontiers of what came to be known as Web 2.0. In late 2004, a group of journalists and technologists at the Berkman Center for the Internet and Society, a curious little association housed in a Victorian building on the edge of Harvard Law School, were playing around, distributing self-made audio recordings online. They called the new medium podcasting. The principle was that any individual could make an audio recording, post it online, and distribute it for free. To me, at that time, it seemed astonishing. Blogging was already well established, but the creators of YouTube were only just starting work in San Bruno, California. Their product was still months away. Between text and video blogging, there seemed to be a window.

I tried to think about the idea using what I had learned in twenty weeks at business school. I began with the consumer. Everywhere on campus, students wandered around with that iPod glaze. Might they not like something else to listen to? Something not sold on iTunes and not provided on any radio station? I asked everyone I knew, what else would you like to have available on iTunes? News? Entertainment? Stories? Audiobooks? Lots of people said they would like to have a thorough news program, such as *The Wall Street Journal*, in audio form, which they could listen to while working out. Others said they would like to hear great lectures or talks they had missed on campus. They wanted to hear businesspeople discussing their greatest deals or surgeons explaining operations. There was no limit to the kind and length of content conceivable in a podcast. You could have anything from a thirty-second poem to a three-hour roundtable discussion.

I thought of my journalist friends. One of the main frustrations of working for a newspaper is the limiting nature of paper and ink. You could kill yourself on a story only for a bomb to go off at 7:00 P.M. right on deadline, and see it shrunk by half to make way for the breaking news. There was also the issue of meddling editors extracting your best lines or most interesting quotes so that your piece could fit in a box hemmed in by advertisements for washing machines. Every journalist I knew had far more material in their notebooks than they could ever get into print. Podcasting seemed like the ideal outlet. It would be easier, after all, just to spin your thoughts straight into a microphone than into more words for a blog.

Bo started riffing about doctors and medical students. They had so little time and yet so much to learn, they would love the idea of receiving information through their iPods. Maybe we could persuade some leading surgeons to spend ten minutes each week talking through a procedure. These people were unlikely to have time to write a blog. But if you made it easy enough for them—perhaps they could make their recording while driving home—they could just talk. The same with lawyers; we could get them to talk about cases, offer advice.

Our idea was starting to take shape. We would create a website that would be a supermarket of audio content. Users could come and find a favorite journalist or a renowned surgeon and download an audio file. We would try to get them to subscribe and download audio files every week— and pay for them. We would then pass on a piece of the revenue to the creators to keep them interested. Our role in this would be to sign up the speakers, help them create recordings, and then manage and market the website. Bo created a spreadsheet outlining our revenue and cost forecasts for the next two years. We were going to be rich!

HBS was a wonderful place to get this thing going. Everyone seemed keen to help. We had lunch with a section mate who used to work in the strategy department at Disney. He warned us about the difficulty of building a content brand. Another, who had worked at Yahoo!, advised us on our website layout and functionality. Finally we created a ninety-second pitch, which we recorded onto Bo's iPod. We took turns speaking and even had a cool soundtrack going in the background. Feeling pretty good about it, we asked for an appointment with Gompers. "This week's crazy, but I have fifteen minutes available in ten days' time," his assistant said. This was absolutely normal at HBS. Everyone was always "crazy." Nine times out of ten, if you asked to meet someone, student or faculty, they always said "things are crazy right now, but . . ." The few who said "great, whenever you'd like" were that much more precious.

So, ten days later, Bo and I turned up to see Gompers in his office in Morgan. He kept us waiting for ten minutes. When he finally waved us in, we set up the iPod and played him our pitch. He fidgeted in his seat for the entire ninety seconds. When the recording was finished, we asked him what he thought. He rambled awhile, sounding unenthusiastic. We asked him how we might find financing. He suggested we bootstrap the business as far as we could. He said that he could not see the potential. We tried asking him a couple more questions, but he excused himself, saying he had a doctoral class to attend. We had received maybe seven minutes of his time, and he could not have been less encouraging. We left cursing his name.

"What the fuck," I said to Bo back in his colossal SUV. "You'd think the entrepreneurship professor might be a little more enthusiastic about his students trying a little entrepreneurship."

"Yeah," Bo said, "but do you think if he were a real entrepreneur, he'd have been a professor all his life?"

"But even if our idea sucks, you might expect him to encourage us a little. Say, 'Good for you for trying to do something.'" I then descended into a minute or two of violent cursing. Bo seemed to enjoy my Anglicized versions of familiar American swear words, and soon we were vowing one day to prove Gompers wrong.

Next we turned to the anti-Gompers. Rodger had been a part of our section for just a few weeks of the first semester, until he dropped out to run his business and take care of his ailing mother. He was an entrepreneur to his fingertips. I had never met anyone like him, someone so obviously jazzed by the idea of setting up a business. He did not dwell on the difficulties or sacrifices, the financial hardship or personal commitment. He looked at potential, the creation of something new and vital, and he wanted in. As far as he was concerned, there was no other business life worth living besides that of the start-up entrepreneur. Rodger was the same age as me, but he had already set up and sold one technology business and was on to his second, a cell phone service for students. He had received funding from Bain Capital, one of the most prestigious venture capital firms. VC firms tend to invest in people more than ideas, so Bain's involvement was a vote of confidence in Rodger's ability to make things happen. The moment Rodger heard what Bo and I were up to, he swung into action. "I'll introduce you to some VCs," he said. "They'll love it."

"But we're just getting this going."

"Just meet these guys. They'll be looking at you anyway more than the idea. If there's anything you can't answer now, just say TBD."

"TBD?"

"To be decided."

Before I could make any further objections, my in-box began to swell with advice and online introductions orchestrated by Rodger. Within a week, we had meetings arranged with three of Boston's most prominent venture capital firms and one in Silicon Valley. It was almost too easy.

Now we had to write a business plan to go with our audio presentation. Once again, Bo swung into action, and overnight he had compiled twenty elegant PowerPoint slides describing us and our plan. Rodger's only advice was that we put our biographies up front, as this was the single most important slide. Cash flow forecasts were necessary to show you had actually thought about the business model, but otherwise meaningless. What mattered was us. Could we make this happen? And happen big?

"Most ideas are good ideas," said Rodger. "The differentiator is how they get implemented. And that's about you. You'll be great. They'll love you."

Bo forwarded me notes he had taken on a speech by two Boston venture capitalists. When pitching to a VC, it was vital to "get them juiced in the first five minutes. Get them captured and fully engaged quickly." I envisaged a spoiled, hyperactive five-year-old deciding our fate. "Make them see the business pain of the customer, then move into why your team is good and so on," the e-mail continued. "Do not start with Macro conditions . . . tell them a story . . . make them understand . . . then move into the opportunity. Customer interviews are great . . . how many customers have you talked to? Is there a real problem . . . how many said they will pay? What is your sales channel . . . direct or indirect . . . how do you get to the end user? . . . Use the HBS platform while you have it . . . aim high, solicit big players for input and advice . . . Sell with personal passion . . . have to make the personal connection." I got the point. Sell yourself. Know your customer. Know what you're going to do with the money. And don't let yourself get screwed.

Word of our endeavor quickly spread. One lunchtime, I fell into a conversation with another classmate, Jon, a phlegmatic New Yorker who before HBS had set up a software applications company and sold it to a large California firm, which appointed him to a senior strategy position. Jon said he had come to business school because he was sick of being patronized by MBAs. He wanted to learn how to patronize them right back by imposing some discipline on the great swath of hunches, instincts, and skills that made up the business intelligence that had carried him this far. Jon told me that meetings with VCs, in his experience, followed a very predictable pattern. During the first few minutes, everyone was excited. He traced a line moving upward. Then the VC started to tire of your presentation. The line began to move down. Eventually you were back at neutral. At that point, the questioning began. How big can this thing be? Rather like Hollywood executives who could envisage new films only as derivatives of others—"It's *Star Wars* meets *Pirates of the Caribbean!*"—VCs liked to feel reassured that the project they were looking at could be the next version of whatever was hot at the moment. "It's kind of a MySpace crossed with Skype."

"This is the moment to strike," Jon said. "Just as the VC is talking about the hot businesses of the moment, you should look off into a corner of the room and smile. Perhaps shake your head. You're trying to tell the VC you've heard all this before and he is no better than the herd. You are disappointed in his lack of imagination. This totally freaks them out." He demonstrated his faraway gaze and the gently exasperated laugh.

As venture capital has become institutionalized, the people in it have become less and less venturesome. Those who visited campus were overwhelmingly male and either white or Asian. Some had worked at a real company before becoming capital providers, but that was no longer necessary. Most had degrees in science, engineering, or business. They liked to think of themselves as renegades and rule-breakers, and yet they struck me as a hardened monoculture. When one of them took up bicycling on the weekend, they all did. If one had pale blond wood in the conference room, they all did.

In the HBS classroom, the future VCs all affected a similar manner, speaking in a measured monotone, keeping their notes in a leather portfolio, wearing chinos, tucked-in dress shirts, and baseball caps. The comments they made were never surprising, sticking close to the frameworks we were taught. Whereas the bankers were often argumentative and difficult, the VCs liked to affect calm under pressure. They loved to poke holes in business plans by saying things like "I'd like to see more customer data" or "I question the founder's motivation." They enjoyed sitting in judgment and looking terribly pleased with themselves, to the point where all you wanted to do was slap them to life and demand they *do something*.

Our meetings bore this out. The rhythm of each was the same. Niceties, excitement, drift, reinvigoration, the promise to stay in touch. Each VC gave the same advice: pick a vertical. "Don't try to accumulate content from all over the place," said one. "The audience for it is too hard to find. Pick something like medical content, focus on getting top surgeons to talk and market it to doctors. It's easier to gain traction and get good at what you're doing if you're focused on a single area from top to bottom. Vertically."

We could not brush off their questions with a TBD, the way Rodger had suggested. They just came back with more. They all asked about video. Why weren't we going into video? Surely it was superior to audio? Bigger market. Cooler. More money. One of them looked askance at me when I said I didn't own a PSP, Sony's new gaming device. Fortunately Bo did, but I had already hurt our cause. The VC looked at me and said, "I don't trust anyone coming into my office to talk about consumer technology who doesn't own a PSP." Luckily, I didn't have a chance to lay out my vision of an office without a computer.

Once it was clear no VC was going to give us a huge amount of undeserved money, we decided to press on regardless. We created a series of podcasts for our section, in which fellow students talked about their lives and ambitions. Every day, we tracked the evolution of podcasting. A team of ex-Google technologists in San Francisco were developing a software product to allow anyone to record and post podcasts online. A group of wine lovers had achieved some success with a podcast called Grapetalk. And a hyperactive DJ based in London, calling himself the Podfather, was garnering a lot of attention. Working each night in front of ESPN, Bo built us a functioning website. He taught me how to make recordings on my computer and post them. My friends on Fleet Street came through like troopers, allowing me to interview them about goings-on in Britain for an American audience. We began mixing music into our recordings, and each day our archive grew.

Then one day we went to talk to Felix, our strategy professor. Unlike Gompers, he was generous with his time and he asked us a question to which we did not have an answer: "How much value are you going to capture doing this?" The barriers to entry were low. People had shown they were reluctant to pay for online content. We would never have a technology advantage, so our only hope would be to build a brand and style of content that people could find nowhere else. He did not say all of this, but once he had asked the question in those terms, we began to figure it out. When we discovered that Kleiner Perkins was investing over $8.85 million in the Podfather and asked ourselves why, we could not figure it out. It was not a good sign for our own business. We had been thinking of spending the summer working on the company, but as the cracks in our model became ever more apparent, Bo stepped up his search for a biotech/venture capital job in Boston and found a great one.

Plenty of businesses started and stopped at HBS. There was no shame in that. I was dreading telling Rodger that we were terminating our efforts, but he said, "No problem. Keep me posted on what you do next." He was an instinctive believer in creative destruction, the constant churn of ideas, some of which worked, others which didn't. The most important thing for him was not sitting on the sidelines.

Approaching the summer without a job was daunting. On the one hand, I knew that the companies that came for hell week did not come to HBS looking for people like me. In their eyes I was an oddity. But it was still depressing to be made to feel like that. One job I interviewed for and thought I had a chance of getting was with *The Washington Post*. But my interviewer, a woman, barely let me say a word as she rattled off the history of the newspaper and descriptions of the kinds of people who succeeded there. When I was not offered a second interview, an alumnus at the company told me that ex-journalists were not thought to make effective executives. The divide between the journalism and business operations was too wide to jump. Now if I had been a banker before HBS . . . This was maddening. But I was not alone in struggling to change my career. Luis, the Franco-Argentine, complained to me that many people felt HBS failed in its promise to give people a new start.

"They say this is your chance to change industry, but very few are succeeding. You see, the problem is that the path of least resistance is to do

banking or consulting. Now, if you wanted to do either of those, you probably could. But if you wanted to get out of them, you really have to fight,"
he said, driving a fist into his palm. "If you don't have experience in an
industry, they don't want you, so you end up going back to the industries
you do have experience in."

My own solution to the problem was to do something I had been trying
to do for years. I retrieved a boxful of notes and books that I had kept in
France and set to work on a novel. Each day I would go to the Boston Public
Library and work, and as Margret moved into the final months of her preg-
nancy, I was around to amuse Augie. By the end of the summer, I had completed a first draft of the book. It was entrepreneurship, of sorts. After
spending so much of the past year struggling with the work and feeling
incompetent, it felt wonderful to be doing something on my own terms
again and reconnecting with life before business school.

As I reflected on that first year, I came across a description of the HBS
learning model written in 1954 by Malcolm McNair, a former professor at
the school. It was in an essay called "Tough-Mindedness and the Case
Method":

> William James, a great teacher of psychology and philosophy at Harvard
> during the early years of this century, made the useful distinction between
> people who are tough-minded and people who are tender-minded. These
> terms have nothing to do with levels of ethical conduct; the toughness
> referred to is toughness of the intellectual apparatus, toughness of the
> spirit, not toughness of the heart. Essentially, it is the attitude and the
> qualities and the training that enable one to seize on facts and make these
> facts a basis for intelligent, courageous action. The tough-minded have a
> zest for tackling hard problems. They dare to grapple with the unfamiliar
> and wrest useful truth from stubborn new facts. They are not dismayed by

change for they know that change at an accelerated tempo is the pattern of living, the only pattern on which successful action can be based. Above all, the tough-minded do not wall themselves in with comfortable illusions. They do not rely on the easy precepts of tradition or on mere conformity to regulations. They know that the answers are not in the book.

This captured much of what I had learned. Despite my frustration at being so far behind my classmates technically and in my basic knowledge of business functions, I knew that my intellectual apparatus had toughened. I saw things in the world that I had not seen before. I looked at facts and numbers in a different way. I recalled Dave Hawkins, my first accounting professor, reading out a piece from the front page of *The Wall Street Journal* and thinking to myself, if I can find that as interesting as he seems to, then I will have learned something. Now, for the first time in my life, I turned eagerly to the financial pages of the newspaper. Business was no longer a parade of dry facts and personalities, but a soap opera. The podcasting adventure, despite its failure, had proved to me how much I had learned. I got a geeky thrill from sitting with venture capitalists and hearing them talk about IRRs and thinking to myself, well, sure, but are you more interested in the internal rate of return or the ROE, the return on equity?

The routine of the section had eventually palled. After so many classes, everyone had his role. We knew who would say what when, who would make the controversial remark, who would have the numbers, who would crack the joke. It had gone from comfortable to dull, and I was looking forward to interacting with different students in every class during the second year. As the winter gave way to spring, we resented the windowless room and the routine of cases and cold calls. We had even given up on the classroom games. The best of it, though, was the easy familiarity with ninety new people from so many backgrounds and walks of life. It was great in the context of a life to have this opportunity to expand one's social circle so dramatically at a moment when most of my friends were feeling their circles contract.

My summer job search had been a shambles. I knew I had not given it my all, and I was angry with myself for that. But I was also aware that my indifference to the work most of my peers would be doing told me something. I knew I would have hated "the stool." My pride could not have taken it. And I knew I did not want to spend the summer away from Margret and Augie, even though many of my married classmates would be separated from their families for ten weeks. Still, standing on the bank of the HBS river as the rest of my class sailed off was uncomfortable. The questions spun in my mind. If I was not going to follow the HBS formula, why was I here? What right did I have to dismiss the stool, or the ten-week placement in corporate marketing? What would be the consequences? Clearly one did not come to HBS just for the education. But was I a fool to think I could take the education and pursue a business career on my own terms, not as yet another corporate MBA?

The final section event of the year was the auction. Each section organized its own auction to raise money for charities of their choosing. Students and professors donated items, and we all dressed up and went to a venue in Boston. We had booked a room above the *Cheers* bar on Boston Common. Marnie, whom I had sat next to during the second semester, organized the event and had asked me to be the auctioneer. Her irrefutable argument was that "all the auctioneers you see on television are English." The items for sale ranged from dinner cooked by our professors to an all-expenses-paid trip to the annual Berkshire Hathaway shareholder conference in Omaha, Nebraska. After nearly two hours of banging away with my gavel, we had raised over $50,000. Then a voice from the back shouted, "I'll pay twenty dollars for Philip to take off his shirt." Several voices joined in until we had a five-hundred-dollar bid. I removed my jacket, tie, and shirt. Then another voice shouted: "I'll give two hundred dollars if Stuart takes off his shirt and is handcuffed to Philip for the rest of the bidding." Stuart was the Wall Street trader known in the section for his mathematical genius and massive physique. He spent every lunchtime pumping weights in the gym. So the idea of me, pale and English, chained to this bronzed Nevadan Adonis quickly sent the bidding up to $2,000. Which was how my first year at the Harvard Business School ended. Bare-chested and handcuffed to a muscular bond trader, surrounded by my braying peers.

Chapter Twelve

CHASING
THE CURVE

If I offered you twenty thousand
pounds for every dot that stopped,
would you really, old man, tell me
to keep my money or would you
calculate how many dots you could
afford to spare—free of income tax,
free of income tax?

—HARRY LIME,
IN *THE THIRD MAN*

After the strictures of the first year, the second year, the elective curriculum, was all about choice. You could take more courses or pursue independent studies supervised by a professor. During the final weeks of the previous semester, we had received a thick booklet describing the second-year courses. We were also given access to surveys of the various courses completed by previous classes of MBA students. This was like a restaurant guide, with formal descriptions of the courses supported by customer reviews. These ranged from superlative, "greatest course at HBS, hands-down," to coruscating, "horrible professor, lame cases, total waste of time." We could see which classes were oversubscribed, which were on the verge of being struck from the catalog. The most popular second-year courses were Advanced Competitive Strategy, Building and Sustaining a Successful Enterprise, and Entrepreneurial Finance. The courses were assigned using a computer algorithm. You ranked your choices in order of preference, one to thirty. The computer then ran through everyone's choices, allotting you as many of your highest-ranked picks as possible. If you chose Advanced Competitive Strategy, it was unlikely you would also get Entrepreneurial Finance. But if you didn't put one of these three as your number-one choice, you would be unlikely to get any of them at all. The challenge of picking the right courses in the right order was time-consuming and became a subject of intense discussion and rumor. Students followed one of three strategies for choosing their courses. The first was to deepen their knowledge in one specific area. If you knew you were going into private equity, you could take extra finance, tax, and corporate restructuring. Bo took a slew of courses in venture capital and health care. The second strategy was to work on your weaknesses. I had so many, it was hard to know where to begin. But I decided to load up on finance and strategy. The final path was to take the easiest courses you could on a schedule you liked. This was chosen by people returning to their old jobs or family firms. One man in our section picked courses that would allow him to commute back and forth to Los Angeles, where his wife lived, and spend just Monday, Tuesday, and Wednesday mornings in Boston.

The algorithm served me well. For the first semester of the second year, I was assigned Entrepreneurial Marketing, International Financial Management, Strategy and Technology, Coordinating and Managing Supply Chains, and Dynamic Markets. Entrepreneurial Marketing and Strategy and Technology were exactly the kind of courses I had come to HBS to study. I chose International Financial Management in order to consolidate my first-year finance and because of the professor, Mihir Desai, who had made such a positive impression all those months ago during Analytics. Coordinating and Managing Supply Chains would be taught by Zeynep, and again, I liked the dirt-under-the-fingernails quality of the subject. It felt far less antiseptic, less virtual, than many of the other aspects of business we studied. Dynamic Markets was a curious choice. It was a course for anyone thinking of joining a hedge fund after HBS. I decided to take it partly because I thought that if ever there was a time for me to learn about hedge funds, this was it, and partly because I realized I enjoyed learning the grammar of finance. A lot of it passed me by, but whatever I did grasp gave me more pleasure than the lessons, say, of marketing. As with Supply Chains, when I studied finance, I felt I was learning something concrete rather than faddish. Not that I wanted to push this too far. There was a student in old Section A, a dashing but arrogant Indian Rhodes Scholar, who liked to say that the only second-year courses worth taking were finance courses. Everything else was a waste of time. I could not agree, but I could see where he was coming from. When he graduated he took a vast salary at a glamorous new hedge fund.

Our second son was born on September 6, the day before the elective curriculum year began. We were summoned to the Brigham and Women's Hospital in Boston at 7:00 A.M. on the due date and spent the day waiting in the maternity ward. Late in the afternoon I wandered down to the cafeteria, and when I returned to our room the midwife, who was wearing a Boston Red Sox shower cap, barked, "Put those down and come over here." I set my coffee and sticky bun down on a counter and grabbed one of Margret's legs. The delivery went quickly, and we named the boy Hugo.

The next morning at eight thirty I was back in class for Entrepreneurial Marketing, with Joe Lassiter. I had read the case several days earlier, but when I came to look at it again—the highlighted passages, marginalia—I could not recognize a thing. The class was packed, and Lassiter came at us like a jet of cold water, rinsing off the last of the summer and bringing us smartly back to our HBS mind-set.

"So how big should this business try to be?" he said, calling on a Vietnamese student in the back row. "Five million dollars in revenue a year, ten million a year, a hundred million a year?"

"I think they should go for five million," said the student. He then described the product, a kind of printer that built 3-D models for engineers and designers. "I think the market is small right now, and the company does not have the resources to go beyond that."

"Come on," Lassiter said. "Look how cool this thing is." He showed us a clip of the machine in action. You fed in an image and within a few minutes it spat out a three-dimensional model made of gray plastic. "Who thinks we can get to a hundred million? And how do we get there?" Several hands went up. "That's more like it," Lassiter said.

He pressed the more gung-ho students to describe the perfect customer for this new product, the one who would persuade all the others they had to have it. And he asked us all to write an elevator pitch, the pithy summary that could win over an investor or customer in the space of an elevator ride. The pitch had to answer these questions: What problem will this product solve? And why should I buy it from you?

Lassiter was an intriguing man. He had been an academic early in his career, then transferred to business for twenty years before coming to teach at HBS in his fifties. He had a natural enthusiasm and sympathy for the challenge of running a business, and this made his course one of the more popular on campus. It sought the answer to a distinct problem. When big organizations decide whether to launch a new product or service, they use the tools of marketing to test and refine their idea before going to market. For an entrepreneur, such tools are far too expensive and time-consuming. So how do you know an idea is a good one, and sell it to others, with limited resources? Later, the course evolved into something even more intriguing, a discussion of what it means to be an entrepreneur. What was it like to pursue an opportunity with only the very scarcest means? What did it take? We heard so often of those at the extremes, the entrepreneurs who had made it big and those who had failed dismally. But what of those who had made a life of pursuing their own ideas, winning their own customers, building their own fortunes beyond the comfortable fortresses of corporate life? It was what I had missed in Gompers's class.

In the first year, we had defined *entrepreneurship* as "the relentless pursuit of opportunity beyond the constraints of the resources currently controlled." We had also been told time and again that entrepreneurship was not about taking risk but about managing it. It was about spotting an opportunity, seizing it, and reaping the rewards. It was a way of managing not only a business but one's own life. Lassiter retooled the HBS definition of entrepreneurship to suit his course. Entrepreneurial marketing, he said, was about the "relentless pursuit of the customers and partners necessary for the people leading the firm to select their business opportunities, to sell their products and services, and to obtain the future resources they desire." It was also about how to gather the information required to make decisions and persuade others to commit to your idea before knowing it would work.

In case after case, we studied small- to medium-size companies struggling to launch a new concept or deciding which new opportunities to pursue. Our key texts were Geoffrey Moore's books *Crossing the Chasm* and *Inside the Tornado*. The challenge Moore addresses is that many new products struggle to move from small markets of enthusiasts over into the mass market. He calls the enthusiasts "visionaries," people who buy on promise, the first in line for the newest gizmos. The mass market comprises the "pragmatists," those who just want the damned thing to work. Among the solutions Moore proposes is identifying those people who affect buying decisions in the mass market. If you are making fancy handbags, the way to go from selling a few to selling millions might be to persuade a Hollywood movie star to carry one. Another way would be to convince the relevant channel of your worth. If Wal-Mart decided to sell your product, you would be almost guaranteed to sell a lot of it, regardless of whether the end consumer had ever heard of you before.

But before getting into the movie star's hand or into Wal-Mart, you need to make sure you have a product the star might want or that piques the Wal-Mart buyer's interest. To do this you need to understand consumers, through interviews, research, even psychological testing. Then you need to develop a product that you hope will meet their demands. This might involve challenging the egos of your gifted scientific team, who left their highly regarded research posts to develop a world-changing dermato-logical treatment only to find that their paychecks now depended on fine-tuning a diaper rash cream, because that is what is going to sell. Also, you need to have enough cash to keep the business afloat while awaiting your first sales. Which brings us back to the key commandment of entrepre-neurial finance: don't ever run out of cash.

We studied the case of IdeaVillage, a company that sold products through television infomercials. Eventually they realized that to sell even more product, they needed to get onto mass market retail shelves. Their breakthrough product was an electric razor for women's facial hair, which sold well enough on television to be picked up by Wal-Mart. Its success had allowed IdeaVillage to move from selling to niche audiences on late-night television to building a permanent presence in Wal-Mart.

Lassiter emphasized the importance of people and connections. It was important to hire not just a great salesman but also one with relationships with the people you want to sell to—either the visionaries who will take up your new product or the influencers who will stir the pragmatists to adopt it en masse. He displayed a picture of a herd of wildebeests. Pragmatists, he told us, find safety in numbers. They watch for what they fear. And when panicked, they stampede. The trick is to identify the pain and rouse the fears that cause the herd to stampede straight into your arms.

What was interesting about Lassiter's course was the way it examined the interaction between entrepreneurs and the people they sell to. It recog-nized the difference between building a small, moderately successful ven-ture and hitting a home run, and it asked the question, what does the entrepreneur do to make that happen? In some cases, it means hiring the salesperson who knows the right person at the big company or government department who signs the first major contract. In others it means focusing on one customer's particular problem so effectively that all of its rivals soon come rushing to the entrepreneur's door. In yet other cases, it means end-less rounds of experimentation, years of thrifty cash management, or a rush of external events. Raising money, Lassiter observed, should never be an obstacle. "Never in recorded history," he told us, "has the supply of capital not overwhelmed the supply of opportunity." Toward the end of the year, Bo told me this was the single most important lesson he had learned at HBS: there is always money for a good idea.

What was also fascinating was how much Lassiter's course left open. There were clearly things one needed to do in getting a new business going, from securing financing to proving your concept to finding the right employees, partners, and customers. But how you sequenced these was always going to be a juggling act. Can you get the money before the proof, or the customer before the money, or the partners before any of it? The only firm decision one could make in embarking on this was the decision to be an entrepreneur. And on this, Lassiter offered the following:

Entrepreneurship, he said, was more than a job. It was a way of thinking, managing, and living. In certain ways it was harder than choosing a corporate career. It would involve more financial uncertainty. But, ultimately, if it meant enough to you, it would be more than worth it. The difference between success and failure, he said, was very fine, very personal, and yet very public at the same time. Ultimately, you had to decide for yourself. These issues had come up occasionally during the course and in conversations with friends, but this was the first time I felt I was hearing them from someone who knew what he was talking about.

Lassiter said that if we still wanted to follow this path, we should pick a place where we wanted to live and try to join a "world-class tribe." He demonstrated his point with a diagram showing all the companies that had spun off from Cascade Communications, a telecommunications equipment maker founded near Boston in the 1990s. The diagram showed eleven companies founded by people who had worked at Cascade. Several of them, notably Sycamore Networks, had been enormously successful. It was a powerful point, especially for a class full of students wondering what to do next. "It really does help to know what you're doing," Lassiter stressed. Constantly moving from place to place, changing careers and specialization, meant you would never develop the reputation and deep networks that helped entrepreneurial ventures take off. Having people know that you know what you are doing really matters. "You really don't know what you're doing until you've done it a couple of times," he told us. "And then the world changes." Even if you've built a reputation and developed experience, you still have to revel in uncertainty.

Lassiter emphasized having people around you who could talk frankly to you in such a way that you would listen. And above all, he said, the coolest thing in the world was to be in love, to be together, and to see your kids grow up. It was a little corny, but it was exactly what I had been longing to hear. It was an affirmation of everything I was feeling. The entrepreneurial life would be hard at times, but there was a way to do it, and it was hardheaded and made a lot of sense. It allowed you to have control over your time and be with the people you loved. This was what I had to come to business school to figure out.

Being free of the section was both a relief and a shock. Ripped from its embrace, we were now exposed to the wolves within our year. It was fascinating to sit in class with new people, to hear new voices, but the mood was less comfortable, more aggressive. In International Financial Management, a small group of Indians who were all returning to jobs in private equity firms formed a clique in the skydeck. They relished challenging Mihir Desai, who always gave it right back, and scorning anything that met their disapproval. In a case involving Nestlé, Desai described visiting the company's headquarters in Switzerland. To make the point about the difference between American and European corporate cultures, he said that at lunch he had been greeted by a wine waiter who offered two kinds of wine. The skydeck roared with laughter. Oh, the decadence! The disregard for the investor! Those European executives quaffing wine with lunch! While the financiers slapped their desks in glee, I was jotting down a reminder to myself to look into careers with Nestlé.

Max Verlander, my German friend, had alerted me to the anti-

European feelings on campus. He pointed me to a speech given by Jeff Immelt, the chief executive of General Electric, at HBS in 2004. "In the United States, when you go see your customers, customers like you talking about how much money you make," he said. "It's a bravado thing. Customers say, hey, that's great, you make a lot of money. If you go to talk to a customer in Europe about how much money you make, they say, that's money you stole from me. You're not supposed to make that much money. You have to alter what you do and how you approach it. There's nuance. Companies aren't sup- posed to make money. It's Europe." You bet there's nuance, I thought.

"It's all India-China, India-China," Max said. "People here think Europe is dead."

The Dynamic Markets class assembled every Monday and Tuesday after- noon to trade stocks, bonds, and their derivatives. Ideally, the course was for people steeped in finance. Graduates of the class joined elite hedge funds or the special situations groups at the top Wall Street banks, where they traded in products the rest of the street barely understood. I was an obvious interloper in this whey-faced and serious group who flicked on their laptops like gunslingers dropping the catch on their pistols. It was such a special class it required two professors rather than the usual one. Josh Coval and Erik Stafford were a curious pair, one small, dark, and restive, the other tall, blond, and artfully laid back, like a Viking at rest. Unlike with every other HBS class, grading was not based on class participation or a final exam but solely on how much money you made trading on a simulated exchange. This was pure. No irritating classmates mouthing off for credit. Just us and the markets. Mano a mano. During the two-hour sessions on Monday, we would trade electronically in a virtual market. On Tuesday, we went through what we had done. Our rankings were posted each week.

In our first class, Stafford strode languidly to the front of his desk and sat down. "Everything we do in this class comes down to one thing," he said. "The law of one price." The law of one price states that in an efficient market, all identical goods must have only one price. This seemed blindingly obvious. Imagine a market where ten different vendors sold bananas. The moment one dropped his price, all the others would have to or else they would have no customers. But there would be a fleeting moment for the buyer who spotted the lower price to buy the cheaper bananas and sell them at the higher price before everyone else in the market saw what was going on and dropped their prices. He would be the arbitrageur. Arbitrage is the making of a riskless profit. You sell one product and immediately buy an identical product at a lower price with the funds from the sale. But here in Dynamic Markets, we were not talking about colorful fruit markets populated by cackling, sun-scorched vendors. We were in the world of stone-hearted Wall Street traders for whom a product is a six-digit number flashing green on their screen, amid hundreds of other flashing numbers and fluctuating graphs. To them a product had no color, taste, or texture. It was something that produced cash flows. It could be stock in a company or a bond. It could be the option to buy or sell that stock or bond in several months' time. What made products identical in the eyes of the trader was if they guaranteed identical cash flows. So you could have a bond that promised to pay you ten dollars in a year and a package of stocks and options, artfully structured, converted into Thai baht via pork belly futures, but if each promised to pay you ten dollars in a year with the same degree of risk, the cost of each of these today should be the same. If they were not, you had an opportunity to make some money.

For the truly red-blooded, there was also risk arbitrage, of which the classic form is merger arbitrage. It involves betting on the likelihood that corporate mergers will occur once they are announced. Company A announces a merger bid for Company B. It is offering a price, X, for Company B, usually above Company B's current stock market valuation. The merger arbitrageur then sets to work. What, he asks himself, is the likelihood that this deal will actually go through? Will the shareholders of Company B accept it? Will the government block it? Will there turn out to be some hideous accounting fraud at Company B? Will the CEO of Company A fall down an elevator shaft, leaving the company in the hands of its president, who never wanted the merger in the first place? During this period, between the announcement of the merger bid and its completion or collapse, the stock prices of the merging companies move around more than usual as investors weigh up the probability of the merger's taking place. The skilled merger arbitrageur will assess this probability, judge whether the stock prices are what they should be, and invest accordingly.

While taking this class, I read the former Treasury secretary Robert Rubin's autobiography. For much of his career, Rubin was a revered risk arbitrageur at Goldman Sachs. He would spend hours sketching out probability calculations on yellow legal pads. It was an approach he brought to government. His entire way of thinking was about understanding risk and reward. When he was Treasury secretary and the Mexican economy imploded, he tried to calculate the scale of the bailout America should offer against the risk of the Mexican economy foundering for years to come. There was no political calculation here. That would be left to others. What Rubin brought to the party was this sense that every risk of every outcome was calculable, and if that was the case, it was possible to limit and prepare for the probability of the worst outcomes occurring. Rubin wrote that the risks most people ignored were the very low probability risks of catastrophic outcomes. They spent an inordinate amount of time worrying about the 20 percent chance of having a bad day and no time thinking about the 1 percent chance of their entire life being turned upside down.

For the risk arb, the 0.1 percent risk of losing $100,000 from your savings is identical to the 20 percent chance of losing your wallet containing $500. The present value cost of both outcomes is $100. Once this way of thinking had burned itself into my brain, it was hard to think any other way. Everywhere I looked in my own life, there seemed to be small risks of total disaster, to which I had never given much thought. Leaving our son with a baby-sitter seemed the most obvious. Perhaps the odds of the baby-sitter turning out to be a kidnapper are 0.01 percent. But what would be the cost of losing him? Infinite. If you thought about this in a Rubin framework, you would only ever entrust your child to someone in whom you had 100 percent confidence.

When people talk about trade-offs in their personal life, they often keep it at a very high level. If I take this job, my salary will be higher, but I'll spend less time with my family. But what if you turn that "less time with my family" into the actual consequences you most fear? Your spouse will leave you. Your children will treat you as a stranger. And then assign a probability to it. Each outcome used to carry a bearable 5 percent risk. Now that rises to 25 percent. How does that $50,000 pay increase feel now that you have raised the odds of jeopardizing your entire family life by 20 percent?

Sketching out these issues, I found, was more than just a handwriting exercise. It forced me to confront the values I placed on the various parts of my life and how irrational these values were. A small risk of disaster equals a moderate risk of something quite bad. A small chance of great riches is equal to a moderate chance of moderate riches. This was how an arbitrageur saw things, and it made an awful lot of sense. Why didn't the whole world think like this?

"People do," Annette told me, "but the reason it doesn't work is that perceived risk and actual risk are very different. You know, nothing seems so bad until it actually happens. It's like being in a relationship when you imagine breaking up with the other person, and then when you do, it's ten times worse than you thought it would be. You have to be really cold to get the probabilities and outcomes right."

Some of this was basic human psychology. People buy lottery tickets despite the staggering odds against them. As an investment on the risk-reward spectrum, it makes no sense. But on the brightening-my-dismal-week-with-the-faint-hope-of-escaping-the-rat-hole-that-is-my-life spectrum, it makes perfect sense. Trying to price out and assess the worst possible scenarios in one's life, however rational, is no fun at all. So we tend to avoid it. Or overpay for insurance. The profits in the insurance business, after all, arise almost entirely from the difference between the consumer's and the insurer's capacities to assess and price risk. I found that trying to apply whatever financial concepts I actually grasped to nonfinancial situations made understanding Dynamic Markets easier.

During the first half of the course, we were assigned a different partner each week and expected to meet before Monday's class to practice executing a different trading strategy on the simulated market. One week we had to derive the value of information in supposedly efficient markets; the next, we considered price and liquidity. We used matrix algebra to create portfolios of stocks weighted so as to minimize risk and maximize return. Fortunately, I was paired up twice during this period with Ottavio, a brilliant Brazilian who had worked as a trader before business school and wanted nothing more than to work at a hedge fund afterward. He left me with little to do but praise the trading models he built in Excel and watch while he went at it.

For the second half of the course, however, we were told to pick our own partners. I knew Ottavio would be teaming up with his fellow Brazilian, Rubens. I also knew that if I were to stand even the slightest chance of survival, I needed a hotshot by my side. The moment Coval said, "Pick a partner," I dashed off an e-mail to Chad, the Section A finance stud. "Chad: You have to be my partner. If not, I am screwed. Completely screwed." I turned around to see him stuffing his hand into his mouth to stifle a laugh. He looked down and nodded. Across the room, I saw another man from our section banging his fist on his desk. He had e-mailed Chad within seconds of me. But he was too late. I had snared the King.

Each team was given a notional $1 million to manage and told to come up with a name, a prospectus, and a fee structure. Chad and I called ourselves Alchemy and pledged to turn base investments into gold. Another team chose the title "Bringing down the house," which indeed they did in one class, taking on such a leveraged position that they crashed the entire computer system, forcing Coval and Stafford to redraft the rules of the game. Chad, as I had hoped, created masterly spreadsheets, embedded with options calculators and winking formulae. He tried once or twice to explain how we would be hedging delta or scalping gamma in the upcoming class, but we quickly resolved that I would be his his data entry goon, trading according to the numbers thrown out by his spreadsheets. Computer trading was an eerie sensation. If this had been real, behind each of those numbers blinking on the screen, those moving charts and shifting spreads, would have been communities, factories, and towns. There were mothers dropping off their children at school and going to work, relying on a company to feed their families. But we would just be buying and selling the assets on which these lives depended, as their prices moved by fractions of a decimal point. Trading felt like the furthest possible remove from the workshop and assembly plant, and it was attracting the very brightest minds at HBS because the rewards for doing it well were so outlandish. Yet one had to truly trust in capitalism to believe that trading like this served the goal of efficiently allocating resources in society. Because there was no obvious proof that what you were doing served any purpose besides enriching the trader and his client. One could argue that trading was an effective mechanism for setting prices and that this affected everyone in an economy. But did the traders really deserve the money they made? The rise of the hedge fund investor often felt to me more like a failure of the market rather than a fair allocation of rewards. Sitting in Dynamic Markets, with so many smart classmates focused on these numbers and moving charts, it felt like clever capital was outwitting honest labor, not sharing in an efficient market.

Over the next five weeks, Chad and I marched steadily to the top of the class. Every so often, when Chad's computer packed in, I would simply eyeball trades for a while, riding up stock or bond prices to make some extra money. This goosed our returns more often than it hurt them. In the final class, we had a chance to vault to the top of the rankings after the Brazilians lost most of their capital on a spread that did not close fast enough. But we never caught up with the leaders, an American man and a German woman. Nonetheless, I walked away with a one from this class. Chad said it was proof that markets could fail. I felt it was my biggest bull run at HBS.

. . .

In 1998, HBS imposed a policy whereby recruiters were not allowed to request a student's grades. At the time, there were two MBA classes in each year, one that arrived in September, one in January. The caliber of the classes varied, and it was felt that it was not fair on students in the tougher class to have their grades compared with those in the inferior one. But since the two classes had been reduced to one, the policy had come under review. Recruiters wanted to know grades, and alumni of the school who had had to reveal their grades felt that the nondisclosure policy diminished HBS's academic standards. At the end of November, we received a letter from Rick Ruback explaining the administration's thinking. "In many ways, non-disclosure is inconsistent with our mission of developing outstanding business leaders," he wrote. "Much of what business leaders do is define, measure, and seek ways to enhance performance." Consequently, HBS was considering optional disclosure starting with the class of 2008. The president of our student association explained to *The Harvard Crimson* that the administration had been worried by a perception that "general academic motivation and rigor has gone down" and that "people are valuing social, networking, and extracurricular activities, rather than gaining general management skills." Ruback countered: "We want to be sure we provide positive incentives for students in a way that helps them make the most of their time at HBS. We also believe students earn their grades, and thus it is fair they be able to use them to highlight their capabilities in a career search, should they so choose."

My own "social, networking, and extracurricular" activities had expanded since the first year to include twice-weekly racquetball games with Oleg, a Russian student in my section who resembled the young Boris Yeltsin, with a heavy, smiling face and a thatch of thick blond hair. Oleg had spent part of his youth in New York, where his father was a Soviet diplomat, which explained his fluent, colorful English. His slow amble onto the court was deceptive. He was a nimble and ferocious player who slammed into walls and cursed enthusiastically. After each game, we chewed over the latest example of HBS insanity.

"I can't see why they're worried about us not working hard enough," said Oleg one afternoon, wiping his brow. "I've never worked so hard in my life. I work and I go home and see my wife. I'm not going to nightclubs in Boston on a Monday. I wish I had time to do some networking. I mean, are you my network, Philip? Fuck. Shit. I'm in big trouble. Come on, you loser, let's play another game."

Grade disclosure unleashed the pent-up feelings among students about the culture of the school, and became a referendum about the school's purpose and methods. Our study groups had broken up after the first year, but I still bumped into Stephen, the ex-diplomat, and he was indignant on the subject. "How can this be a safe learning environment if students have to worry about grades all the time? You remember Analytics? We knew nothing. Then the next thing, we're being put on a forced curve with a bunch of bankers and consultants who could pass the first-year exams in their sleep. It's ridiculous. And look at the way they're just going to try to impose it on us. Didn't they read their own LEAD cases about building consensus?"

"But it's not going to affect us," I replied. "We're safe."

"That's not the point," he said, angrily. "The point is that the students at this place are not respected. The only people whose opinions they care about are the recruiters and the alumni, because they're the ones who give all the money."

I agreed with him. The grades were useful for me in terms of telling me how I was doing, especially in the more technical courses. But the fact that I earned ones in LEAD and Dynamic Markets and twos in Biggie, the macroeconomics course, and LCA, was trivial. It was no indicator of how good a businessman I might be.

Grade disclosure forced us to consider the purpose of a business school. A senior journalist on the *Financial Times* once told me that the real secret to making money was wanting to make money. Not in the sense of "oh, I'd like to make a bit more money." But every day waking up and thinking, right, look at all that money sloshing around out there. How am I going to divert as much of that as possible into my bank account? He, of course, had become rich by marrying a European heiress and was marking his retirement by building a large house overlooking the Mediterranean. But his point was that business success, all other things being equal, was a question largely of motivation. His proof lay in the range of people who made great fortunes, from Mafia bosses to Stanford computer science Ph.D.s, from the men selling vegetable peelers on late-night television to the quantitative geniuses who traded derivatives. People who are barely literate can do much better than those with an alphabet soup of graduate degrees. Business in this sense is not like law or medicine, where every practitioner needs to know a certain body of facts. At most levels, it is a more primal pursuit, requiring character, guts, instinct, leadership, and the application of pure common sense. The last thing it is about is frameworks, spreadsheets, and academic papers. These are just tiny props in a far bigger drama. Consequently, many people have argued that business cannot be taught, only experienced and learned.

In his book *What They Don't Teach You at Harvard Business School*, the late sports agent Mark McCormack wrote, "In fairness to Harvard Business School, what they don't teach you is what they can't teach you, which is how to read people and how to use that knowledge to get what you want." He said that early in his career he made the mistake of hiring Harvard MBAs, assuming they would have the confidence and expertise to solve certain problems. Instead, he found them to be "congenitally naïve or victims of their business training. The result was a kind of real-life learning disability—a failure to read people properly or to size up situations and an uncanny knack for forming the wrong perceptions." McCormack concluded that graduate degrees were no guarantee of "business smarts."

McCormack isn't the only one to have relished attacking Harvard MBAs. During the summer between my two years at Harvard, I spent an hour with an investment banker in Boston who spent the entire time referring to the business school as "Cambridge Community College," and finding it funnier every time he said it. Scarcely a week went by at the school without some business titan coming through and saying Harvard MBAs were all well and good but they needed to talk less and do more. The school needed to produce more problem solvers and fewer windbags.

In early December, Ruback attended a student debate on grade disclosure. The argument in favor of it was that it would refocus students on their academic work, and mark a return to a policy that had worked for the school's first ninety years. The argument against was that it would discourage students from taking academic risks—my taking Dynamic Markets, for example—and diminish the importance of extracurricular activities. It would also be unfair to nonnative English speakers, given the emphasis on class participation; to anyone from nontraditional HBS backgrounds, for whom all the material was new; and to those trying to switch careers, who would no longer be able to conceal poor finance grades while they tried to find jobs in, say, banking. The final speaker made the point that if HBS admitted students on the basis of their range of achievements and brilliant leadership qualities, why would it then put them all on a forced curve based simply on academics and have that as the only grade they received?

The vote went forty-four to six against grade disclosure. In the end it did not matter. The administration decided to go ahead anyway, and the dean wrote to say that "Harvard Business School's reputation is deeply rooted in the transformational experience we provide in our classrooms, an experience that is vitally dependent upon maintaining high academic standards. The relatively recent policy of prohibiting disclosure is inconsistent with our commitment to these standards."

The experience reminded me of the anecdote Ruback had told in the first week about the angry student being warned he was not the customer at HBS but the product. But it also reminded me that however much I was enjoying business school, I was too old for a lot of its culture. I did not need any additional motivation to do the work. My motivation came from having left my job and incurred large debts to come to the school with a family.

Once I had gotten over the insecurities of the first semester, I had given up worrying about grades as a reflection of what I was learning. I knew what I was learning, and that was enough. When I heard that HBS was now considering admitting more students straight out of college and fewer over thirty, it made sense in terms of creating a more controlled, teachable student body, but no sense in terms of including the widest possible range of experience. What would all those case discussions have been like with a class half full of twenty-two-year-olds with minimal work experience?

During my time at HBS, I often ran into Bob, my first-semester section neighbor. All my early fears about him had dissolved. Behind the glacial Air Force exterior was a warm, funny man with an elegant mind and a keen ambition to do the best for his family. When we talked about our futures and the opportunities presented by HBS, we would always remind each other that the class of 2006 was not our peer group. Their average age on arrival was twenty-seven. They had not done the same things as we had. In many cases all we had in common with them was HBS. We were not the classic HBS product, and if we tried to compete with those who were, we would be rejected. As we struggled to figure out our route back into real life, we had to bear that in mind. Staring up the curve would kill us.

Chapter Thirteen

BIG HAIRY
GOALS

Absurdly profitable company seeks
journalist with ten years' experience
and a Harvard MBA for extremely
highly paid, low-stress job in which
he can wear nice suits and loaf around
in air-conditioned splendor making
the very occasional executive decision.
Requirements: acute discomfort in
the presence of spreadsheets, inability
to play golf, poorly concealed loathing
of corporate life, knowledge of
ancient Greek.

—THE HELP WANTED AD
I SOUGHT BUT NEVER FOUND

It was mid-January and we had not seen the sun in Cambridge for months.
From our apartment high above the Charles River, all I could see were
clouds and slush stretching to the Boston skyline. And I still hadn't a
clue what I wanted to do. Everyone else on campus seemed to be fielding

multiple job offers and bidding wars for their services. The careers service was telling us that this was the greatest job market they had ever seen. I just wasn't sure I wanted an MBA job. But graduation was bearing down on us, I had two young sons, and I needed to figure this out. I e-mailed a journalist friend in Washington. Any bright ideas? He e-mailed back: How about being a foreign correspondent in Paris? Most days, I would scan the online HBS Job Bank, where companies posted their positions. Every single job, it seemed, wanted people with "2–4 years in investment banking or management consulting." My decision not to take one of these jobs over the summer seemed ever more foolish. Would it really have hurt to institutionalize myself for ten weeks? I scrolled listlessly down the screen. Even the nonprofits seemed to want ex-consultants. The only job that seemed to match my qualifications was with the CIA.

The company presentations on campus slid me into an even deeper funk. The low point was a presentation by a big publishing company from New York, led by a large woman in a blousy suit emblazoned with orange flowers. She had the complexion of a forty-a-day smoker and a sour smile, and spoke in such a stilted, corporate way that I imagined her getting home each day and unleashing her frustration with a string of violent expletives and punches to the kitchen wall.

"We are passionate about our work," she said in a listless monotone. "Passion affects everything we do." The fruits of this passion were laid out on a table before us: financial information, educational and business books, some of the most sleep-inducing magazine titles I had ever seen. One by one the publisher's recent MBA recruits got up.

"It's been really exciting," said the first, without conviction. "On my first day, I got to work in Manhattan and they told me I had to visit a warehouse in New Jersey. And that's where I spent the next few weeks. I've already presented to senior management, and they acknowledged my proposals."

The second recruit, an African American woman, was aggressively peppy. "The great thing at our firm is the passion. Everyone here really wants to do the best job they can and improve not just the company but the world around them. I've been on a rotation in all the different divisions of the company—marketing, finance, strategic planning—and I get up each morning and really want to go to work."

The cursing smoker intervened. "We're looking for people who are really smart, passionate, and committed—the very best—to work here." I was fidgeting furiously with my ballpoint pen and wanted to grab this monster by the neck and scream into her yellowing eyeballs, "And what are you going to do with all these smart, passionate, committed people? Plug them into your dull, trivial culture and waste their lives on the hamster wheel of corporate life?"

To my self-disgust, I had capitulated, and deposited an application with the consulting firm McKinsey. They made it easier than buying an airline ticket. All you needed to do was fill out an online form with some personal details, which I did late at night after completing my cases. I told myself that if I were a consultant in New York focused on media, I could do it. It would be good for my future. I could put up with the long hours, the weekends in the office, because right now, I needed to earn a living. I could not come out of HBS with nothing. At that moment, all that I had told myself mattered—evenings with my family, the control over my time—went out the window. That was the pressure I was feeling.

Ben, the parks official I had sat next to in Analytics, offered to help me prepare for my McKinsey interviews. He had spent the summer between the first and second year at the firm's Boston office and enjoyed it. More than that, he said he had never met such an intelligent, admirable group of people, or been in a company that cared so deeply for its culture of knowledge, education, and improvement. He saw that the hours could pile up and the work might become repetitive, but he was impressed, and I respected his opinion.

We met over breakfast in Spangler, where he pulled out a large file of caselets—mini business scenarios that consulting firms used to test potential recruits. The interviewer, he said, would begin by offering me a few details about a case. "The client is a beer company whose new light beer is failing to sell in key markets. The company has a history of success and cannot understand why this beer has not succeeded." A few numbers would follow. When the interviewer stopped talking, you were supposed to begin asking questions. But first, Ben said, you had to ask for a moment.

"Yeah, right, a moment," I said.

"No, seriously, you have to say, 'Would you mind if I took a moment here?'"

"Those words exactly."

"Pretty much. You have to show you're digesting the information. Then you should repeat the scenario to make it clear that you've understood it."

"So, I say, 'One moment please,' then say, 'We're dealing with a beer company that can't sell its light beer.'"

"Exactly."

"No deviation."

"Best not."

Once you had taken your moment and repeated the problem, you were then expected to start asking questions. "What's their marketing strategy?" or "Does their beer taste good?" The interviewer slowly revealed facts and numbers as you asked for them and required you to do some quick calculations. What's the break-even on this business? What's the market size? The whole exercise would take about twenty minutes. After Ben's briefing, I attended a special McKinsey-run interview practice session on campus. Eight of us sat around a table while an exhausted-looking junior associate peppered us with caselet questions. Every time she laid out a scenario, the student answering her would say, "Would you mind if I took a moment here?"

My McKinsey interviews occurred at the Doubletree Hotel, an ugly cube just a short walk from the business school. Arriving in the lobby, I saw scores of students from my year, even people who had vowed never to go into consulting. They were all wearing suits and carrying leather folders containing a notepad and pen. It was like arriving in some deviant sex club and finding all your religious friends gawking at the act. Everyone made excuses: "Oh, I'm just doing it for the experience." "It's a fall-back option if the private equity job doesn't come through." "It's the only firm offering to send people to South America." I even caught Bo there: "I'm just going to meet some dudes in the healthcare practice," he said, looking uncomfortable in his dark suit. "I mean, we're at HBS. Gotta have a McKinsey interview at some point. It's part of the experience."

"You traitor," I said.

"Well, look at you," he shot back, poking me in the shoulder. "So much for Mr. Entrepreneur."

One by one, we were summoned up to a hotel suite with a McKinsey employee. In the first interview, an associate quizzed me about what to do with a failing drugstore. It all came down to adapting the product selection and range of promotions to the needs of the customers. It seemed to go well. In the second interview, a partner at the firm asked me to develop an approach for an investment fund manager with lower margins than its rivals. We were sitting in armchairs and I realized now why everyone had those leather folders. I had to lean my piece of paper against my knee to scribble my notes. I failed to ask for my moment, and flunked the answer. The partner took pity on me. The light had gone out in the sitting area of his suite and I could see through to the rumpled sheets in his bedroom. The room smelled faintly of cigarettes. We sat there in the semidarkness like a pair of guilt-stained adulterers and he asked me what I thought of HBS. I said what I usually said, which was that I felt I had learned a lot, even though the place was a little loopy.

"I hated it when I was here," he said. "Compared to being an undergraduate at Harvard, the intellectual experience was nothing." He asked me where I had last gone on holiday and whether I made a good colleague. These were clearly not the questions he reserved for likely hires. We were just killing time. After twenty minutes, he got up and we parted ways. That evening, he called to say I didn't seem like the right fit. I agreed.

. . .

Peter Drucker, the great authority on late-twentieth-century management, wrote that "An employer has no business with a man's personality. Employment is a specific contract calling for specific performance . . . Any attempt to go beyond this is usurpation. It is immoral as well as an illegal intrusion of privacy. It is abuse of power. An employee owes no 'loyalty,' he owes no 'love' and no 'attitudes'—he owes performance and nothing else."

Why was it then that every speaker who came to Harvard Business School demanded we be "passionate" about our work? There were several ways of looking at this. The first was that the speakers genuinely cared about our enjoying our professional lives. In that case, advising us to follow our passion made a lot of sense. Loving what we did would make working that much less hellish. Another interpretation was that the word *passion* was just another form of corporate coercion. It was no longer enough simply to do a job that you found okay for a reasonable financial reward. You had to say you were passionate about your work even if you found the work meaningless and unsatisfying. And then, of course, if it was your passion, why wouldn't you want to stay in the office until late at night and all weekend long? Didn't you say it was your passion? Then why are you going home so early? Not playing on the softball team? Skipping the company barbecue?

Visitors to campus would say in that manic, evangelical way, "Business outsourcing is my passion"; "I have a passion for delivering product to customers"; "Here at Widgets Incorporated, we are passionate about enterprise resource management systems." But isn't the truth that passion is a fleeting sensation, one that most humans are lucky to feel even once in their lives? In love, we speak of the first flush of passion, which dims to become something else. We talk of the passionate intensity of composers, artists, and freedom fighters. Perhaps the very greatest businesspeople, the ones whose lives are dominated by their work, share this passion. But the rest of us?

A third explanation was that businesses used the word *passion* because it reflected what they wanted their employees to feel. Work at its best should be about passion, not just drudgery. A few lucky souls might feel genuine passion for their work, but companies used the word so freely, I sensed, because it set a loftier goal for their activities than mere profits. To be in the business of business was not enough. You had to be about something bigger. But where did businesses go after passion? Was it only a matter of time before the head of the Boston Consulting Group told an MBA class, "We bring a panting, sexual intensity to our work." Or the recruiter from Fidelity: "Our analysts share a knee-trembling, quivering, orgasmic degree of focus on company fundamentals." Or the CFO of Goldman Sachs: "In the people we hire, we expect to see a stalkerish obsession with financial performance and a downright creepy fascination with the office and all that goes on there, to the total exclusion of anything else, which might bring moments of serendipitous joy to their dreary lives. Going home at any time of day or night signals to us a lack of absolute, maniacal commitment. We demand total devotion." What would sound like the ravings of a madman coming from, say, Kim Jong-Il had become perfectly commonplace coming from business leaders. The obsession with a single firm-wide culture. Discipline. Order. Unrelenting assessment by one's peers. The fear of denouncement. A cult of the leader.

A new and potent recruiter on campus was Google. A delegation from the company had visited in October. A recent hire from HBS got up and said that her day consisted mostly of dealing with e-mail and going to meetings. She added that because the company was growing so fast, she often didn't know what the meetings were all about. Then she handed out pens and T-shirts with the slogan "Do you feel lucky?" and a stack of papers describing jobs the company needed to fill. Almost all of them required either a degree in computing or several years of work experience at a technology company. I passed.

But during my early January slump, I returned to Google's online job site. I had fond memories of my visit to the firm during the Westrek. I found a posting for a job marketing Book Search, Google's effort to digitize and make searchable all of the world's books. The requirements were experience in the media or publishing industries and an MBA. The job was based in New York and would involve talking to libraries, publishing houses, authors, and readers trying to get everyone excited and in legal agreement. Book Search was one of those products that had run into trouble because of Google's lack of focus. Google had a powerful vision: all the world's books readable and searchable online, available to every man, woman, and child with an Internet connection, regardless of their location or educational or economic situation. It would be the library of Alexandria made virtual and accessible to all. But well-organized opponents of the plan said Google was trying to seize control of the publishing industry, to impoverish authors and publishers, to take the whole cloth of books and chop them into incomplete threads of information. Authors like John Updike accused Google of trying to destroy the pleasures of holding a book or wandering the aisles of a secondhand book shop hoping to make a serendipitous discovery. Google, they said, was going to fragment our attention spans and overturn centuries of the printed word. It was a debate I could get into.

Everyone who had applied for jobs at Google told me the interview process was a shambles. Decisions were hard to elicit. E-mails and telephone calls were ignored. You had to speak to ten or more people, who had to reach a consensus before sending your case up to Larry Page, one of the company's founders. Even though Google now had more than five thousand employees, he still liked to vet every single hire. One of my section mates had received his job offer at two o'clock on a Saturday morning, in an e-mail sent from a Google executive's BlackBerry. Knowing all this, I thought I'd just Zen out and see what happened.

Three weeks after I sent in my application, I received an e-mail inviting me to interview by telephone with a product manager at Google's headquarters in Silicon Valley. The interview would last half an hour. The first few minutes were personal stuff—"why had I gone to business school" questions. In the second half, my interviewer set what he called "big, hairy, audacious goals" and asked me how I would reach them. For example, how would I develop an electronic reading device, market it, and get it into the hands of five million people in three months. Google, he said, liked big, hairy goals. I told him I'd try to do a tie-in with Oprah's Book Club or perhaps an educational book publisher and popularize the device on college and high-school campuses.

Ten days later, I received another e-mail. Would I be available for another telephone interview? I prepared for more big, hairy goals. I saw them in my mind as enormous sea urchins, black and prickly, dripping with slime, floating out in space with one gloopy eye on the lookout for approaching business school students, primed to zap them with foul-smelling musk. This interview ran for forty-five minutes, but the interviewer sounded glum. It turned out he had owned his own technology company and sold it to Google. He hadn't made as much money from the deal as he had hoped and was locked in for another couple of years. "I'd say I spend ninety percent of my day dealing with internal meetings and e-mails," he told me. I imagined him in his cubicle at the end of another day in Mountain View, California, his ever-blinking in-box draining all that was left of his strength. A week later, in late February, I heard that the company wanted to fly me out to California for a full day of interviews.

It was a bright afternoon in San Jose when I arrived. The sun was a welcome change after the gloom of Boston. The hotel Google had booked for me was full, so I was sent to stay in a motel beside a shopping mall. The room was dark, overlooked a car park, and had that slightly sweet funk that made me think of businessman after businessman lying on the bed watching pornography. I dropped my bag and went out. I found a branch of Jamba Juice and sat outside, freezing my brain with a Passion Berry Breeze and flicking through the paperwork sent to me by Google. The documents read as if they had been written by a particularly grating high-school student. One sheet contained instructions for reclaiming expenses: "If you eat at a restaurant, be sweet and leave a tip of no more than 15%, just be sure to indicate it on each meal receipt . . . Be sure to submit your expenses within 15 days of incurring them . . . You snooze you lose! . . . We firmly believe paperwork is your friend . . . As such we may request additional clarification and detail on any business related expense in question—don't be offended, just chalk it up to paperwork love." Sitting there in the sticky warmth of the California evening, reading this and watching the cars drive in and out of the parking lot and the traffic lights swinging overhead, I felt a long, long way from home.

The next morning at nine, I stood outside the hotel waiting for a shuttle bus I had been promised would take me to Google. I had had a fitful night under a thin blanket, disturbed by the sound of my neighbor's television burbling through the thin wall until two o'clock. A white stretch limousine pulled up in front of the hotel, and a young man in an embroidered gold waistcoat hopped out.

"Mr. Broughton?"

"You must be kidding," I said, staring at the car.

"Our normal SUV has some problems, so we're having to use the wedding limo." A piece of cardboard was flapping from the roof. "Sorry about this. The sunroof's broken." I clambered in the back. A row of dirty scotch glasses clattered in a rack as I closed the door. I couldn't believe it. I was going to interview at a company that prided itself on being egalitarian and unshowy, where the employees dressed in T-shirts and flip-flops, where the company motto was "Don't Be Evil," and here I was showing up like Dr. Dre at the Vibe awards.

Google's headquarters, 1600 Amphitheatre Parkway, was a sprawling glass-and-metal complex originally built for Silicon Graphics, a pioneering 3-D computer graphics firm that had hit hard times. It sat in the middle of nowhere in particular, hemmed in by roads and freeways. The buildings curved and swerved around open-air volleyball courts and trees. Linking them were walkways that rose and fell gently from the ground as if lifted by a breath of wind. It felt like a college campus or the headquarters of a progressive church. Through every window you could see someone working, many staring at two screens simultaneously. The people were eclectic, from long-haired Viking look-alikes and surfer dudes to buttoned-down white men in striped shirts and khakis, all carrying their ThinkPads under their arms. But first I had to get in. The white limo passed security and tried to negotiate a small, tight traffic circle. Behind us waited a line of humble Toyotas and Hondas, each containing a Google zillionaire. As we pulled to a halt, I heard a crunch from the front bumper. The driver backed up. Crunch again, this time from the side. He nudged forward, then backward again. I could see the sweat pearling on his forehead when he turned to try looking out the rear window.

"Let's try this again," he said. *Sccrrunch.* "We may be just a little bit stuck here."

"I've got to get out," I said, gathering up my things. I tried opening one door, but it was jammed. I pushed open the other door and ran up a flight of steps away from the limo, just as two security guards approached to assess the developing crisis. I glanced back briefly to see the traffic into the Googleplex stretching all the way down a street lined with palm trees. I ducked into Building 42. Above the receptionist a screen showed a real-time selection of search requests made by Google users: lawnmowers, tennis, Bush, anal, Omaha steaks. I grabbed one of the free fruit juices stacked in a refrigerator by the door and plunked myself down on a purple sofa to recover and get my head right. Eventually I was shown to a small, windowless meeting room painted pale gray, with just enough room for a round table and two chairs. This would be my home for the day. I wedged my bags and myself into one corner and waited.

It was 10:00 A.M. and my schedule was full until 5:30—seven interviews in a row, with a break for lunch. The first one began with the usual questions. Why Google? Why business school? Why marketing? Yes, why exactly marketing?

Lots of people at business school had very precise ideas of the kind of function they wanted to pursue. When I turned up at HBS, I did not even know what a business "function" was, let alone which one suited me best. Was I a finance person, or more suitable for marketing, or product management, or strategy? I hadn't a clue. During long discussions on the Spangler sofas, I had learned that product managers at technology companies needed to speak at least two, and possibly three, languages. They needed to talk to software engineers and understand their peculiar whims and desires. But they also needed to talk to users and consumers and understand what they wanted. Somewhere in the middle, they had to talk business and make money from their product. The main challenge in this job was communication. You had to persuade engineers, whose characters tend naturally to the perfectionist and obsessive, that at some point they must tailor their work not to some technical ideal but to actual consumer wants. At the same time you had to help educate consumers and develop a business model.

At companies like Google there were fleets of gleaming MBAs all product-managing like crazy. A few managed entire products, such as Gmail, Google's e-mail service, or AdWords, its advertising service to businesses. But most served on product management teams, where they managed tiny pieces of a product and spent a lot of time e-mailing one another. Lurking below the product managers were the product marketing managers. At a company like Procter and Gamble, which made commodity products such as toothpaste and toilet paper, marketing was king. You were never going to distinguish your toilet paper from a competitor's on functionality alone. It was all about the brand and the way you marketed it. The most senior managers at P&G tended to rise through marketing and sales, and it is what drove the business. At Google, marketing was treated as an afterthought. The marketers fought fires as they arose, tried to offer some customer feedback and ideas for launching new products. But the department was mostly ignored and understaffed. Engineering was where the action was. It was understandable. Google grew to be a multibillion-dollar company without spending a dime on advertising. The excellence of its search product spoke for itself. Such success was a computer scientist's fantasy. Build a wonderful product and people use it in droves. No need for the fluff and hype of advertising. These were deeply practical people who loved things that worked, hated things that didn't, and were not going to be swayed by a twenty-foot-high billboard telling them a brand of underpants would make them more attractive to women.

The problem was that as Google's success attracted envy and competition, it had to engage in marketing. It could no longer hide out in Mountain View making billions and ignoring the world. As it built its business in China, stored personal data in the United States, and took on industries ranging from book publishing to telecommunications, it prompted suspicion and accumulated enemies. Still, this did not mean the company had to like marketing. One woman in my section turned down a marketing job at Google because she said she would be standing on the other side of the fence from the rest of the company just waiting for them to toss over a sack load of products when they were ready for release. Marketing would never be part of how Google developed products. The department was just there to keep the various freaks and misfits who populated the engineering department from ever having to deal with the world. As far as I was concerned, as a Google marketing manager, you got paid, were issued some of that precious stock, and got ignored by some geeks. It could be worse. I told my interviewers that Google had a serious public image problem waiting to explode, much as Microsoft's had, and that it needed good communicators like me to help defuse the bomb. I said I was a keen Google user, which I was, and that I believed Book Search was a thrilling concept, which I did. As each interview progressed, we tried out some big, hairy goals. So, if you like photo-sharing, what would you like to be able to do that you can't do now? How would you launch that feature? How would you get ten million people using it in six weeks? How would you get print publishers to use Google as a medium for getting advertisers? What exactly would you do? What kind of events would you organize? So you would invite all these publishers to Silicon Valley and then what? As a journalist, what article would you most like to write about Google? Is it evil not to disclose our cut of advertising revenue to our publishing partners? It was all rather like business school, the persistent search for answers and action plans as well as analysis.

My interviewers were uniformly nice. There was a woman in her twenties who had joined the company as an administrator well before the IPO and had risen up. I suspected she had made an awful lot of money, as she didn't seem to much care about whether product marketing worked. There was a man in his late thirties who rushed in from the gym, still sweating and gulping from a water bottle. He had been in sales all his career and talked quickly and nervously. He asked me to explain the network effect of Google's business, how more users meant more advertisers meant more users meant more advertisers, and so on and so on, to incalculable profits and overwhelming market share. There was a woman who had been handling the marketing for Book Search over the past few months, when publishers and authors had turned on it. "I told them we had a problem, but they didn't believe me until it appeared in *The Wall Street Journal*," she said, but she didn't seem too concerned.

In between interviews, I would go to a nearby snack area, stuff my pockets with free malt balls and yogurt-dipped pretzels, and throw back a large espresso. By the end of the day, my breath must have stunk like Satan's bowels.

A number of people had told me that the fizz had gone out of Google since the initial public offering had made everyone so rich. I certainly got that feeling. Apart from the sales guy, there was none of the oomph I had been expecting. Perhaps it was just a California thing. Maybe the software engineers are so brilliant that the rest of the company can just ride their coattails. Or maybe I was just shocked that really, honestly, they weren't evil.

I emerged into the fading sunset, my mind drained of every scrap of technology knowledge it had ever contained. The white limousine was waiting for me on the street, a scratch down its side. The driver started to edge into the parking lot, but I waved him back, running across the traffic circle where we had been wedged nine hours earlier. I yanked open the door and hurled myself into the backseat, arms out in front of me like Superman, hoping no one saw me. Later that night, I was delayed in Las Vegas airport. From 11:00 P.M. to 1:00 A.M., I waited in a departure lounge, beneath the ten-foot-wide cleavage on a strip club poster. Across the hall was the crowded smoking area, full of desperate-looking souls. All around me were the foot soldiers of American business: men in raincoats fidgeting with their cell phones, glancing up at the boarding announcements for the flight that would take them home or off to yet another hotel room with yet more pornography on demand. They were like ghouls, haunting me whenever I wavered, urging me not to go corporate, not to give up my life to travel schedules and airports and sales meetings and bad food and a paunch and boasts about frequent flier programs, scratching at my face and mewling diabolically into my ears: Don't do it!

Three weeks later, in mid-March, I heard from Google again. They liked me, but could I do one more interview on the telephone? We had already been at this for two months. How could a tenth interview hurt? I took the call in one of the HBS study rooms overlooking the warehouses and depots that stretch out behind the school. The sky was an Etch A Sketch of skidding, bursting clouds, with lightning bolts in the distance. Above me a fluorescent light flickered before dying halfway into the interview, leaving me talking in darkness. My future now lay in the hands of a voice three thousand miles away, a calm, friendly voice but still just a voice. At the end of the interview, she told me I should hear back within a week or ten days.

After two weeks, I e-mailed my recruiting manager and heard nothing back. After three weeks I called. Nothing. I called two more times. Nothing. "Call them until you get an answer," said a friend Google had already hired. I sent an e-mail to all four of the recruiting managers I had dealt with. Finally, a month after my final interview, three months after I first

applied, I received a call. The job had been filled, but I was being put back
into the general pool. Would I be interested in working as a product manager for technical solutions? In Mountain View?

With my pride now dragging along the ground, I approached an HBS
graduate at Google and asked what I could do. She arranged another round
of interviews for me, this time in New York. In sales. "Sales is where it's
at," she told me. It's where the money gets made. So off I went to Manhattan for my eleventh, twelfth, thirteenth, and fourteenth interviews. There
were the familiar lava lamps and play areas, the Foosball tables and refrig-
erators full of fruit juice. There was the same assortment of people I had
seen in Silicon Valley, chatting on the iron stairways, leaning into one
another's cubicles. But this time, I felt queasy the moment I arrived. I knew
I was in the wrong place.

"We've got a big funnel of people trying to work here, and only a few
get through," one of the sales managers explained. "What makes you think
you can?" My interviewers had been in sales their entire careers. When I
asked one of them how he had reached his present position, he started
drawing a diagram, writing out his list of jobs and then linking them with
arrows and boxes. "I've done really hard-core sales," he said forbiddingly as
he scanned my résumé. "Have you?" I could scarcely bring up the *Truck
Driver's Handbook* from all those years ago. As I gave my answers, I could
feel the case I had made to myself that I could work at a place like Google
collapsing, destroyed by reality. I could no more do sales at a technology
firm than I could scale the north face of the Eiger.

By the time I got home to Boston that night, I decided I was going to
quit before I was pushed. I e-mailed Google and told them that after four
months of interviews, I no longer wished to continue. They told me they
were sorry and that I could always come back. But I wanted the company
expunged from my life. I wanted to scrub away the mask I had worn for
them all these months. I uninstalled all the Google features on my computer and made Yahoo! my default search engine. I took the thick folder of

notes and articles I had assembled on the company and tossed them in the bin. My HBS job search had reached its sticky end. I had played the game atrociously. Margret came through with a beer.

"How did it feel?" she asked.

"Wonderful."

Chapter Fourteen

"WATCHING MY CHILDREN GROW LONGER"

An unexamined life is not worth
living.

—SOCRATES, 399 BC

Living an examined life sucks.
—YVON CHOUINARD, FOUNDER
OF PATAGONIA, TO THE
HBS BUSINESS OF THE
ENVIRONMENT CLUB,

2006

In the car park of the St. Moritz Toboggan Club in Switzerland, the home
of the Cresta Run, there is only one reserved parking spot. It is for a fabled
German bobsledder who coaches first-timers down the jaw-rattling ice
chute, and is marked with a homemade sign that reads "Guru." At Harvard
Business School, as in St. Moritz, there was but one true guru. The Guru
was urgent in everything he did. Despite a bad right leg, he walked fast,

leaning away from the weight of his battered, bulging brown leather briefcase. Other professors would slink into the classroom, hang their jackets in
a nook, and wait for the students to file in. The Guru had an entourage who
swarmed the room before he arrived like a presidential security detail. One
of his assistants set two cans of Diet Coke on his desk, his caffeine ration for
the next two hours. He needed them like baseball players need ampheta-
mines to stay awake during long, hot days in the field. His uniform was a
blue woolen blazer, light gray trousers, and a silk tie, though he put on a
suit for visiting heads of state. His once-blond hair was whitening now and
worn swept across his head, a frosting of elder statesmanship. His pale blue
eyes stared out from behind clear horn-rimmed glasses. When he became
excited, you thought his eyeballs would burst through his lenses and clatter
to the floor like marbles.

"So what explains Finland's success in telecommunications?!"

He strode up and down the steps in the classroom, his arms turning like
a windmill, his trousers covered with chalk dust. This was the fourth time
he had asked the question, but he was still unhappy with the answers.

"Come on. What explains this small Scandinavian country's becoming
the dominant player in this field?"

Michael Porter was a high-school sports star, and it was easy to imagine
him in one of those old-fashioned uniforms, eyes darting, the ball bouncing rhythmically beneath his hand, slashing his way up and down a basketball court in New Jersey, where he grew up, directing the action from
beneath a mop of blond hair, turning his back to a defender and then
flicking the ball over his opponent in a perfect arc, like Pistol Pete Mar-
avich. After high school, he attended Princeton, where he played NCAA
golf and earned his BSE in aerospace and mechanical engineering in 1969.
He then brought his game to the study of business at Harvard, earning
his MBA in 1971 and his Ph.D. in 1973. He was now one of seventeen
University Professors at Harvard, the highest academic position available, and one of only two at the business school. (The other was Robert
Merton, a finance professor who won the Nobel Prize in 1997 for his work

on valuing stock options.) The *Times* of London ranked Porter as the most important business thinker in the world. His official biography listed honors ranging from Catalonia's Creu de St. Jordi to Nicaragua's José Dolores Estrada Order of Merit, not to mention a slew of honorary doctorates and academic honors from around the world. The only thing missing was a Nobel Prize, which, if everything went to plan, could not be too far away.

Porter began his career thinking about companies and the way they compete. His ideas were the basis for the RC strategy course. These days, he was applying himself to entire countries and regions. He was advising the government of Libya on a program of national economic regeneration, while his latest book was about reforming America's healthcare system. In his spare time, Porter served on company boards and as senior strategic adviser to the Boston Red Sox. He gave the impression that no problem was so vast or slippery that it could not be attempted with the pitons, ropes, and pickaxes of a Porter analysis. It turned out to be a wonderfully optimistic way to think about the world, and exactly what I needed at this point in my MBA experience.

Porter's class was the only one at HBS for which you had to apply. Some people groused and said they would never "kiss the ring" as if Porter were the pope and we mere supplicating sinners. I had no such problem. In my application letter, I said I was keen to learn about applying what I had studied at HBS to problems larger than those of companies. I had grown up in the United Kingdom where I had witnessed the extraordinary influence of economic policy in creating the European Union and helping to bring an end to the civil war in Northern Ireland. But I had also seen how a rotten set of economic policies had destroyed Burma, my mother's home. I wanted to discover more about business as a driver of social progress. Roughly half of the applicants to the course were accepted, and I was delighted to be one of them.

The course was called Microeconomics of Competitiveness, though that makes it sound less interesting than it was. What it really dealt with was the big, gnarly question of how to spur economic development at local, regional, national, even continental levels. It was about how you coordinated business and government, schools and universities, road-builders and everyone, really, in a society to pull themselves up the economic ladder. Porter's analytical approach began with what he called the diamond. This was a way of assessing the quality of an economic environment by putting all the forces that affected it into four separate buckets and analyzing how they helped or hindered one another to create a good environment for business. It allowed you to get beyond the natural advantages of any particular economy—large oil reserves, for example—and start to understand the causes of sustainable competitiveness. You took a country, region, or city and looked at the rivalry between companies, the demand from consumers, the availability of skilled labor or capital, and the supporting network of industries. Each corner of the diamond could be unpacked and investigated, but overall it allowed you to see through to the potential sources of competitive advantage. Porter believed that the fundamental unit for thinking about competitiveness was not the individual company or sector but the "cluster." To understand the success of Wall Street, for example, it was insufficient to credit the banking talents of a few executives, or the organizational setup at a few firms. You had to look at the presence of so many firms and financiers working in such a tight space, all the terrific universities in and around New York City turning out gifted graduates, the proximity of first-rate corporate lawyers, the courts and the legal framework, the exchanges, the Federal Reserve Bank of New York, the range of other businesses and corporate headquarters in the city. Together they made Wall Street what it was. It was the strength of the cluster, not the individual firm or sector, that mattered, and the strategist aiming to spur economic progress should work to develop every part of the cluster.

At the core of Porter's thinking was the belief that competition was the engine of productivity growth and that every business, town, or country should be seeking out a competitive advantage and developing it. But he had evolved this into something more humane than it first sounded. The cases we studied ranged from Finland to Rwanda to the slums of St. Louis.

Porter was willing to address himself to any problem, however hopeless. He was not just another business school professor trying to figure out how to drive an ever-wider wedge between cost and willingness to pay. He was taking the best of HBS and applying it in areas too often starved of such intellectual horsepower. In the Rwandan case, for example, we studied a country that after the genocide of the mid-1990s had to rebuild from next to nothing. But by the end of the class, and after watching a video of the country's president, Paul Kagame, who had come to speak to a previous year's class, we had laid out a detailed strategy for Rwanda to build its competitive advantage through scientific education and lightweight exports, which could be flown out of the country rather than having to take the dangerous land routes to the ocean. Was it implementable? Well, it was a start.

Porter's class consisted of forty MBA students and forty students from the Kennedy School of Government. While the MBAs would waltz into class in T-shirts, having walked through the tunnels linking the buildings on campus, the Kennedy School students arrived stomping snow from their boots, their faces raw from the wind lashing the Charles. The gulf between the business and government students was also apparent in how we approached the class. The HBS students would opine authoritatively, working solely from data in the case, while the Kennedy School students would squirm under Porter's questioning and then come up with big, broad remarks such as "this is the problem when business and government work together." But Porter's goal was to meld the cultures and approaches of the two schools by pushing us on, urging us to consider how we would revive the Estonian economy or expand a washing machine business in Latin America. In the washing machine case, we were discussing whether the business should try to survive in the face of low-cost Asian competition when I put my hand up and was called on. I said the owner of the business should sell out now. He was not playing to his competitive advantage. It was the right answer for the business school. But Porter stared at me, folded his arms, and looked around the class. "Who thinks he should sell?" A student from the Kennedy School raised her hand and said that perhaps the owner of the business should keep going and that if Latin America was ever to have a home-grown appliance business, it needed to persevere and not sell out at the first opportunity. This was what Porter had wanted to hear—not my blinkered, manufactured MBA answer. I had been thinking solely of the competitiveness of the business, not of the people, country, and region it represented. I should have known better. Had I built a washing machine manufacturer from the ground up in Costa Rica? Had I defied all the odds to spend twenty years building factories, hiring employees, and developing a supply chain and marketing strategy? No. But I felt comfortable enough advising the founder to sell out rather than try to build something he and his country could be proud of. This was why people hated MBAs. Too much cost-benefit analysis, too little humanity.

I had recently visited a prominent journalist who was researching at the Kennedy School. We talked about the future of newspaper publishing, and he told me that newspaper owners would simply have to accept lower returns than they were used to. Instead of 15 to 20 percent, they would have to get used to 8 to 10 percent. And wasn't that enough? His economic logic was driven by his desire that newspapers survive and not be destroyed by the rush of advertisers to the Internet. Before arriving at Harvard, I would have agreed with him. Of course that was the answer. Newspapers survive but make a little less money. What a perfect solution! But it was an emotional response. The rational one was different. And as he spoke, I thought, "if only you understood . . ." Margins don't just fall a bit and then settle at a lower level. They could just fall and keep falling until there was no economic reason to be in newspapers at all. Business school had taught me a way of thinking about problems that was useful, often correct, but not always comfortable. I once asked a hedge fund manager in New York about the reckless way credit was sold to people who could ill afford it. I said they would be ruined. They would lose their homes and their possessions. Where were the checks on all this? Who was helping to teach people about responsible borrowing? What would happen to all these firms lending like crazy when people stopped paying back their loans? The hedge fund manager looked at me like I was a madman and said, "It's just economic." He meant that over time these borrowers would learn their lesson. The bankrupted lenders would be bought cheaply by other investors and turned around. The economic wheel would keep turning, no matter how many lives had been crushed against it. However true, it was also unpleasant. In Porter's class, I realized that my response to the appliance company's problem had placed me on the dark side. However technically correct an analysis might be, it could also be too rational. Achieving the balance between reason and emotion would never cease to be a challenge.

Jack Welch, the former head of General Electric, visited campus during the second year to promote a book he had written. He came to a packed Burden Auditorium to be interviewed by Rakesh Khurana, a professor who had criticized the cult of the superstar CEO, which Welch embodied. Khurana began one of his questions: "Business is too important an institution for us not to pay attention to its leaders—" Welch butted in. "No, it's *the* most important institution. It all revolves around that. Government generates no revenues. Government lives off taxes generated by business and people that work in business. Don't ever forget that." How any businessman, not least the most fêted one of the past thirty years, could say this astonished me. Did he seriously believe that business could run without sound government? Were the two not mutually dependent? What about clusters? Was Welch's narcissistic view representative of America's corporate elite? And what of people who went into government after a Harvard graduate education? Were they just mugs? It was one thing to say government should be run more like business, with more efficiency and accountability. But to say that business was *the* most important institution seemed unhinged. It was the kind of view that could prompt a revolution. The great unwashed would punish Welch's hubris by desecrating his homes and country clubs. Porter's course, I found, was a useful counterweight to

Welch. It showed that business was not the sole driver of a society and that it was possible to come out the other side, to have an MBA, to put competition at the center of one's beliefs, and yet not be a completely heartless scumbag.

My fascination with strategy led me to take two more courses in the subject during this final semester. One was the most popular course in the elective curriculum, Advanced Competitive Strategy, with Jan Rivkin, a small, wiry South Carolinian with a badger's brush of gray hair. Rivkin resembled a NASA rocket scientist of the 1950s or a member of Robert McNamara's inner circle in the 1960s Department of Defense. His shirts and suits were perfectly pressed. Before the start of every class, he lined up three small bottles of apple juice on his desk to keep himself energized. His color-coded notes were laid out meticulously well before any of us arrived. His CV was a litany of academic scholarships and awards, and he had been a repeat winner of the teaching award voted on by students. He brought such intensity and enthusiasm to his classes, you felt obliged to return the compliment with preparation and thought.

The premise of his class was that knowing the principles of strategy was one thing, but being able to apply them was quite another. His course was about decision making in pursuit of strategic goals. Peter Drucker, the revered management guru, wrote that "executives who make effective decisions know that one does not start with facts. One starts with opinions." Opinion sets the criteria of relevance for facts. But a single opinion was never enough. "A decision without an alternative is a desperate gambler's throw, no matter how carefully thought through it might be." The goal of Rivkin's class was to learn how to think through the choices and consequences attached to multiple opinions and only then make a decision. He showed us a slide of a three-dimensional graph. It resembled a mountain range, with jagged peaks and troughs, all of different sizes. Each point on this chart, he said, represented the outcome of a particular set of strategic choices. A trough was bad. A peak was good. But not all peaks were the same height. You could set off up one mountain, making a certain set of decisions, and reach the top only to see a higher peak in the distance. But to get to that higher peak, you had to scramble back down and start again. It was a twist on what we had learned in the first-year strategy course. Strategy was not one thing. It was many things, and in particular how they fit together. When you made a set of strategic choices, you were ascending what you hoped would be the highest peak. But how could you know? You couldn't, but Rivkin hoped to give us a means of making a more educated guess.

The first step was to dig deep into the issues of cost and willingness to pay. By calculating these, you could begin to see the sources of a company's competitive advantage. We dissected the cost structures of beer, laminate, and motorcycle manufacturers. Our goal was always to break a business down into its separate parts, all those functions we had studied in the first year—accounting, production, marketing, finance, negotiations, organizational behavior, leadership—and then identify connections between them. How you integrated them was what mattered. The next step was to develop multiple integrated options for the company. If we move production, what does this mean for the culture? We studied a technology firm, Lycos, during its acquisition of a smaller partner in a different location. Did it force all the employees to move to the company's headquarters? Or did it allow them to stay with their own culture and set of norms? What were the alternatives? As we kept developing these integrated options, we listed the unknowns and set up tests and the forms of proof we would need to make a certain decision. But every time we did this, the first thing Rivkin insisted we do was "follow your gut." There was plenty of room for instinct in his approach. Once your gut had given you a direction, then you delved into the problem.

We studied companies such as Sears and IBM as they struggled to adapt what had once been very successful, well-integrated business models. We saw how they tried at first to tinker with one aspect of their business—sales, for example, or pricing. But it was only in the face of crisis, the threat of bankruptcy, with their pants on fire, that they undertook dramatic changes to their entire business, unpacking every aspect of it and reassembling it to pursue new strategic goals. It was at these moments that the strategist was paramount.

Rivkin told us that in order to influence company strategies early in our careers, we should learn about all of our employer's operations, especially those that drove the business or faced change. We should find companies where new ideas were encouraged and developed and stay close to the people who were in charge. Finally, he told us that to be a great strategist required intellectual restlessness paired with a grounded competence. You needed to understand your business from top to bottom, but also be ready to tear it up and start again, to listen to evidence that challenged your biases and ceaselessly revise your judgments. He was telling us that however secure we felt, we should always be alert for tremors.

I heard this same lesson in a very different form from Dan Gilbert, the founder of Quicken Loans. I had not planned to hear him speak, but I was doing my usual Spangler shuffle between the frozen yogurt machine in the basement and an upstairs study room when I thought I could use a voice from beyond the HBS walls. I wandered over to Aldrich and sat in the back of a sparsely filled classroom. Gilbert had started his first mortgage company aged twenty-three, while in the first year of law school. Twenty years later, he and his friends had bought their hometown Cleveland Cavaliers basketball team, which they had transformed from an NBA basement dweller into a glamour team with the drafting of Lebron James. Gilbert was much wealthier than many of the investment banking honchos who came to campus with their entourages and limousines, but he wore a fleece top and khakis and looked like he might have just dropped in from IT support. He was a compelling talker.

"We really became philosophically driven real early," he said of his company. "It all starts and ends with culture, environment, philosophy. It's all about who we are versus what we do." His biggest challenge "was just getting people to pay attention. It's seventy percent of the battle." He repeated what I had heard on the venture capital circuit when Bo and I had been floating the podcasting venture. Most ideas are pretty good ones. It all comes down to execution, staying alert, paying attention. "Except for companies that have a certain patent, it's about thousands and thousands of little things." This had also been Zeynep's lesson in TOM and Podolny's in LEAD. Process matters as much as outcome. In fact, process determines outcome. Toyota worked because every single worker kept his eye on the process and had the right and obligation to improve it and even shut it down if there was a flaw. "There is nothing more important you can do," Gilbert said, "than to ingrain a culture where everybody is looking and has the power to make changes." This was the crux of Rivkin's course: always be alert to a better way of doing everything, never stop innovating. The example Gilbert gave to demonstrate the endless potential for improvement was pumpkin carving. At Halloween, most people hollow out their pumpkin by slicing off the top and scooping out the contents. One year, one of Gilbert's employees had recommended a different method. Why not slice off the bottom? The contents fall out more easily. It's easier to light a candle placed on the bottom and then to put the pumpkin over it than to light a candle from the top. You can then carry your pumpkin around using the stalk at the top, which remains attached. Who would have thought that after all these years of conventional pumpkin carving, there was a new and better way to do it?

If there was one thing we should remember coming out of HBS, Gilbert said, it wasn't the weighted average cost of capital or the four *P*s of marketing. It was to return calls and e-mails in a timely way. That would put us 99.9 percent ahead of our competitors. "People are shocked, people are in awe. They can't believe it. And we can't believe that people can't believe it because we think everybody should do it." The e-mail auto-reply function, he said, was the equivalent of giving your customers the finger. He emphasized the difference between the victims at a company, those who blamed others and felt sorry for themselves, and those who tried to make things right. Identifying the victims, or "spectacle makers," was vital, or else they would contaminate everything you did. To illustrate the polluting effect of a whiner, he said, "if I had my favorite bowl of ice cream over here and a bowl of shit over here, if I took one speck of shit and put it in the ice cream, would you eat the ice cream?" Numbers and money follow, he said. They do not lead. After so many months of agony with Excel and watching the ex-bankers let their fingers pirouette across their keyboards, Gilbert's words were like a drink of cold water. They cut to the heart of what had nagged me about finance: the fact that every model we built seemed rooted in backward-looking assumptions and diminished the essence of every business, the very people who ran it. We were told again and again that finance was really all about the assumptions you made about the future, but when it came down to it, we all spent far more time tinkering with the details of these models than developing the quality of those assumptions. Models felt real. You could feed in one set of numbers and get another. Assumptions? Well, those were debatable. Anyone could assume things. How could you build a proprietary advisory service around assumptions? Where was the high-priced voodoo in that? Financial statements, Gilbert said, were "a little fantasy exercise we all do," while budgets were pretty much a "bunch of bureaucracy. We're not in boardrooms looking at pie charts analyzing capital expenditures for 2008 to 2009." It was crucial to stay in the "bowels of the business."

He went on to say that you could tell everything about a company from its top line, its revenue. All of its creativity, innovation, and processes were there in that top line. Revenue was proof of your ability to win customers, which would determine your success more than your ability to squeeze a few pennies out of your costs. He recommended we ditch our copies of *Crossing the Chasm* and *The Innovator's Solution* and read *One Smart Cookie*, the biography of Debbi Fields, the founder of Mrs. Fields cookies. She was a young mother, with three children by the age of twenty-one, and loved cookies. She knew nothing about finance or business. It all came down to people who were excited enough about an idea to make it happen.

. . .

The last of my strategy courses was Strategies Beyond the Market, with our RC strategy professor Felix Oberholzer-Gee. Unlike many at the school, Felix seemed to look at the world not as a vast problem in search of solutions, but rather as a glorious mess to be wallowed in, enjoyed, and, perhaps, if you were lucky, dimly understood. His course dealt not with the rational practices of the market, but with the murky dealings that lay beyond: duplicitous lawyers and self-interested politicians, corruption-fighting mayors and investors who made the most of their ethnicity, corporations being held up by nongovernmental organizations and a rabid, misinformed press. It was riveting stuff, a world away from the preachy discussions in LEAD and LCA.

One of Felix's favorite tricks was to show how some piece of deep economic research could uncover a hidden truth. In order to understand which companies were most dependent on the Suharto regime in Indonesia, for example, rather than relying on street gossip or public reporting, he had examined the stock price movements of the companies listed on the Indonesian stock exchange on the days when Suharto was hospitalized. Fortunately for Felix's research, Suharto was often being wheeled in and out of the hospital. While the entire index dropped to a certain degree, the same few companies dropped more than the others. These, he concluded, had the deepest links to Suharto.

Felix encouraged a counterintuitive view of business opportunities. We studied a pharmaceutical firm that had almost gone under because it had filed a patent for its most important drug, thereby attracting a spurious lawsuit that bogged it down for years. It was too simplistic to regard patents as the best means of protecting one's intellectual property. The recipe for Coca-Cola, for example, had never been patented, which would have involved a public filing, but was simply kept secret. Stealth and secrecy could be better methods of protection than laws.

We looked at how some companies used regulation to their advantage, by cooperating with lawmakers or appealing to voters, while others railed against it. All too often, companies treated their legal and regulatory departments as problem solvers, when in fact they could be used to serve strategic ends. We also studied the effect of social pressure on companies, how campaign groups out to make a name for themselves often went after the biggest targets they could with the most embarrassing issue they could find. Environmental groups, for example, did not always tackle the worst offenders but rather the ones most likely to be embarrassed and to bring their cause the greatest attention. Companies that yielded and collaborated with these campaign groups often emerged better than those that tried to argue with them on the facts.

For the second half of the course, we were required to write a paper. I had already written three papers during the second year, all on media companies. Now I wanted to find a subject in which the business world I had discovered at HBS clashed with the nonbusiness world I knew from before. In June 2003, my newspaper sent me to cover the protests against the G8 summit in Evian. While my political colleagues had sat in the air-conditioned cool of a local swimming complex, which had been transformed into the press center, I had trudged around a nearby airfield filled with anticapitalists, anarchists, groovers, and dope peddlers. As I picked my way through the tents and VW camper vans, the raggedy-haired jugglers and shirtless falafel chefs, all heady on clouds of hash smoke, I remembered feeling grateful that these people were here. Democracy needed them. What other check was there on the men in suits who carved up the world to suit their needs? So they smelled a little riper. And swore at me and called me names for working for a conservative British newspaper. And laughed at my questions in the sweltering DJ tent. Many of them, I felt sure, had attacked policemen in their time, maybe even smashed up some stores and been denounced by politicians as troublemakers. Still, I thought, good for them. The forces of capitalism needed scaring now and again. Who else would keep them honest? Certainly not the poor consumer/voter, prostrate and voiceless in his credit-induced serfdom. Whenever I expressed these feelings to my friends in London, they would laugh at me. "Oh, right, Philip, you're a real hero of the barricades. Man of the working classes." But why couldn't I be a capitalist skeptic? Why did it always have to be one or the other?

On the Sunday morning of the summit, I marched with the protesters from Geneva toward the French border, where we were to meet another group of marchers coming from France. It was a sunny day and everyone sashayed along to reggae and chants of "Kill George Bush." Among the twenty-five thousand marchers were Zapatistas from Mexico, Maoists from Italy, French high-school teachers, Palestinian nationalists, and a twenty-four-year-old investment banker from London who said he was there to "fight the extremes of capitalism, the misapplication of capitalism," especially the mismanagement of poor countries by the International Monetary Fund and the World Bank. A large British contingent organized by the *Socialist Worker* newspaper was furious about the war in Iraq. A hospital worker from Oxford said he was marching for "peace in the world and to stop the privatization of everything." A Belgian kid in a Jacques Chirac rubber mask said he was there to celebrate the "good dope coming out of Afghanistan" since the American-led invasion. The mood was briefly disturbed when news reached us of the Auto-Gnomes of Zurich, a group of disaffected Swiss anarchists. They had smashed their way into a gas station and stolen dozens of bottles of mineral water. It was a very Swiss heist. The police had vacated their posts at the border, so the marchers were free to climb on top of the control booths and dance. When I returned to the press center and saw the politicians passing through, numbing the three thousand journalists into a collective coma, I knew whose side I was on.

So after three semesters diligently studying the way of the capitalist, I was persuaded by Felix's course that I needed a fresh dose of anarchy. I found it in a small village in Maine, so small in fact that I missed it twice while driving through it.

Arthur Harvey's house was a rickety-looking construction that seemed held together with spit and chicken wire. It was two hours northwest of Portland, tucked away in the woods of rural Maine. Two old Volvos with logs strapped to their roofs squatted close to Harvey's front door. Rust-colored paint was chipping away from the walls and door frames, and an unsteady wooden banister led up a set of rough stone steps to the entrance. A single solar panel provided enough electricity to power a laptop computer and a telephone. Any more electricity, Harvey said, would open a Pandora's box of convenience leading to idleness and disconnection from the world. Light came from oil lamps, heat from a wood-burning stove. The only way to get hot water for a bath was to heat it, saucepan by saucepan, on the stove.

Harvey lived here with his wife and a cat, whose likeness he had printed onto a gray sweatshirt. Harvey had a thick white beard, a bald head, and wore wire-rimmed glasses. With some padding round the belly, he would have made a passable department store Santa Claus. For several months a year, he farmed nearly twenty-five acres of local blueberry fields, which he had acquired in pieces over the past thirty years. When he was not farming, he was visiting other organic farms as an inspector for a certifying agency and challenging the government in court.

As the parents of two young children, Margret and I had become aggressive buyers of organic milk and vegetables. But our knowledge of what exactly *organic* meant was vague. The more I investigated, the more I found that this was in large part intentional on the part of food manufacturers. If you could persuade consumers to pay more for foods marked "organic," why fuss too much over specifics? Arthur Harvey, I had discovered, was a stickler. With no legal education, beyond the training he received as a member of his town's planning board, he had launched a case against the U.S. Department of Agriculture, accusing it of breaking the law and ignoring key precepts of the Organic Foods Production Act of 1990. He had won a number of court victories, but these were reversed by Congress under pressure from the major food companies. But his fight I found inspiring.

Harvey had been challenging authority for as long as he could remember. He was born in Hackensack, New Jersey, where his mother worked in the cooperative movement and his father, a mathematician by training, handled tax-delinquent properties for a real estate company. He almost failed to graduate from high school after refusing to sign a loyalty oath to the laws and Constitution of the United States. "I could support the Constitution," he said, "but I certainly wasn't going to support all the laws. They told me I was failing the rest of the students in my home room. But I didn't have much loyalty to my home room." Eventually the school gave him his diploma anyway.

"When I asked my mother why I should go to college, she didn't have many answers," he said, so he set off instead for Michigan, to work on cooperative farms and later to join the peace movement. In Michigan, a man who had recently returned from India lent him a book by Gandhi. He was immediately struck by Gandhi's arguments in favor of self-reliance and against excessive consumption. In the late 1950s, Harvey spent six months in prison in Sandstone, Minnesota, for invading a missile base in Nebraska with a group of fellow peace activists. "Prison was a blast. I was in there with one of my very best friends and we played horseshoes and Scrabble and spent lots of time in the library." His tenure as library clerk ended when he refused to compile a list for the prison authorities of the books each prisoner was borrowing. After prison, he traveled to New Hampshire, where he took shelter in a dilapidated chicken coop and tried to live as lightly off the land as he could. He bought a mimeograph machine and printed *The Greenleaf,* a newsletter in which he wrote about peace and self-reliance. He soon became a magnet for young people who had refused the draft, spent time in prison, or yearned for a simple life close to the land.

By 1975, Harvey was overseeing four picking crews, fifty-five people, working in apple orchards in New England. He imposed strict rules on his crews, including no alcohol, drugs, or nonmarital sex. "That was pretty tough on some people," he says, "but I just happen to think that's the way people should behave. As for alcohol and drugs, that's an open-and-shut case. They are harmful to people. As far as sex goes, well, it just seems to me that the raising of children and the relations between a man and a woman are fundamental to everybody." In 1976, Harvey married one of his crew supervisors and they moved to Maine, where they acquired their house "virtually for free" and began farming blueberry fields for local landowners. It was around this time that Harvey had what he calls "some enlightening experiences." On one farm, he found blueberries covered with white dust. It turned out the farmer was spraying his fields with DDT to kill birds. "That sure gave me food for thought. I wasn't anti-pesticides then. But I did notice that wild blueberries weren't inferior and did not require expensive chemicals."

Whenever government inspectors visited the blueberry farms, Harvey said they all told him that for blueberries to be sold legally they could not contain more than five maggots per quart. It seemed an arbitrary number to him, so he decided to investigate. He went to the library in Portland and looked up "blueberry" in the USDA book of regulations. He could not find it. So he telephoned the USDA and asked them about the five-maggot rule. After months of inquiry, he was told that inspectors were permitted to make on-the-spot decisions with regard to tolerable maggot quantities. But why, then, did they all agree on five? He never received a satisfactory answer and concluded that the inspectors were intentionally frightening farmers into buying expensive and unnecessary chemical treatments. Harvey's suspicion of the USDA had taken root. He began what became a lifelong effort to keep the USDA honest.

During the winter, Harvey continued his work trying to safeguard organic standards. When I visited him, he was trying to organize a network of students in every state to write to their congressmen to defend the standards. On his solar-powered computer, he went to Amazon.com to find the most popular books about organic food production. He then ordered copies of the books directly from their publishers and offered them for sale. When the orders came in, he sent out the book along with a letter explaining his efforts and asking for support.

He was rueful about the final outcome of his legal campaign against the government. "A lot of my fellow inspectors are aware of the imperfections of the organic regulations but they continue to work because they say these are the growing pains and that eventually they will restore integrity. That's true to a certain extent. But the dominance of the manufacturers at a legislative level complicates the picture. The next two years will tell us whether or not we're on our way to a complete dismantling of the standard or not."

Harvey, I felt, had been caught in the maw of business and politics and emerged with his dignity. He represented something missing from HBS: the unmanageable, unembraceable, unsackable, incorruptible quixotic. He did not use quotes from Gandhi, as Gompers had done, to spice up an entrepreneurship class. He lived what Gandhi preached. He did not seek profit or competitive advantage, but he had managed to scare multibillion-dollar companies and the U.S. government. He was as far from the HBS formula for success as one could imagine, which was why I had sought him out.

The search for the formula for success was a theme of a course called Professional Services. Our professor, Ashish Nanda, was a tremendously enthusiastic Indian who thundered around the classroom like a bee-stung elephant, pushing along rows, pounding on tables, and urging us to consider the implications of a merger of accounting firms or the ethical dilemmas faced by management consultants. For most in the class, this was jaw-dropping stuff. Such issues lay in their immediate future. I had signed up for the course because it had terrific reviews and I felt I had spent too much time considering finance and corporate strategy. I wanted to try something more human resource-y. The course certainly provided that, but not nearly in the way I had imagined.

Early in the semester we were presented with this equation:

$$\text{Change} = f(d \times m \times p) + E$$

It meant that the amount of change you were able to effect in either a company or your own life was a function of your current level of dissatisfaction (d), the new model being put in place (m), and the process by which this new model is being implemented (p). Plus E (error), or all the other stuff that might come into play. My first thought was this was not very useful. In fact, more than just not useful. It was actively designed to confuse the issue. It was taking something so obvious—that you would change something only if you were unhappy with it, and the unhappier you were, the more change you would want—and overcomplicating it so that MBAs could charge a fee for offering it in a consulting presentation. Quantification had overstepped its limits.

Nanda was evidently a brilliant man, a graduate of India's finest colleges, a popular professor. Early in his academic career, he had chosen to specialize in the practices of professional service firms. He was an authority on hiring practices at consultancies, staffing at investment banks, growth strategies for law firms. During his class, we studied the role of accountants and consultants in the Enron debacle and how they had betrayed their professional standards to gorge on fees. We learned everything you could ever want to know about McKinsey. We studied a fictional HBS MBA who became a successful investment banker only to work murderous hours and lose touch with his children. Most of the students in the class had already signed up for jobs in finance and consulting, so for them this class was a long exercise in trying to feel better about their decision. Once again, the national differences were blindingly apparent. The Americans seemed resigned to a fate of endless hours and slavish toil, their only hope being to find a suitable mentor who might lead them through Hades. The Europeans and Latin Americans felt that at worst, these jobs were a temporary fix and that soon enough they would be heading back to civilization. During one class, the senior partner of an American accounting firm that had merged with a French rival explained the difficulty of negotiating with Europeans. "It's like the difference between American football and soccer. In American football, you drive down the field, play by play, until you score a touchdown. In soccer, you flick the ball around from player to player until you see an opening, and then you strike." He was clearly very pleased with his comparison. But immediately, Xavier, a Frenchman, and one of the older students in the class, raised his hand.

"Yes, you say this about the different sports," he said, "but a game of American football takes three or four hours, while a game of soccer is over in ninety minutes." Touché. The Europeans laughed while the consultant looked shifty and cross.

Whenever Nanda organized a speaker, he also arranged a breakfast so we could meet the speaker in a more informal setting. One gray morning, I found myself sitting next to a management consultant called Sherif Mityas. He had grown up in Wisconsin, the son of Egyptian immigrants, both scientists. Mityas trained as an aerospace engineer but soon found that knowing engineering alone would not take him to the top of his industry. He needed to know something about business. So he went to Kellogg, Northwestern University's business school, in Evanston, Illinois. Upon graduating in 1994, he decided to become a consultant and had remained one ever since, rising to the top of his profession. Mityas spoke of the intellectual thrill of his work, descending on a company, figuring out a problem, and proposing a solution. He enjoyed the variety of moving from industry to industry, problem to problem, and never spending more than a few months gnashing over the same issues. But then he mentioned the snow globes.

Someone had asked him how he made the best of the relentless travel involved in consulting. How did he maintain his morale? A woman who had left HBS the previous year to become a consultant told us in an earlier class that the two most important things for a new consultant were a good suitcase and a dependable dry cleaner. It was not a pretty picture. Mityas said he would keep his team buoyed up by every so often letting them off an evening working session and taking them to a good restaurant. In order to stave off hotel fatigue, he might go to a local grocery store and buy some fresh fruit, anything to reconnect him with the world beyond the conference room. And each time he went somewhere new, he would buy his daughter a snow globe. She now had quite a collection. I immediately started thinking of my own son and the idea of returning home on a Thursday night in a crumpled suit, wheeling in my case and handing him a snow globe of the Woonsocket skyline. The thing was, Mityas seemed to be very happy with his lot. His work had its issues, but whose didn't? He was excellent at what he did. He liked his colleagues. He had provided a more-than-comfortable life for his family. Why was I getting so hung up on the snow globe?

Another visitor to the class was a graduate of the HBS class of 2005 who had gone to work at Morgan Stanley. He had been in the military before HBS and had decided that investment banking, at worst, would facilitate his transition from soldier to businessman. At best, it would be interesting, financially rewarding work. He told us that during his first year, he had once spent 127 hours in the office in a single week. Weeks had gone by when all he saw of his two children were their outlines under their blankets when he left in the morning and when he returned late at night. "I've been watching my children grow longer," he said. His life was the reality for most MBA graduates. The degree enabled them to get jobs that robbed them of their private lives. The consolation was that the experiences and money they accumulated would eventually allow them to live the lives they wanted. But there was no fixed timetable for delaying satisfaction and living the life you wanted. Would there always be one more promotion, one more pay raise, one more bonus? When would be the right time?

Nanda and I finally crossed swords over another equation. I had been growing impatient with the course as it descended into a therapy session for future consultants. How will I find a mentor? How will I get any work-life balance? How do I make sure I don't get sacked after two years? It was obvious that most of those choosing consulting as a career were doing so because they were not yet sure what they really wanted to do. Consulting, despite the punishing workload, gave them more time to consider their options.

One day we were grappling with the staffing requirements at a consulting firm. There were two tiers of consultant: associates and partners. Associates did most of the donkey work, while partners made presentations, managed existing clients, and solicited new ones. Most firms used a version of the forced curve, which they called "up or out." Every few years, you were reviewed and either promoted or fired. This created a pyramid structure with associates at the bottom and partners at the top. One of the main challenges for these firms was having the right number of people to do the work. Too many, and they would cost too much and be bored. Too few, and the work suffered and you could not grow. Then what did you do in times of boom or bust? Did you hire dozens of people in boom times knowing you might have to lay them off when the bust came? Or try to keep an even hiring pattern, thereby missing out on the upside of a boom economy?

Nanda had applied himself to this problem and produced a formula: $g = rp - \delta p + \sigma \lambda$. He wrote it on the blackboard with a flourish. From my seat in the back row, I squinted at it. G stood for the growth rate of the firm. Rp was the recruitment rate of partners and δp the attrition rate of partners. Sigma was the fraction of associates who made partner and λ was the ratio of associates to partners. All of which seemed a fussy way of saying that your ability to grow was determined by the number of partners and associates you had to do the work.

"Why are you making that face?" Nanda said, thundering up the steps of the classroom toward me.

"I'm trying to understand your equation," I said.

"Tell me what it means."

I went through the various terms, apparently to his satisfaction. But I was still clearly looking a bit funny.

"And what's your problem with it?" he bellowed.

"I just don't find it"—I rifled through my mind for the right term—"meaningful. I don't find it meaningful."

"What don't you find meaningful about it?"

"It seems too self-evident. It's like saying that when General Electric makes lightbulbs, it needs enough raw materials and production capacity to make the lightbulbs."

"Well, perhaps we can find someone who does find it meaningful," Nanda said, shooting me a filthy look and turning to the class.

A man who was sitting across the aisle from me, and who had served in the Special Forces in Afghanistan before HBS, gave me a thumbs-up and mouthed the words "this is a joke." But there was no shortage of hands, and soon the discussion was back to familiar territory. Quite justifiably, Nanda gave me my worst grade, a three.

Chapter Fifteen

GRADUATION

> People are delighted to accept
> pensions and gratuities, for which
> they hire out their labor or their
> support or their services. But nobody
> works out the value of time: men use
> it lavishly as if it cost nothing.
>
> —SENECA, *ON THE*
> *SHORTNESS OF LIFE*

At the end of the final semester, Section A reunited for one last class. We voted for Felix to oversee it and our assigned reading was Peter Drucker's article "Managing Oneself." The main idea in the piece was that in a knowledge economy, we would have to do far more than previous generations to manage our own careers, education, and development. We should recognize our weaknesses, then focus on our strengths and develop them. We should work on our lives outside our careers in order to pursue a meaningful life even while our careers were sputtering. It was an idea that explained much of the personal development focus at HBS, the attention to "transforming" us into leaders. Earlier graduates could join a large company and stay there for their entire careers. We would have to take care of ourselves as individual assets, unique fragments within the business universe, moving from company to company, place to place, responsible for ourselves.

The question that prompted the sharpest debate, however, was on a different topic. It was posed by a student who would be returning to Wall Street to sell bonds: "How will we know how much is enough?" The benchmark for being truly rich while I was at HBS was having your own jet. This would probably require a net worth of over $100 million and separated you from the merely wealthy. Lisa, the ethical jihadist, said true wealth would come from having a work-life balance and a happy family. The skydeck strained to contain their smirks. A woman going to a New York hedge fund said that enough was knowing she could live comfortably without ever having to work again, which she intended to achieve long before the usual retirement age. The question encapsulated the fear to which all the cases and discussions had provided no answer. The world was still full of uncertainty. Sure, we were now better equipped to navigate that uncertainty, to weigh up a variety of choices. But the great existential questions remained unanswered. Who are we? And why are we doing this with our lives? How much will ever be enough?

Overall, the section reunion was flat. All the forced section bonding of the first year had forged friendships within small groups of people. But now we looked at each other for what we were: a random group of people brought together in an educational experiment and now being flung back into the world as individual atoms. The prospect of returning to work weighed on the room. The bankers and consultants were coming to the end of their two-year vacation. Those changing careers were nervous about what that change held in store. After two years of looking at the world as barons and generals and CEOs, most of us would be forced back into the trenches, where a LEAD or Strategy frameworks would be as much use as an ermine cloak. The HBS bubble had protected us. For two years we had been treated as people of extraordinary promise. Now we would have to perform.

The final weeks of HBS were an unsettling experience. I had achieved a status as the only person in my section without a job offer. The rest of the class was off to Google and Yahoo!, Merrill Lynch and Lehman Brothers, McKinsey, Bain, and the Boston Consulting Group. Annette continued to resist the wads of money Wall Street waved at her and pressed ahead in the fashion industry. A couple were off to China and India—but surprisingly few, after all the noise made about the two countries over the past two years. Bankers who had vowed never to return to Wall Street were now doing so, incapable of resisting the pay. One woman was returning to her job with a West Coast private equity firm despite the fact she had spent most of HBS saying how miserable she had been there. But she had concluded that she had a rare talent for finance, and that in ten years, by her late thirties, she would have all the money she would ever need and could do something she liked. Her family was not rich, and she had the opportunity to make a serious amount of money. However wretched each hour and day might be, she was not going to throw it away. Justin had decided to spend more time in the belly of the beast and would be returning to the investment bank where he had spent the summer. Two years, he said. Then the conversion begun at HBS would be complete. He could then do anything he wanted to. Business and government alike would have to take him seriously after two years on Wall Street. Bo had bought a house in Kansas City, where he would be working for a foundation whose mission was to study and promote entrepreneurship through education programs and academic research. His job would involve touring universities, investigating how entrepreneurship was taught and how researchers and entrepreneurs collaborated to bring ideas from laboratories to the market. It was an ideal place from which to keep searching for that killer start-up opportunity. Cedric had accepted a job at a nonprofit that helped small enterprises in emerging markets, but he was already plotting to join an investment bank that would send him to Africa.

The careers service kept making announcements: "95% of the class of 2006 have accepted job offers!" One week later: "97.6% of the class of 2006 have now accepted jobs!" I was part of a very small and fast-dwindling group. I'd like to say I was cool about it. That I was sticking to my guns. That I had paid attention to what every single guest speaker had said. Do what you love. Don't settle. Take risk now, because it will be much harder later in life. Your family is more important than your work. Don't do anything for the money. If you love what you do, the money will follow. But I wasn't cool. I was freaking out. As the end loomed, I felt like a man edging toward the end of a plank.

My biggest worry was that I had wasted the experience. And what greater proof was there than my looming joblessness? I knew people would think less of me. "You went to Harvard Business School and couldn't find a job?" A clear hierarchy had also emerged within the class. At the top were those going to the private equity firms and hedge funds on salaries of hundreds of thousands of dollars a year. People called them "studs," as in "he's a total finance stud, going to Blackstone." Then there were those going into investment banking and consulting, cliquey groups all swapping notes on which office they would be heading to, which partners they would be working for. Five percent of the class was going to McKinsey, around forty-five students. Among those interested in technology, several had snagged jobs at the top venture capital firms in Silicon Valley and Boston. Seven more were off to Google, nine to Microsoft. Once you added them up, finance, consulting, and major technology firms had taken 69 percent of the class. Right at the bottom of this hierarchy were those without jobs or even offers: me.

The international students were split between those going straight home and those who wanted to spend more time in America. The Latin Americans tended to want to get a blue-chip American firm on their résumé before going home. A few years with Citibank or Goldman Sachs would not only help pay down those loans but give them even greater credibility. Most of the Europeans were heading straight back across the Atlantic, many to London. A new trend among the Indians was to go immediately back to India. One of the smartest finance students in our entire year gave up a place at Goldman Sachs's top internal hedge fund in

New York to set up a private equity fund in India. The Chinese were the same. The opportunities for them as HBS graduates in China were far greater than if they had become yet more MBAs scurrying around New York. Aside from the explosive economic opportunities, they would be special at home in a way they were not in the United States.

Whenever I started feeling the anxiety, I turned to Margret. She reassured me. I had not wasted my time. I had worked hard. Read every case. Never gone to class unprepared. Attended talks. Made time for the section. Tried my hand at a start-up. Gone for interviews. I just hadn't found the right thing. But as the weeks slid by, she admitted that she, too, was getting anxious. We had two young sons. We needed an income. At some point, the agonizing was going to have to stop and I would have to choose. The loans I had accumulated were now starting to weigh on me. I had spent pretty much exactly what HBS told me my education would cost, including tuition and accommodation, health insurance and living costs for me and my family. The total bill was $175,000. Much of that I had borrowed, and the first payments would come due six months after graduation. Max, the German entrepreneur, told me not to worry. "They're all flexible, and you can delay and reduce the amounts. Think of it as easy credit, debt on your balance sheet. You're leveraged. It's what we've been taught to do." I was not consoled.

The evening after the Managing Oneself class, I went around to Bo's house for dinner. When I arrived he was busy inserting a Budweiser can up a raw chicken, which he then rested on top of his grill. "We're having beer chicken," he explained. "Real juicy." When I told him of my anxiety, he threw himself down in one of his large recliners and ruffled the hair of his two dogs.

"PDBizzle," he said, using his, and only his, nickname for me. "When are you going to stop thinking of these people as your peer group? They're this weird, self-selected group of people. Most of them want to be bankers and consultants. They are not like everyone else in the world. I know this, so listen to me: you would hate working with them. You would hate working at a large company. You might think that because you enjoyed a few courses here, you would enjoy it. But you would not. Business and business school are totally different things."

And yet, it required more inner strength than I could muster that March and April not to measure myself against my business school peers. Every company that came to campus seemed to want candidates with "two years of management consulting or investment banking." Still I applied and was frustrated when I was rejected. I imagined that an MBA would be proof enough of my interest in business and of some basic competence. But for big companies with a number of MBA résumés to choose from, HBS alone was not enough. You needed to have been following the path to these companies long before. Whenever I called an HBS alumnus for help or advice, he was invariably interested and helpful. He'd pass on names of other people to call, suggest ways into companies or sources of finance for ideas. Many alumni told me that it was far better to take a great job in September than one I would hate just to have something at graduation. My deeper problem was that I still didn't know what I wanted to do, and I was starting to feel pretty pathetic about it.

I realized I was torn between extremes. At one end was Joseph Galli, at the other Alice Trillin. Galli had visited campus one dark winter afternoon during the second year, several months after being fired as CEO of Newell Rubbermaid. He had been appointed to this job at the precocious age of forty-two, after a successful career at Black and Decker. But he lasted just four years and failed to turn the company around. He was clearly feeling chastised after his failure at Newell, but retained this manic quality, as though he were in withdrawal from the CEO life. "I've had the benefit of taking four months off," he said, talking at a blistering speed. "For four months I've gotten to know my family, relax, read the books I've always wanted to read." I wondered, could it take just four months to do all that? Later, he said, "I don't think you can be a good CEO and spend time with your family, play poker three nights a week, join a golf club, go to Myrtle Beach with the boys, hit the strip clubs. Something's going to have to give."

He said that he did not know his eighteen-year-old daughter until she was twelve and admitted he "blew it." But as I sat there listening, I wondered how he would have spoken if he had succeeded at Newell. If his professional life had continued on an upward trajectory, would he be telling us about his relationship with his daughter? Galli, I felt, along with all those businesspeople who boasted of attending their kids' sports games, as if that were the ultimate sign of good parenting, had made their choice: work first, family second.

A friend from the section who had found a job at a blue-chip investment bank told me that he had had this weird conversation with the head of his bank when he came to speak at HBS. They were standing around before the talk, the CEO was staring at his feet, so my friend struck up a conversation. "Any regrets about being a banker?" he said. "Well, it's exhausting," said the CEO, without looking up. "And I barely talk to my son." My friend related this story as if it were one of the most pathetic things he had ever seen. But he still took the job.

Alice Trillin was the wife of the writer Calvin Trillin. She died in 2005, and Calvin wrote a beautiful reminiscence for *The New Yorker*, which I read at the end of my time at HBS. Alice, he wrote, had a very strict view of parenting. Either your children were the center of your life, or they were not. Everything else was commentary. The words electrified me. It was a truth I had known coming into HBS but had slowly lost grip of. You could not have multiple centers in life. It would only lead to confusion. There was no balance, there were no trade-offs. Just elementary choices about how you lived your life. You had to pick.

One evening, a friend who had graduated from Georgetown's business school and started a hedge fund that closed within two years took me for a drink at the Racquet Club in New York. We sat on the balcony staring up at the office buildings on Park Avenue, which hummed with light and life. "I'll tell you what your problem is," he said, pointing at me with his cigarette. "Your problem is this: You wanted to make all this fucking money and you went to Harvard Business School so you'd have the opportunity.

But all the time, you couldn't quiet the voice inside your head telling you that just making money is a ridiculous way to spend your life. I know this is your problem, because I suffered from the same thing, before I got over it."

The previous summer in London, several friends had bombarded me over dinner, saying I was selling out by going for a highly paid job, asking me why, since I had so many of the pieces in place to live exactly the life I wanted, wasn't I grabbing it? Why was I trying to rejoin the herd at the very moment I had a chance to escape? "You've managed to stay off the hamster wheel this long," one of them said. "Don't for God's sake go jumping on now."

We had a month-long break between the end of classes and graduation. I returned to England for a week, and we also spent some time in New York. One day, I was sitting on a bus going down Lexington Avenue around lunchtime when I looked out to my left and saw a stocky little figure in a camel overcoat cut to mid-thigh fidgeting on the sidewalk. The way he stepped from foot to foot, he looked as if he were desperate to pee. His large head was shaved and his face was pinched into a sour pout. Beneath his coat he wore a pair of expensive-looking jeans and pointy black leather shoes, all of which looked made for a much younger man. A few steps in front of him stood another, much larger man in a long black raincoat, holding his finger to an earpiece.

The bodyguard looked up and down the busy street, maintaining an invisible cordon around his ward. It took me a moment to recognize the man in the camel coat. And even then I didn't quite believe it. Why was Ron Perelman, all seven or eight or nine billion dollars' worth of him, depending on where the markets were that day, standing on a street corner in the middle of the day? Didn't men of this stature have people to stand on street corners for them while they gobbled up companies?

The first time I ever read the name Ron Perelman was in an issue of *Vanity Fair* in 1995. He was photographed sitting in a Porsche near his

summer home in the Hamptons. At that point, he still had some hair clinging like lichen to the outer surfaces of his lumpen head and he had just
wriggled free of his second marriage to embark on his third. In the photographs, he looked extremely pleased with life, as well he might, and either
oblivious to or contemptuous of what the rest of the world thought of
small, tubby, middle-aged men with Porsches, blond wives, and billions in
the bank. It felt like he was grinding his good fortune like one of his dead
cigars into the ashtray of the reader's face.

During the 1980s, when Perelman made the bulk of his money, he was
considered a renegade, a thug holding up corporate America. He looked for
companies he considered undervalued, bought them with large amounts of
debt, and then broke them up for a profit. The debt was often provided to
him by Michael Milken of Drexel Burnham Lambert, who later went to
jail for securities violations. Since it was poorly secured, the debt carried
high rates of interest and came to be known as "junk." But the term *junk*
never made sense to me. The risk of a loan derives from the probability of
its being paid back. Now you can assess that probability based on the physical assets securing the debt and the cash flow they generate. But you can
also assess it based on the personality of the borrower.

Ordinary banks use individual credit scores to size up borrowers. But a
sophisticated lender looks more deeply. What drives this person? How
much does he want to succeed? If I were a lender presented with the red-
hot ambition of a Ron Perelman, all of that seething insecurity, that
extraordinary will to power, that unquenchable need for cars and women
and status, I would lend and lend again, and the last thing I'd call my loan
would be "junk." I would be delighted to have the opportunity to lend to a
man so motivated to make money. J. P. Morgan said something along these
lines in testimony to Congress. Morgan was being questioned by Samuel
Untermeyer, a relentless corporate lawyer. Untermeyer asked Morgan if
the main criterion for lending was the money or property of the borrower.
"No, sir," Morgan shot back. "The first thing is character." "Before money
or property?" Untermeyer asked. "Before money or property or anything

else," Morgan said. "A man I do not trust could not get money from me on all the bonds in Christendom." The financial system turns on personalities as much as anything else.

Anyway, somehow time and events have cleaned any stain from Perelman's methods. Today he would be fêted as a private equity genius, maybe even touted as a future Treasury secretary. The heirs of Perelman and Milken are today's financial mainstream. Leverage has gone from dirty word to byword. Firms like Blackstone borrow cheaply to buy undervalued companies and then reorganize them at enormous profit to themselves with barely a whimper from Perelman's erstwhile critics. The predators have become the establishment.

So there stood Ron on the street corner, one hand in his coat pocket pressing, perhaps, on that bursting bladder. I stared and stared, while the bus stopped to let people on.

It took Perelman until his mid-thirties to really get going, which gave me some hope. I still, just, had time to catch up. But once he got going, he was unstoppable. A multimillionaire by the time he was thirty-six, a billionaire soon afterward. Along with the billions came the divorces, four in total. My first reaction, after recognizing Perelman, was delight. How ordinary he looked! How miserable and shifty-looking on this gray Manhattan morning. The last thing I wanted a multibillionaire to look was happy.

But almost immediately I wondered, what was my problem? What had Perelman ever done to me? It is not as if I had never wanted to be rich like that. So why was it that every time I encountered someone with enormous amounts of money, my first instinct was to think, "well, of course, he must be miserable," and then seek out the frailest shred of evidence to support my assumption. So you need to pee, do you, Perelman? Hah! Fat lot of good those billions are doing you. Here I am in my nice warm bus, a paperback in my pocket, happy as only a soon-to-be-jobless Harvard MBA can be. Give me a billion dollars and I'd know what to do with it. Let's just say paying a bodyguard to walk me across Lexington Avenue would not be top of my list. You're a loser, Perelman. Go ahead, count your billions and your blondes. Doesn't change anything. You're still a fat man in a tight coat looking anxious on a street corner.

But why on earth had I put myself through Harvard Business School, of all places, an institution whose purpose was teaching people how to amass and deploy vast resources? Why did I still experience this emotional whiplash in the presence of the very rich? If I admired them so much, then I should simply try to emulate them, not yearn for their misery. Was I just jealous? Or was I experiencing the deformed emotional offspring of my encroaching awareness that for lack of ability, personality, and hunger, I would never experience that kind of wealth? As a twenty-year-old, I had imagined I might be Jimmy Goldsmith. Now here I was thirty-three, no closer than I had been thirteen years earlier, with any hope of achieving that ambition shriveling with every passing day.

I recalled a morning in Aldrich Hall, when Cedric and I were passing the time between classes talking about French politics. Jacques Chirac, he told me, was rumored to consult West African marabouts, witch doctors. These marabouts, it was said, would help a man achieve great power only in return for enormous personal sacrifice. In 1988, after Chirac lost the presidential election, it was said he summoned a marabout to Paris. If he wanted the presidency, the witch doctor told him, he must sacrifice one of his daughters. Soon afterward, Chirac's younger daughter, Laurence, began suffering from extreme anorexia, from which she has never recovered. In West Africa, Cedric assured me, this outlandish story was accepted as gospel.

This tale struck me as a twist on the Faustian pact. If you are ready to give up your soul or, failing that, a child, the devil will give you anything. Perhaps an economist will do the work one day. How many very rich or powerful self-made people have suffered a terrible personal loss? And do they suffer more than average? But watching Perelman, I thought about Faust in a different way. Instead of being a morality tale, perhaps the story was just a reflection of how the less fortunate have always consoled themselves. No one could be rich and happy. It was one or the other. It had to be. Didn't it?

Graduation was a washout. The rain began to fall a couple of days before and refused to let up. Baker Lawn resembled the deck of a cruise liner passing through a hurricane, with rows of red folding chairs facing a forlorn, tented stage whose roof sagged under the weight of water. My parents and my aunt valiantly drove up from Washington, D.C., but by the time they got here, all they wanted was to see me receive my diploma and then go and see our children. They had not the slightest interest in Class Day, the day before graduation, when a student and a guest speaker gave us some final thoughts on the whole shebang. So I went alone. Burden Auditorium was full, so I trudged over to Aldrich, where a sodden spillover crowd watched the speeches on a large screen. The first speaker was P. J. Kim, a student chosen for his eloquence from a large pool of applicants by a panel of section officers. P.J. was an Asian immigrant whose family lived in south Texas. Like me, his job search had not gone as smoothly as others', but he was charming about it. "Not having a job in your last semester at Harvard Business School," he said, "is like being at a really great party when everyone else has paired up and you're sitting alone in the corner eating potato chips."

He said he had canvassed his friends for advice to offer the class and come up with three key points. Justin once pointed out to me that at HBS you could explain the meaning of life, the universe, and everything in paragraphs, and no one would pay you any attention. But say you have a list and everyone bolted upright and prepared to take notes. P.J.'s list was:

1) When we look back, the big things will look small and the little things will look big.
2) Comparison is the death of happiness.
3) We are all we have. No one else will rescue us.

I liked the second one in particular. Measuring oneself against one's friends or peers could only lead to misery, because always, in some area of life, there will be someone doing better than you. It was the misery of the curve. I had been good at what I did before HBS. I had a role, some status. But while at HBS, even as I learned so much about business and myself, I had been beating myself up with comparisons to others.

The second speaker was Hank Paulson, an HBS alumnus who had recently left his job as CEO of Goldman Sachs to become the Treasury secretary. He was an awkward man with huge boxy shoulders and a shaved head. He spoke in a gravelly voice, his throat doubtless rubbed raw by hours bellowing at lawyers in airless conference rooms. The world, he said, was richer in economic opportunity than he had ever seen it. But it was also more uncertain. The victors would be those who "made change their friend." He had four pieces of advice:

1) Resist the temptation to be a short-termist.
2) Be honest with yourself about what jobs are the right ones for you.
3) Keep your moral compass.
4) Maintain the proper balance between your professional career and your personal life.

He urged us not to be "career engineers" but simply to learn and grow at every opportunity. "The only thing you cannot afford not to do is learn." On the second point, he said that today everyone he met seemed to believe they came out of their mothers' wombs to invest or trade large private pools of capital. But not everyone was suited for this, and there were plenty of other worthwhile careers to pursue. Professional happiness, he said, would come from being very good at something difficult.

Concerning the moral compass, he said it was important both to do the right thing and to be seen to be doing the right thing. He warned us of the dangers of groupthink and peer pressure in pushing otherwise good people to participate in bad things. Bad people doing bad things and good people doing good things were easy to understand, he said. It was more important to learn why good people did bad things and to avoid that fate ourselves.

On the question of balance, he said that as a young banker in Chicago, he had spent far too much time in the office when his children were young. Eventually, his wife ordered him to be home for their bedtime. He caught a train late in the afternoon to be home by six to read them stories. But he was so used to the pace of work, he would rattle off the stories as if reading a stock ticker. His wife told him to slow down, but his daughter told him not to listen to her mother. She liked him reading fast. No company, Paulson said, was going to help us with balance. We had to learn how to say no, how to juggle our schedules to make time for our families, friends, and private pursuits.

The following morning, at dawn, was the university's commencement ceremony. I had planned to go, but it was raining and I woke up needing some time alone. Despite all the work I had done, all I had learned, the friends I had made, my uncertainty about my future left me feeling a failure. I knew how ridiculous this was. HBS was not about getting a job. It was about putting up the structure for a more interesting life. The statistics showed that a large number of graduates left the first job they took out of HBS within the first year. The crazy environment and tight parameters of a business school forced people to make bad decisions, which they quickly rectified once back in the real world. But this was no help. I thought that by this point in my life I would have more answers and that by continuing to drift and agonize and wonder I was letting a lot of people down.

Early that morning, while the rest of the class prepared to go to Harvard Square, I dressed Augie and the two of us drove over to Boston's North End. We often came here on Saturday mornings for cannoli while Margret and Hugo slept. We took our usual table in Caffe dello Sport, beneath a giant TV screen that showed soccer matches from Italy. I read the newspaper while Augie slurped and crunched through his cannoli. Then we went for a walk in the drizzle. We turned up Paul Revere Mall, past a statue of Revere and up along a line of trees. The red brick was damp, the air heavy and quiet. We were the only ones there. We walked along to the fountain just below the Old North Church and sat down. While Augie played with a toy car, I walked over to the wall to read the plaques commemorating famous residents of the North End. There was Revere's. "Paul Revere 1735–1818. Patriot. Master Craftsman. Good Citizen. Born on Hanover Street. Lived on North Street. Established his bell foundry on Foster Street and died on Charter Street." He had lived a good life, an important life within a knot of narrow streets. I read the plaque again and again. Its simplicity galvanized me. He had not traveled to find his fortune. It reminded me of Lassiter's advice to find a world-class tribe and stick with it. The North Enders at the time of the American Revolution had certainly been that. I thought of the friends Revere must have had, the deep family ties. And then I thought of my classmates, disappearing to the ends of the earth in search of opportunity, worrying about work and life, and I felt better not to be among them. Not to have committed myself to something I knew I would not enjoy. After so much wandering, I coveted the life summed up in that plaque. I realized that if I kept searching, with the education I had, it was well within my grasp.

Chapter Sixteen

A FACTORY
FOR
UNHAPPY
PEOPLE

"Do you know what the margins are on popcorn?" It was a year since we had graduated, and Oleg was calling from St. Petersburg, where he was running a chain of multiplex cinemas for a private equity firm. "Two thousand percent. Can you fucking believe that? Two thousand percent! You think running a cinema is about movies, but then you find out it's about popcorn."

He said he had just spoken to a classmate of ours whose family owned cinemas in the Middle East. "In their cinemas, they have breaks during the film so people can go and buy more popcorn and drinks. So I'm trying to figure out a way to have breaks here. The problem is that in Russia, if you put on the lights during a film, everyone starts shouting and throwing things because they think the projector's broken." Oleg sounded ebullient. He was delighted to be back in Russia, his wife was delighted, and he was loving his work. I asked him what he remembered from HBS.

"I remember it was like a fucking boot camp. It was really tough in terms of the workload. I remember when I went there thinking, this should be a walk in the park. But I wasn't even a little bit aware of what I was letting myself in for. But then, today, I download an HBS case nearly every week and read it for inspiration. And I would gladly talk to anyone who was there with me. I think really highly of the people there, and generally I'd be very happy to see anyone from the school, which makes me think they did a good job."

He said that the most important thing he had learned was that "you never should consider yourself the smartest guy in the room. I was surprised how valuable the input during the class discussions was." It wasn't that all the comments were brilliant, though a few were. It was more the range of perspectives that surprised him. "Now I never make a decision without asking what the other guys think. Although people can be annoying, it's still worth listening. I was a pretty reasonable guy before going to HBS, but now I always have questions, I never make a statement."

Now that he was running his own operation, he thought back again and again to the cases. "It was very valuable to see a lot of business situations. Now, being a CEO, I know that this shit happened to every other guy who was a protagonist in those cases. We saw a lot of businesses from the inside, so business doesn't seem like rocket science anymore. It's just about finding the right approach. The veil has been removed. The practical knowledge, you forget most of that anyway. You can pick up the models from a textbook. But seeing all those situations and listening to other people's opinions, that was the thing."

Soon after returning to Russia, he was put in charge of a small amusement park. One of the rides, he discovered, was structurally weak. Despite the financial pressure, he ordered it to be shut down. "I kept thinking of the Tylenol case in Leadership and Corporate Accountability. When that guy at Johnson and Johnson had to ignore the immediate financial implications and pull the drug because it might be unsafe. He had to do the right thing. I thought about that a lot, and it helped me make my decision. I stopped the ride. I said, I'm not going to run this thing until I'm sure it's safe for the people." Another case that stood out in his mind was the introduction of the Mercedes Benz A-Class, which we studied with Felix in

Strategies Beyond the Market. Mercedes had invested a fortune in its first small car only to find just before its launch that it failed a certain safety test. The executives at the company had to decide what to do. "You remember that guy who had to make a hard decision by himself and stick to his guns? I liked that shit."

Oleg had found his calling, but it had taken a few months. Straight out of HBS, he had taken a consulting job in London. "If you're not sure what you want to do, or if you want to win some time to get some options, consulting opens some doors. I spent five months, and even after such a short time, I was getting a lot of calls from headhunters. It's like a continued job search. Especially when you change countries. They treat you very nicely. They find you an apartment, transfer all your stuff, they give you a signing bonus, they give you time to look for a better job. For people who are afraid to make choices, it's a safe place."

I met Cedric for lunch in a noodle bar close to his office in Manhattan. He had gotten the job he wanted, at the investment bank, and would soon be off to Africa. The moment we came in from the cold street, we were engulfed by warm steam. We took a small table in a corner by a window covered with a bamboo shade. The last time we had seen each other was during the France-Brazil semifinal in the soccer World Cup, which we had watched amid packing boxes in a room on campus. We began talking about everyone in our class and how they were getting along. Several had already left the jobs they had taken upon graduating, while others were seriously considering doing so. Why, I asked Cedric, had they taken these jobs in the first place? It's not as though we didn't know what they would involve.

"HBS," he said, hoisting a ball of noodles to his mouth, "is a factory for unhappy people. We have so many choices, and yet so few people seem happy about that. It just makes them anxious. And more anxious. And then they make terrible decisions about their lives. But," he added, "these are mostly very good people. People from good families with good values. I can't figure out what happens. I think they just get desperate."

I called Nate, a member of Section A who had lived in the same building as we did during the second year. He was now working for a biotech firm in the Pacific Northwest. He had joined his company when the stock price was over seventy dollars and now it was around seven dollars. He had witnessed rounds of layoffs and serious business reversals. But he was as sanguine and upbeat as ever. "It has been difficult here, but I've learned a ton." The single biggest thing he had taken from HBS, he said, was confidence. "At conventions, I'll just go up to CEOs of other companies and just start talking. HBS gave me the confidence that I have a right to be wherever I am. In a meeting, speaking up, talking to a CEO. Maybe that right's not justified, but I definitely feel it. Just don't ask me to do a discounted cash flow or tell you the three *P*s of marketing. Or were there four *P*s?"

Looking back, the thing Nate enjoyed the most was "the quintessential Cambridge educational experience. I loved just waking up in the morning knowing I was at Harvard, seeing people rowing sculls on the river, the first snow of winter." Having experienced academic hysteria firsthand as an undergraduate at Stanford, he made sure not to get caught up in it at HBS. But he was disappointed to find a different kind of hysteria, a herd mentality focused on financial rewards. "It is like if you play ice hockey, the trick is to skate to where the puck is going to be, not to where it is. I felt at HBS, everyone was skating to where the puck, or the money, was—private equity, hedge funds, real estate—without thinking where it was going. Lots of people seemed more interested in a number, the amount they would earn, than the life or future that would entail.

"And yet, when I think back to every case we studied and every protagonist who came to class, every visiting speaker, it seemed like all of them said 'I was a bad spouse' or 'I was a bad parent.' Not one of them could say, 'my family was a smashing success.' I remember going to hear this panel of

HBS alumni in the second year. One said her husband had had a brain seizure, the other spoke about how his daughter didn't remember his name. And then there was this top Goldman Sachs executive who came to talk about leadership and values, and I just remember this look of total defeat on his face when he said how he had four ex-wives. But then when you saw how our class made choices, you saw they would do what these people do, not what they say. We didn't want to hear about their lives. You can measure who is the second wealthiest person in the world, but not who is a good husband. It's like *Death of a Salesman*. Who appreciates the average family guy?

"It was a surprise to me how making the right choices coming out of HBS would require real intestinal fortitude, a real functioning moral compass, because the forces pushing you to pursue success in a very specific way were overwhelming."

I met Annette for a drink near Central Park, close to her Midtown office. She was still at the fashion company she had joined upon graduation. She still thought of the Wall Street money she had passed up to take this job, but she was happy about her choice. She was learning and could see a number of different paths open to her. Every day she used something she had learned at HBS, whether it was calculating the correct batch size for an order or digging into a financial projection.

"After doing this job for a year, I feel I'm on my way to being able to run my own business. I could advise other brands. I could acquire a business. I feel like I can manage people in a way I never would have had the chance to on Wall Street. But then I look at my little brother, who is really into his music, and he keeps telling me he's going to make it big, and I think that for all my HBS education, he's more of an entrepreneur than I am. You have to be kind of risk-averse to go to HBS. The whole thing about the network and the transformation, it's for people who want to minimize the risk in their lives when they go after opportunities."

. . . .

Luis, the Franco-Argentine, had returned to Madrid, where his wife was from, and was now working with a group of investors identifying and acquiring underperforming businesses. He was back in his element and delighted to be so. He said that any negative feelings he had about the school had quickly evaporated. He had loved the case discussions and found himself thinking back to them almost every day.

"I learned to think in a very different way. The way I explain things and break down an argument is different. In the beginning, when we first had thirty seconds to make a point in class, you didn't get anywhere. By the end, you know how to say things quickly and you learn to think before you talk. But now my friends tell me to stop speaking like I'm in business school, always saying 'there are two or three ways to look at this,' even when we're deciding where to go for dinner. It's a very structured way of thinking. Maybe overstructured."

Hasan was now a banker living and working in the Middle East. He had disliked the section, finding it repetitive and conformist. He would rather have spent the first year going to different classes with different people. But he had loved the academic work. "Strategy really stuck with me. It totally changed the way I think and analyze. The use of detailed analysis to make macro-decisions. Before, I'd assumed that macro-decisions required macro-analysis. Here I found the level of detail you have to get down to to make macro-decisions. You have to think about things all the way down.

"Entrepreneurship was a life-changing experience for me. It eased a lot of fears I had about entrepreneurship and taught me that it's not about taking risk but about managing risk. The course triggered the observation that everything is possible. I learned about the power of leverage, how to raise money and structure your financing deal. It gave me the window on unlimited possibility." The way the professional world was set up these days, he said, "switching gears has become such a costly process." HBS was an efficient way of "retooling" and changing careers.

He had found the school more parochial in its view than it had promised. "HBS is an East Coast, conservative institution. It's not really an international school. For example, you had to seek out the international courses in the EC, and once you got there, you realized that all the other students were international! Internationalism was a fad. If Goldman Sachs or other big American companies weren't going big into China, the school wouldn't have been as interested in it." He found the school's approach to ethics "fundamentally puritanical. It put an American spin on every case. If you tried to apply the frameworks we learned and tried to succeed in Dubai or Nigeria, you would never succeed, I tell you." Hasan admired the American way of doing business for its obvious success, but he resisted the sense that it should be applied to every culture and country.

He had finally chosen the Middle East over California, where he had worked before graduate school, to be closer to his family and because the Harvard MBA meant more there. American companies had come to view the MBA as a filter, a requirement for senior management. The degree had become a commodity. Internationally, a Harvard MBA was much rarer. The networks of international alumni tended to be smaller and stronger, especially in Latin America, Africa, the Middle East, and Asia. There were entire industries in these regions, Saudi oil, for example, that had yet to be taken over by the MBA class. Men like Hasan were preparing to change that.

The job statistics for our class showed that 42 percent went into financial services, ranging from investment banking to private equity, venture capital, and commercial banking. Twenty-one percent went into consulting. There was then a steep drop to technology and telecommunications, with 6 percent. Pharmaceuticals, consumer products, retail, and other manufacturing each drew less than 5 percent. Nonprofit and government accounted for less than 3 percent, half of whom were part of an HBS program that placed students in nonprofit and government jobs and subsidized their salaries to bring them in range of the for-profit sector. Eighty percent of the class took jobs in the United States. The median total compensation for my class in its first year out was $138,125. Ray Soifer, a graduate of the class of 1965 and a banking analyst, had been keeping track of the relationship between the condition of the American equity market and the percentage of Harvard MBA graduates choosing careers in financial services. Ten percent or less was a long-term buy signal. Thirty percent or more was a long-term sell. The choices of the class of 2006 told you the markets were soon to crash.

My first few months out of HBS were difficult. We returned to New York to be near friends and family and to find work. An old friend of Margret's told me that while I was still waiting to become a titan of business, I may as well do something I knew I enjoyed. So each day, I took the subway up to the library at Columbia University and wrote fiction and articles for newspapers. I then decided to flesh out a business plan I had started while at HBS. It was Margret's idea, for a very high end laundry firm. She had needled me for months to look into it. Now I had the time. I identified the customer pain and established the probable market size. I scoped out competitors and contacted laundry firms, asking to visit their plants. I flew to Kansas City and stayed with Bo while visiting the country's leading high-end laundry. I took detailed notes on the company's operations, the route laundry took through the plant, the use of employees, the way specialist tasks such as repair or stain removal were incorporated into the work flow. It was all good TOM stuff. The owner of a commercial laundry in California showed me his meticulously kept books, and I pored over them, scribbling down numbers I could use later to do some ratios. The owner explained how he kept his prices and margins above those of his rivals, how everything his firm did—from the trucks he used, to his policy of giving employees stock, to the long-term relationships he had with his customers—helped drive open that wedge between cost and willingness to pay. It wasn't one thing, as we had learned in strategy, but how everything worked together that gave you a competitive advantage. The research took me back to my journalism days, but now the questions I was asking, the range of subjects I was interested in, were so much broader. I found the minutiae of these businesses fascinating, and it was wonderful to speak to business owners and see them light up as they described their operations, the joy they felt at creating jobs, the satisfaction at installing a piece of equipment that speeded up their operations. I could ask a question about through-put rate, and they would be thrilled that someone was interested in the details of what they did.

After looking closely at the business, Margret and I decided that it could work. But it required one of us to commit ourselves to it full-time. And there would be no guaranteed income for at least several months. One thing I had learned from studying so many entrepreneurs was that if you were going to start up a business, you had better be ready for a lot of thankless hard work while you got it off the ground. I also knew that whatever happened with the business, I would want to have enough cash set aside to pay our bills for a year. We did not have those kinds of means, so we decided to wait at least until our younger son was into nursery school. But the exercise of researching the opportunity and putting together a plan had reminded me of how much I enjoyed thinking about business challenges.

I had been warned that as a recent HBS graduate on the loose, I would get all kinds of strange requests. And sure enough, I did: Friends of friends wanting help with business plans. Small firms wanting strategic advice. It was those three letters, MBA. I spent three months advising a British media firm trying to launch a service in the United States. They had a decent product, but the company was divided between those who wanted to build it fast and sell and the founder, who wanted to go slower and enjoy the status the company gave him. The different ambitions were always flaring to the surface, forcing me back to think of LEAD and the importance of aligning interests and visions early in any undertaking. I used Excel every day to organize data that had been sitting in unsorted piles in the company's databases. I dug out my Entrepreneurial Marketing notes to think about how the company could "cross the chasm," trying to identify the influential visionaries who might goad the wildebeest herd to stampede in our direction.

When this project wound up, I received a call from a film production company I had written a paper for during Lassiter's class in my second year. My paper was about film distribution and the impact of new technology. The company wanted me to raise corporate sponsorship for one documentary and to distribute another. I would have to figure out everything from DVD manufacturing to marketing and sales. When I told my grandfather in Washington, D.C., he burst out laughing. "You are in the film business like Daw Ma Ma," he said, referring to my Burmese great-grandmother, the one who had brought American movies to Rangoon. I had picked up the single entrepreneurial thread in our family, the one story that had been told time and again—how Daw Ma Ma had been widowed at thirty-five with nine children and started a film distribution company to keep a roof over their heads. Here I was, more than forty years after my mother had watched *Ben-Hur* from the family box at the Palladium Cinema in Rangoon, Daw Ma Ma's great-grandson, in my grandfather's eyes at least, following a family tradition.

Looking back on HBS, I was happy I went. Business was no longer a closed world to me. I had the brand on my résumé and access to the network of alumni. I had learned the language of business, the modes of thinking. I knew about risk management and strategic planning, hedging and diversification, returns on assets, sales and investment. I knew about BATNA and ZOPA and the importance of aligning incentives. If a banker started talking about "bips above the curve," I knew he was comparing borrowing rates to the Treasury bill yield curve. I had learned about the importance of process in every aspect of a business, of not just getting the right outcome but doing it the right way so that you could achieve the right outcome again and again. Businesses needed to develop good processes in the ways baseball pitchers or golfers needed to develop muscle memory so they could perform the same physical action repeatedly. For the first time in my life, I understood how capital was allocated, whether it was a company building a new factory or venture capitalists backing the next big thing. This was empowering, because it taught me about the availability of money for good ideas and how and where you went to find it.

I had also been convinced of multiple-option decision making. Every single case we had studied had required us to come up with different alternatives and a decision. But Jan Rivkin's class had added depth and color to this method. You trusted your gut and then you developed options, digging in as deeply as you could, asking what would need to happen, what proof you needed in order to do x or y, and only then picking a course of action. I was surprised by some of the cases that stuck with me. In RC marketing, we had looked at an English shower maker called Aqualisa Quartz, which was trying to decide on the best channel for marketing a new line of showers. It had never occurred to me that if you were in the shower-selling business, the people you really needed to persuade were not the end consumers but the plumbers. The case taught me that the best sales channels were not always the most obvious ones. I had gained a respect for management as a science and the challenges of directing an organization. Porter's class had shown me how broadly the techniques of a business analysis could be applied. And then, of course, there was the confidence. Every HBS graduate mentions this. You emerged from the school unintimidated by business and its practitioners.

But HBS had also challenged me in ways I never imagined it would. I never thought I would be pushed so aggressively against the window of my soul. Until I was there, I had underestimated capitalism's power to sow such insecurity, even among people with the skills to do anything they liked with their lives. Why were my classmates straining so hard to secure jobs they knew would make them miserable? It was more than just the money. They believed that there were well-trodden routes to worldly success and if they absorbed the pain for long enough, such success might make them happy. Satisfaction delayed was better than none at all. I was shocked at how easily I was drawn into this mind-set. My emotional experience of going through HBS was like swimming across a broad river. I had started out from one bank, confident in my own strength and with a clear view of my destination, only to be swept up in unseen currents. It was a fight to get to the other side. When I did, I was humbled, gasping and spitting up water. Only when I had caught my breath and looked back did I realize what I had done. The words *master's in business administration* captured so little of what I had learned.

If I were dean for a day, however, there are changes that I would make to Harvard Business School. The first would be to bar professors without business experience from teaching entrepreneurship. Critics have accused the MBA of teaching academic rather than practical business skills. Or, as one of my classmates put it, we were being taught to be expert diners rather than chefs, always ready with criticism, useless with a chopping knife. But in my experience, the case method, the frequent visits from businesspeople, and the opportunities in the second year to write papers on businesses and industries provided a good balance between the academic and practical. If I had had to endure any more Crimson Greetings games, I might not have lasted at the school. It was fine to be taught finance, strategy, accounting, and process by academics. I could not imagine a better guide to supply chain management, for example, than Zeynep Ton, and she had risen straight through academia. On balance, though, I preferred the professors with experience beyond academia—Oberholzer-Gee, Riedl, Porter, Lassiter—and entrepreneurship was the one subject that could not survive being taught by a walking textbook. It required professors with credibility to describe the visceral aspects of business survival.

My second change would be an overhaul of the way finance is taught at the school. The bankers and hedge fund managers who came through Harvard complained that the problem they had in hiring HBS MBAs was that they thought they were smarter than they were. Wharton and Tuck graduates had them licked on the technical stuff. For those who wanted it, I would introduce more purely technical courses and let the rocket scientists wallow in them, while giving novices like me a more classical training.

Next, I would get rid of grades altogether. The school seemed to view grades as a means of keeping students focused on their work. If they selected the right students, who were serious about learning what HBS had to teach rather than about just networking and getting the Harvard name on their résumé, there would be no need for grades. It would make for a much healthier environment and would relieve some of the pressure to conform.

Fourth, I would commission cases and courses on the proper scope of business practice. I would begin with Jack Welch's claim that business was more important than government and would require professors and students to argue this out. The HBS mission, to educate leaders who make a difference in the world, supposes that business leadership is the kind the world needs. And after two years there, I was not convinced. Democratic societies tend to allocate resources to business and government based on which they believe will do a better job. At its simplest, business is considered more efficient, government, fairer. Voters and consumers are constantly adjusting the dial, one day preferring efficiency, the next, fairness. But at HBS there was a belief that if only everything was run by business and businesspeople, the world would be a better place. It was the duty of businesspeople not only to manage businesses but also to take over nonprofits and cultural institutions, to bring their leadership to bear on every area of society. Michael Bloomberg was often cited as an HBS alumnus who had successfully transferred his leadership talents from business to New York's City Hall. President George W. Bush, however, was rarely mentioned. Though I often asked professors and my fellow students why this was so, I never received a satisfactory answer. Some said it was purely political.

Harvard was historically Democratic. Others said, look at his record. Was it anything for HBS to brag about? Still, I thought, he is the president in a time of war, and he had written favorably of the school in his autobiography, saying the MBA had been a "vocational training exercise in capitalism." At an institution that said its goal is to "educate leaders who make a difference in the world," should Bush not have been invoked more frequently? I began to think that the school's unease with Bush had nothing to do with his politics or his record. It was that here was the first HBS alumnus to enter the White House, and he had never been much of a business-. man. Through family connections, he had been able to make a small fortune as a part-owner of the Texas Rangers baseball team. But it was as a politician, albeit starting with those same family connections, that he had achieved the most powerful job in the world. I believe HBS would have much preferred it if its first president had been a Bloomberg or a Mitt Romney, someone who could point to their business record, their swollen personal accounts, and walk into the Oval Office and say "I'm going to run this country like a business." That would be the apotheosis of the HBS way, the triumph of business leadership. Instead Bush's success seemed to have come in spite of the school. He appealed to a constituency the school did not much care for. He disdained the Northeast and the quantitative method. However, certain HBS traits had never left him. He saw his main role as making decisions. He was "the decider." And as the general manager, he focused on strategy, the big goals of his presidency, leaving the tactical minutiae to others. But he was not of the business class. He was not of HBS.

I often thought back to Warren Buffett's visit, when student after student rose to ask him how he would resolve the situation in Iraq or global warming. We all knew there were bigger issues in the world than the current stock price of Berkshire Hathaway, and we yearned for Buffett to apply his mind to them. The idea of Bill Gates, mandated by his wealth, diverting his personal billions to healthcare issues was more exciting to us than the prospect of using what we had learned at HBS to improve the process of delivering AIDS vaccines. This was evident during the final semester, when I attended the school's Social Enterprise conference. There were eco-conscious coffee growers and World Health Organization physicians, the CEO of Timberland shoes and drug company executives—just not many of my classmates. The large audience came instead from the rest of the university, from the law school, the Kennedy School, the undergraduate college, and from the broader Cambridge community. At the end of the day, I bumped into Justin.

"You'd think after all the talk in class, there would have been more of us here," I said.

"If you want to change the world, get on a plane to fucking Darfur," he said tersely. "HBS is about making money. There are going to be a small handful of terrific people in our class who actually do this good stuff, but most of us are like everyone else in business. We talk about it because it makes us feel better. How many people in our class wrote in their applications that they wanted an MBA so they could do micro-finance in Uganda and are now going into investment banking?"

Which brings me to the fifth, and perhaps most important change I would make during my day as dean of HBS. I would change the mission statement. HBS does not need to promise to "educate leaders who make a difference in the world." It suggests that business, with its priorities and decision-making approach, has a right to impose its will on the world. But business needs to relearn its limits, and if the Harvard Business School let some air out of its own balloon, business would listen. HBS need only promise to educate students in the processes and management of business. It would be a noble and accommodating goal and would dilute the perception of the school and its graduates as a megalomaniacal, self-sustaining elite. For the school's graduates, past and future, the effect would be refreshing. We could end the charade that each of us is a representative of a hallowed brand. HBS can stop saying it "transforms" its students, as if it then had a lifelong claim on them.

Harvard taught that the most admirable lives were those lived in two parts. The first consisted of accumulating resources, the second in distributing them, or "giving back." The first part might involve being rapacious and pushy, the classic HBS elbow-thrower. During the second part you could be gracious and statesmanlike, have your name carved in stone and give speeches about the importance of philanthropy and sharing. Andrew Carnegie articulated this view in his book *The Gospel of Wealth*. He wrote that it was "the duty of the man of Wealth" to live modestly, to provide for the "legitimate wants of those dependent upon him" and then to distribute the rest of his money "to produce the most beneficial result for the community—the man of wealth thus becoming the sole agent and trustee for his poorer brethren, bringing to their service his superior wisdom, experience, and ability to administer—doing for them better than they would or could do for themselves." Even while he wrote these words, Carnegie was squeezing his employees with lower wages and poorer working conditions. His philanthropy was justification for the very worst business practices. Carnegie's assumption that "the man of wealth" makes for a better trustee of the common good than any elected government or private individual is shared by the HBS mission. It is the moral justification for the concentration of capital in ever fewer hands. Unfortunately, I do not think this makes for an admirable society. It venerates those who have amassed the most resources, whether money or power, almost regardless of how they did so, and diminishes those who have not. It places too much emphasis on that which can be counted, the quantifiable sum of those resources, rather than that which cannot, the unquantifiable sacrifices made by thousands of people so the few can accept their laurels of praise. It was disingenuous of Hank Paulson to say that it was up to individuals to make time in their life for their family, having been chief executive of a company, Goldman Sachs, that famously drives its employees to work endless hours. The MBAs who run these big companies are responsible for more than profits and losses, their own compensation and returns to shareholders. They set a cultural tone that affects everyone. Their disrespect for people's time and personal lives has enormous consequences. The world is not simply the apparatus to be used by MBAs to buff up their personal brands. It is not just a stage for them to display their decision-making prowess or leadership skills.

Business today clearly aspires to be something more than it is. It wishes to be recognized as a force more powerful than any government, nation, or individual society, and a good force at that. And the job of Harvard Business School is to provide its leaders. But just as governments and politicians can be undone by the different requirements of achieving power and wielding it, so businesses and businesspeople will forever face the conundrum of how to survive in a capitalist market while doing the right thing. At HBS, you add to this a very American twist: How do you manage to remain the most powerful, the richest and most successful, and also the most morally good? As consumers, citizens, even potential employees, we have the right to be both cynical of the profit motive underlying the piety we hear from business leaders, the talk of sustainability and "doing well by doing good," and yet also grateful that the capitalist supertanker can be diverted toward the greater good.

One of the most famous alumni of Harvard's MBA program is Robert McNamara, the U.S. secretary of defense during the Vietnam War, and member of the class of 1939. In his book *In Retrospect*, reflecting on the war, he wrote that while at Harvard he had developed "an approach to organizing human activities." There were three steps: "Define a clear objective . . . develop a plan to achieve that objective, and systematically monitor progress against the plan." This was still the essence of the HBS method: strategy, planning, and measurement. Of course, McNamara's methods came to seem macabre when he applied them to counting bodies in Vietnam. When asked about McNamara, a South Vietnamese officer replied, "Ah, *les statistiques*. Your secretary of defense loves statistics. We Vietnamese can give him all he wants. If you want them to go up, they will go up. If you want them to go down, they will go down." It was a line that often passed through my mind during my time at HBS, whenever I felt our calculations were missing the point. *Ah, les statistiques.*

The journalist David Halberstam wrote that McNamara mistrusted people who did not speak his language of statistics and hard data. If it ever came down to one person saying something "just didn't feel right" or that it "smelled wrong," McNamara would always go with his facts over their feeling. Fatally, in the case of Vietnam, the data he received were not accurate, and yet he trusted more in the illusion of reality generated by the faulty data—the clean, impersonal, objective facts—than in the messy yet accurate eyewitness reports brought home by journalists and soldiers. Interviewed later in life about the tension between his private reputation as an honorable, modest man devoted to public service and his professional reputation as a ruthless, data-driven boss, he said, "there is no contradiction between a soft heart and hard head."

When you see how businesses function today, it is hard not to feel that McNamara was wrong. When you see the allocation of financial rewards in a system nurtured and sustained by MBAs, you see there is nothing soft about it. Is this just capitalism at work? Or has society allotted too much authority to a single, narcissistic class of spreadsheet makers and Power-Point presenters? What is interesting when you read about HBS over the years is that these questions have always been on the minds of those who have passed through the school. How can I succeed financially without losing my soul? How can I work at a company without becoming a corporate stiff? Raise a family given the hours demanded of me? Can I be good and successful in business? Can I live decently, honorably, and completely in a world which makes that so difficult? You know these are vital questions because companies themselves make a lot of noise about them, pretending to have answers, which they don't. Until business and the MBA class resolve them, or at least demonstrate a fuller understanding of the problems they cause, they should drop their claim to leadership in society. And when incoming classes arrive at HBS, McNamara, not Coburg and his serfs, should be the first case they study.

AFTERWORD

Shortly after this book was first published in July 2008, the global economy cratered. The entire credit market, it turned out, was built on rotten timber. For several years, Americans and many Western Europeans were being lent money to buy homes they could not reasonably afford. And the only way these loans could work was if the prices of homes kept going up when sooner or later they were bound to fall.

When this happened, it was not just the home owners and their immediate lenders who suffered. It was the whole financial system, which had been trading these bad loans in their many derivative forms. With incredible speed, vaunted financial institutions revealed that the assets on their books weren't worth nearly what they thought they were. And one by one, they toppled, either into bankruptcy or the arms of their rivals or the federal government.

But it was not just the big banks and home owners who were caught up in this. A financial era ended in the summer of 2008, one built on the availability of credit and the ability of an ingenious elite to exploit it. This elite consisted of investment banks, private equity firms, and hedge funds. Their business models were based on their ability to borrow extraordinary sums against mere shards of their own money. The slightest positive move in their investment created terrific returns on equity. When the credit markets froze, the age of the leveraged return came to a close. Stripped of the fun house mirror of borrowing, which had given these firms the illusion of size and strength, we could now see most of them for how small they were.

Throughout these weeks and months of crisis, the Harvard Business

School's alumni were exactly where the school wanted them to be: in positions of leadership. They were president of the United States, Treasury Secretary, head of the Securities and Exchange Commission, CEOs of banks, and senior partners in investment firms.

Which begs an obvious question: What exactly had Harvard been teaching them?

When I wrote this book, I was very conscious of not being too critical of free market capitalism. I still believe in it as a system, as a superior means of creating opportunity and prosperity for everyone in a society. I also remain a great admirer of those who build businesses, who innovate, create jobs, and improve our lives.

But I see now that I was too timid. I worried that the aspects of the school which unsettled me were only unsettling to me because of who I happened to be. I realize now that they should have been unsettling to everyone: the narrow thinking, the greed, the disinterest in politics, the contempt for the nonbusiness world, and most of all the complete unwillingness to accept responsibility for its mistakes.

In October 2008, HBS held a global summit to mark its one hundredth birthday, inviting hundreds of alumni to Boston. Beyond the conference hall, financial chaos raged. No bank, it seemed, was safe and the government was slashing rates and ordering bail-outs in what often appeared like a blind frenzy. Inside, the tone was set by Jay Light, the current dean of the school. In his speech to the summit, he described how an increasingly complex financial system had collided with the popping of the housing bubble to create the economic crisis:

> We all failed to understand how much that system had changed in the past fifteen years or so and how fragile it might be because of increased leverage, decreased transparency, and decreased liquidity, three of the crucial things in the world of financial markets. We all failed to understand how that fragility could evidence itself in frozen short-term credit system, something that hadn't really happened since 1907. We also probably

286 AHEAD OF THE CURVE

overestimated the ability of the political process to deal with the realities
of what could happen if real trouble developed. What we have witnessed is
a stunning and sobering failure of financial safeguards, of financial markets of financial institutions, and mostly of leadership at many levels. We
will leave the talk of fixing the blame to others, that is not very interesting.
But we must be involved in fact in fixing the problem.

To get this straight, Light, the head of the most famous business school in
the world, was saying that having failed to spot the looming disaster, he and
his crack team of business academics should now be included in the efforts
to resolve it.

He was like a drunk driver emerging from a wreck asking for the keys
to the police car so he could drive home. Don't worry about who's to blame,
let's just all run along, shall we?

A couple of speakers at the summit, however, did seem to get it. One
of them was Michael Porter, by whom I had the good fortune to be taught.
Hosting a panel on the future of free market capitalism he asked again and
again why business leaders had lost the trust of their fellow citizens. It was
an obvious question, but he alone seemed to understand its importance.
The world needed free market capitalism to work, he argued, to create
wealth and prosperity. But it could not work if its consequences include
dwindling fairness and the rush of wealth only to the upper reaches of
society.

The deeper problem, he said, was illustrated by the fact that in recent
years, America has destroyed and created 30 million or so jobs every year.
Globalization had forced this churn upon the economy. And while it was
useful for business to have such flexibility, it was devastating for the individuals who could no longer rely on the certainties an earlier generation
had enjoyed.

Government and business had to figure out ways to ease the impact of
this economic hurly-burly. To ignore it or to tell people they were on their
own in the global economy was to stoke the kind of resentment we see

today. Global market capitalism had created very specific and human problems and it was up to business leaders to address them.

But what had they done? When Porter was helping Massachusetts introduce a universal health care plan, he said, the state's businesses fought bitterly to avoid putting any money into it. They could not see beyond their short-term self-interest to how the plan might help them by creating an ultimately lower cost system and giving workers a greater sense of security.

It reminded me of all the wealthy New Yorkers I had encountered who do everything they can to avoid state and federal income tax and yet demand to be feted when they make tax deductible donations to charity. Their sense of "society" is limited to that which they choose to see and find interesting. The rest, the portion funded by taxes, they regard as an inefficient abomination.

The other speaker able to describe the broader picture was Larry Summers, the former Treasury Secretary and president of Harvard, and who would soon become head of President Obama's National Economic Council. He noted that under the system which had endured in America for the past three decades income inequality had widened, as had the gap between the financial prospects of the children of the rich and the children of the poor, a crucial indicator of the legitimacy of a democratic society. Even the health of the less well off had worsened relative to that of the well off. Twenty-five years ago, the rich lived on average two years longer. Today, they live four years longer. Money in this society does not just buy you a better life. It buys you life itself.

During the two years I spent at Harvard Business School issues such as these were almost never raised, either by faculty or students. In fact, the perpetrators of the economic fiasco were talked about and welcomed to campus as heroes.

I remember Stan O'Neal, the man who led Merrill Lynch to near collapse, arriving in a caravan of limousines surrounded by flunkies and telling us all about the importance of ethics and understanding globalization. I remember so many of my classmates enthusing about the genius

288 AHEAD OF THE CURVE

of such and such a hedge fund manager or private equity investor while never questioning the means by which they achieved their outsized returns. If you did question the means you were assumed to be too dim to understand them. I can't recall a single class in which we talked about what to do for workers once you had fired them—how to retrain them, provide them with benefits, or sustain the communities on which companies depended.

Light was wrong to say "we all failed" in the run-up to this crisis. It is a line I've heard often from those in positions of authority as they try to shirk their responsibilities. We did not all fail. Innocent people who trusted that the markets were efficient and fair and honest as they bought homes and saved for retirement did not fail. The stewards of these markets failed. The intellectual feeders of these markets failed. They failed in their very specific role of managing the economic aspects of our society.

It should be a profound embarrassment to the faculty of Harvard Business School that for the second time in less than a decade it failed to identify an economic catastrophe in which its alumni played a starring role. First there was Enron, led by Jeff Skilling and fleets of other Harvard MBAs. And now this latest financial crisis. Not to mention the long-brewing sense that global capitalism has left so many in worse shape than before.

If the business school's faculty is so smart, how come they didn't see all this coming? Why didn't they warn about it and even try to stop it? Here was a large group of supposedly brilliant business minds, well paid, lavishly resourced, with time and access to every corner of the economic universe—and they missed it.

Light's dismissive attitude to fixing the blame, "not interesting," is insufficient. The institution he runs failed to show the leadership it claims to teach, and despite its unique vantage point and status in the business world, it failed to cry wolf until the chickens were being slaughtered in the coop.

Was it ignorance? Greed? A lack of worldliness? Whatever it was, Light would do well to fix some blame before pressing on to make the same mistakes again.

Of my classmates, the happiest two and a half years after graduation, are definitely those who took the unconventional paths. The ones who joined big, old-fashioned corporations rather than financial firms; nonprofits instead of management consultancies; small entrepreneurial outfits rather than technology giants. These were not easy decisions to make in 2006, when over 40 percent of our class was going into financial services and hedge fund managers walked on water. But in 2009, they seemed like genius.

Of my friends who did go into financial services, the stories are almost universally grim. The hours have been as murderous as they had been warned. But add to that the utter turmoil in the markets. Deals dried up and colleagues were fired. Bonuses were a fraction of what they anticipated. The mortgages they took out to buy homes in cities they scarcely liked now exceeded the value of the real estate. Several spoke of taking antidepressants and other stress medication to make it through the day. Here were people who two years earlier could have taken any job they wanted now feeling scared and paralyzed by their situations.

Those who went to Google found that the options they were given when they joined were now worthless. In January 2009, the stock was trading for 25 percent less than it had when they graduated in 2006. Without the hope of a large stock gain, Google was just another big technology company stacked with MBAs all jostling to work on minute pieces of the business.

By contrast, a friend who spurned a job trading commodities on Wall Street for a corporate job in a Midwestern industrial firm now finds himself running the agricultural arm of an Indian conglomerate and enjoying a fascinating and rewarding life in Mumbai. Another who took a job selling medical products for a small firm in the southwestern United States cashed in when the firm was bought eighteen months later by a pharmaceutical giant. Bo Fishback has thrived at the Kauffman Institute in Kansas City, promoting entrepreneurship in the United States and the world, while squeezing out the time to be involved in as many start-ups as he can, one of which, I'm sure, is bound to make him stinking rich.

As for me, I'm edging toward the life I described in my first semester LEAD class. I live in the country, a couple of hours outside New York. I have an office at home which looks out onto a garden. I am still married to Margret and our two sons are growing up in a clean and healthy place. I don't yet own a handful of media properties, but I'm writing a great deal and spending three or four months a year on business development projects ranging from media to finance. I often think about what I learned during my MBA and remain happy I did it. It has helped me to live without an employer—having no job to lose can be a great relief—and most important it has given me control over my time. At a personal level the MBA has been richly rewarding.

But does this mean the world needs Harvard MBAs running everything after we have seen the consequences of business interests pushing every other interest in society aside? At the Harvard Global Summit, Jay Light said yes. "The need for leadership in the world today is at least as great as it has ever been. The need for what we do is at least as great as it has ever been." To which hundreds of millions, including me, might reply: please, spare us.

ACKNOWLEDGMENTS

Thanks first of all to the Harvard Business School for letting me through the door, to the faculty, staff, and Section A, class of 2006, especially those who relived their experiences with me while I wrote this book. They are an epic vintage. To Stephen Robinson, Alec Russell, and Charles Moore, my editors at *The Daily Telegraph*, for writing my references, and to Quentin Letts, who first showed me how journalism was done and, ten years on, contributed to my reflected best-self exercise. To Richard Perry for his encouragement and advice. To Trattie Davis for the desk in Long Island City and for the hours of moral support. To the friends who read and commented on my drafts: Christopher Coleridge, Barnes Martin, Harry Mount, Andrew Stuttaford, John Brodie, Mungo Wilson, Daisuke Iwase, Mark Kahn, Guy Paisner, Paul Hardart, and Pauline Piechota. To the Bombay Club club, Oakes, Osgood and Steinberg, and, of course, to Bo Fishback.

To Svetlana Katz for reading the novel I wrote during the summer when I should have been interning on Wall Street, and passing it on to the incomparable Tina Bennett, who became my agent. To Scott Moyers and Ann Godoff for seeing enough in the proposal to pay me an advance, and to Eamon Dolan for his provocative editing. To Laura Stickney and everyone at Penguin who ushered the book into print.

To my parents for their love and patience and for not dropping the ball. To Cindy for defying every mother-in-law stereotype. To Augie and Hugo for being such delightful company and efficient alarm clocks throughout graduate school. And most of all, to Margret, a beautiful, brilliant, warmhearted woman who puts up with my nonsense.